CHASING THE DEVIL

Born in 1967, Tim Butcher was on the staff of the *Daily Telegraph* since 1990 to 2009 serving as chief war correspondent, Africa bureau chief and Middle East correspondent. His first book, *Blood River*, was a number one bestseller, a Richard and Judy Book Club selection and was shortlisted for the Samuel Johnson Prize. He is currently based in Cape Town with his family.

TIM BUTCHER

Chasing the Devil

On Foot Through Africa's Killing Fields

VINTAGE BOOKS
London

Published by Vintage 2011

2 4 6 8 10 9 7 5 3 1

Copyright ©Tim Butcher 2010

Tim Butcher has asserted his right under the Copyright, Designs
and Patents Act 1988 to be identified as the author of this work

This is a work of non-fiction based on the experiences of the author.
In some limited cases names of people have been changed to protect
their privacy. The author has stated to the publishers that, except in
such minor respects, the contents of this book are true.

First published in Great Britain by Chatto & Windus in 2010

Vintage
Random House, 20 Vauxhall Bridge Road,
London SW1V 2SA

www.vintage-books.co.uk

Addresses for companies within The Random House Group Limited
can be found at: www.randomhouse.co.uk/offices.htm

The Random House Group Limited Reg. No. 954009

A CIP catalogue record for this book
is available from the British Library

ISBN 9780099532064

The Random House Group Limited supports The Forest Stewardship
Council (FSC), the leading international forest certification organisation.
All our titles that are printed on Greenpeace approved FSC certified paper
carry the FSC logo. Our paper procurement policy can be found at:
www.randomhouse.co.uk/environment

Mixed Sources
Product group from well-managed
forests and other controlled sources
www.fsc.org Cert no. TT-COC-002139
© 1996 Forest Stewardship Council

Printed and bound in Great Britain by
CPI Bookmarque, Croydon, CR0 4TD

In memoriam Silk

Contents

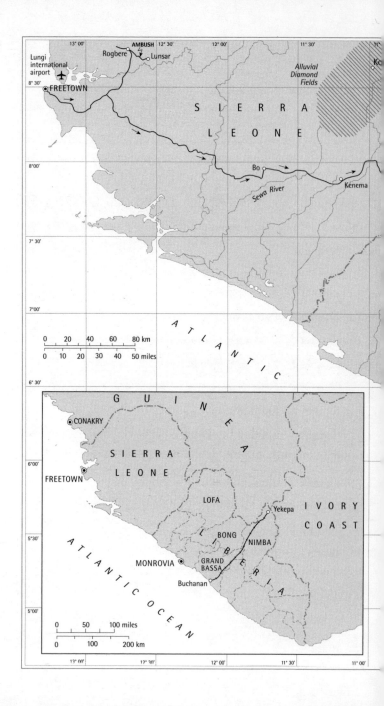

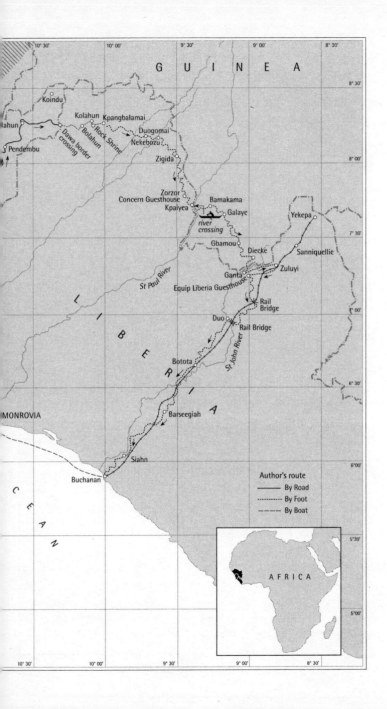

GUINEA

Koindu

Kolahun Kpangbalamai
Rock Shrine Duogomai
ahun Bolahun Nekebozu
Dawa border
Pendembu crossing Zigida

Zorzor Bamakama
Concern Guesthouse Galaye Yekepa
Kpaiyea river
crossing

L Gbamou Diecke Sanniquellie
I
B St Paul River Ganta Zuluyi
E Equip Liberia Guesthouse
R Rail
Bridge
Duo Rail Bridge
I
Botota St John River

A
MONROVIA Barseegiah

Siahn
Buchanan
O
C
E
A
N

Author's route
—— By Road
········· By Foot
— — — By Boat

AFRICA

Jungle Trail,
Lofa County, Liberia

Prologue

The jungle was getting thicker and the path fainter but I could still make out the figure of the young guide up ahead. He was moving quickly and surely, making steady progress along a track my tired eyes could barely pick out from the confusion of trees and undergrowth. Every so often he would slip out of sight, swallowed by the African bush, but then the blade of his machete would ting as he hacked his way clear of the thicket, surfacing once again just a little further ahead.

It was a battle to keep up. Clubbed by the heat and humidity of West Africa, I struggled to keep my footing on the uneven ground, my boots snagging on exposed roots and fallen branches laced with ivy. After sleepless nights in huts alive with rats, my limbs felt leaden as I wrestled through curtains of thorny creeper that tugged at my filthy clothes and left my face a fretwork of gritty grazes. White rings bloomed on the buckled brim of my sunhat, tidemarks for each of the sweaty days of trekking it had taken to bring me this far, and every footfall brought fresh pain from my blisters. Even my swinging arms hurt, chafed raw on their underside as they faithfully kept the staccato rhythm of my march.

But slowly a change took place. Nervousness started to take hold of me, weak to begin with but welling so forcefully it overwhelmed all sense of physical discomfort.

I was walking across Liberia, one of the most lawless and unstable countries in Africa, a nation left in ruins by a cycle of coup and counter-coup, rebellion and invasion, that had festered for decades. Its conflict helped spawn many of modern Africa's most troubling icons – child soldiers, blood diamonds, fetishistic killers – and although the war had officially ended, its jungle hinterland was still regarded by many as off limits.

The crisis came four days into the trek when my local guide and trusted friend, Johnson Boie, could walk no further. Hobbled by blisters, he reluctantly agreed to take a lift on a motorbike to the village of Duogomai where I was determined to spend the night. The bike trail would take Johnson the long way round but I wanted to keep going on foot along a more direct path through the jungle. This meant trusting someone new, a stranger, to help find the way.

Using the rather prosaic English he had learned at a mission school before it was closed by war, Johnson begged me to reconsider. 'Please, Mr Butcher, sir,' he whispered, looking askance at the man I had chosen as a temporary guide. 'Do not become separated from me. I do not know this man or his village. It is a major concern for me if I cannot be with you to guarantee your safety.'

At first I shrugged off his warning, said I would see him in Duogomai by nightfall and got ready to set off. But there was something in Johnson's nervous tone and worried eyes that troubled me, stirring a sense of unease that gnawed away at my confidence as, for the first time, I entered the Liberian forest without him.

Suddenly the new guide began to look suspicious. I recalled he had taken a little longer than he should collecting his gear from his hut and, when he had finally emerged, the long blade swinging in his hand looked more like a weapon than a tool. Then he had seemed to dawdle unnecessarily, whispering to a group of young men at the edge of the village, each of them also carrying a machete. The gang then greeted me a little too effusively and made as if they were going to follow us. I convinced myself a plot had been hatched to lead me round in circles before delivering me to an ambush.

When I had set about preparing my trip through Liberia I was warned repeatedly it was too risky. This had always been a remote enough region but years of warfare had left only a vestigial system of law and order. While the country was officially now at peace, stories of murder and violence continued to leak out of the heavily forested interior. And what gave the warnings added menace was that much of the lawlessness was framed by darkly magical phenomena derived from the very powerful but secret local tradition of spirit worship. Ritual murder remains common in West Africa, nowhere more so than in Liberia, and among the various risks I had been warned of were trophy-hunting killers known as 'heartmen'. They stalk human prey before attacking and removing the heart or another body part, taken specially for use by members of secret societies to imbue potions with magical powers. Heartmen are not imaginary bogeymen whipped up to keep unruly children in check. In rural Liberia they are very real.

In my increasingly jumpy state, thoughts of ambushes and heartmen began to mug my common sense as I set off without Johnson. The date was Friday the thirteenth, a fact that suddenly began to feel significant. With the guide charging ahead, fresh and on familiar ground, I blundered along behind, looking over my shoulder to see if we were being followed by the blade-wielding gang from the village.

I took out my compass and, through eyes smarting with sweat, watched in confusion as the needle span. To reach Duogomai we should have been tracking south-east, but the haphazard jungle route the guide was using swung due south, then west, then north, back in the direction from where we had come. A cock suddenly crowed. That made no sense since domestic fowl are only found where people are found. I began to convince myself the guide was leading me straight back to his village.

Wired through adrenalin, I had failed to notice a group of farmers who had set up a temporary settlement, complete with chicken coop, in the forest. My mind was playing tricks, fitting what it actually saw or heard into a matrix of fear and prejudice. Convinced an ambush was coming, I tried to calculate what I should do.

Did I have time to run into the forest and make my way back to the motorbike trail where I might somehow get a message to Johnson? No, that plan would not work because untracked bush in Liberia is so impenetrable I would soon get exhausted and disorientated. Maybe I could slip away, hide through the night, and then try to find my way back along the footpath to the bike track near the village at daybreak. But we were passing junctions where numerous bush trails star-burst in different directions and to find the way back would be almost impossible. The only idea I could come up with was to surreptitiously mark our way by breaking branches next to the trail, hoping they would be my 'ball of string through the maze' if I had to make a run for it.

I spent two panicky hours following the guide, looking over my shoulder for demons given life by my prejudices. But the more I peered into the jungle looking for heartmen, the more it became obvious there was nothing there and the fear was entirely of my making. When the guide eventually delivered me safely to the end of the trail I shook his hand firmly, paid the agreed fee and nodded a silent apology that I had ever doubted him.

After nightfall, I caught up with Johnson among the unlit hovels of Duogomai. He looked relieved to see me but not entirely at ease. I was about to mumble something about how safe the trek had been and how we must not let our fear of the unknown play tricks with our minds when he said a few words that silenced me. He was standing outside a mud hut with pale painted walls bearing a large, crude picture of a strange un-human creature. I asked him to repeat himself so there could be no misunderstanding.

'This village has some interesting traditions,' he said quietly, his eyes scanning the gathering darkness. 'You see, this is the house where the devil lives.'

CHAPTER I

A Stone in my Shoe

Route taken by
G & B Greene · 1935
xxtxtxtxtxx train
- - - - - - - lorry
xxxxxxx foot
~~~~~ boat

AFRICA

I think you may be interested in glancing through the attached draft telegram to Monrovia and ~~draft~~ letter to Mr. Graham Greene, who is shortly proceeding on a visit to Liberia to collect material for articles in the "Times", and eventually a book. His expenses are being paid by his publishers, and the Anti-Slavery Society are much interested in Mr. Greene's plans.

Mr. Greene called on me the other day and I undertook that we would do everything possible to ease his path. He is a young man and unfortunately does not give the appearance of being of particularly robust health. Quite frankly, I think he is running a considerable risk in making this journey, on which he is apparently being accompanied by a lady cousin. I rather deprecated the proposal that this lady should also trek ~~to~~ the interior from Sierra Leone down to Monrovia, and Mr. Greene, I am glad to say, hinted that she might elect to remain at Freetown and proceed down the coast by steamer. I don't imagine that Mr. Greene has any experience whatsoever of the tropics. There is, however, nothing we can do to prevent him going on this journey if he is determined to do so. *May I have these papers back soon, please?*

G. Thompson.

20th December, 1934

Sceptical Foreign Office assessment of Graham Greene's plan to cross Liberia

I can clearly remember receiving my first death threat. In thirteen years as a journalist covering foreign crises I had had plenty of brushes with unsavoury regimes. The Angolan government had taken against me for reporting on presidential corruption and told me I would never again receive a visa to enter the country. The official government newspaper in Zimbabwe had denounced me by name on its front page. And the daughter of Radovan Karadzic, the Bosnian Serb warlord, had once sought to have my press credentials cancelled when I described her as over-promoted.

But the phone call I received one morning at my home in South Africa was much more serious than any of these previous spats. On the line was a diplomat friend from the British High Commission in Pretoria with word from Liberia, the small, troubled West African country then ruled by one of Africa's more unpleasant warlords, Charles Taylor. It was July 2003 and Taylor's regime was in its death throes, with hostile rebels occupying much of the country and attacking the capital, Monrovia. In spite of all this, his regime still made time to pursue vendettas with foreign correspondents.

'Tim, I have to let you know that our representative in Monrovia has picked up a threat against you from the authorities there,' my friend explained.

'What sort of threat?' I asked.

'The most serious type,' came the diplomatically understated but unequivocally clear reply. We talked a little more and it became clear that, for the time being at least, it was too dangerous for me to go back to Liberia.

A few weeks earlier I had flown into Monrovia to report for the *Daily Telegraph* on the rebel advance. I was then the paper's Africa Correspondent and was aware that, although Taylor's regime had suffered many serious setbacks since fighting its way to power in the 1990s, the attack in the rainy season of 2003 was the beginning of its end.

Reaching Monrovia had not been easy. West Africa's notoriously unreliable airlines routinely refused to land in Liberia during periods of unrest so, with rebels menacing Monrovia city centre, flights had become rare. When I turned up for the scheduled flight from Ghana, I was hardly surprised to be told that day's Ghana Airways service had been cancelled. I spent the afternoon killing time and spotted a story in a local newspaper describing how all Ghana Airways staff had recently taken part in a three-hour-long prayer session asking for God's help to keep the airline afloat.

I was not sure if prayer had made the difference but during a lull in the rebel advance, Ghana Airways did eventually get me to Liberia's main international airport at Roberts Field, once one of Africa's busiest and most strategically important transport hubs. Back in the 1960s and 1970s the stability of Liberia's then fiercely pro-America government and its position underneath the equatorial flight path used by spacecraft meant NASA planners had ordered the runway at Roberts Field to be made ready as a possible emergency landing site for the Space Shuttle. Liberia and its main international airport had briefly played a supporting role in one of the great technological projects of the twentieth century.

The NASA connection was part of a long-standing link between the United States and Liberia, a parent–stepchild relationship that was close but not without occasional tension. A bilateral treaty had allowed American military aircrew to run Roberts Field during the Second World War, an agreement that led to a local town being given a most peculiar name. Smell-No-Taste, located next to the airstrip, was created to house Liberian labourers who migrated there in the 1940s to develop the facilities in support of the American war effort. American airmen did not want to eat local food so they flew in everything they needed, including vast steaks for the barbecue. The resulting aroma and the fact that the Americans refused to share their food with the local workers gave rise to the town's name.

The dominant smell I found when I finally got to Liberia was one of decay. It came from the corpses rotting among the spent bullet casings on Bushrod Island, the closest point then reached by the rebels to the centre of Monrovia. And it came from raw sewage clogging the streets from broken drains overwhelmed by Liberia's notoriously intense rainy season. But most of all it came from Taylor's regime whose last months in power resembled the gore-stained finale of a gangster movie.

After so many years paralysed through conflict, Monrovia was a zombie city, a living-dead sort of place. Cars were a rarity and commerce barely functioned so its population was condemned to plod around the damp, dilapidated streets on a treadmill of survival. Some sifted through rubbish in search of anything of value, some collected rainwater in old bottles and others lived among the dead in shanty towns built between headstones in a city-centre graveyard. There was no mains electricity so during daylight hours government secretaries moved their manual typewriters from dingy rooms out on to potholed pavements where officials would queue to dictate letters. Cloudbursts led to a flurry of typewriter ribbon and carbon paper as the alfresco typing pools fled for cover. The wet season meant dark clouds dominated a sombre city skyline etched in green and russet – green from tropical undergrowth enveloping abandoned buildings and russet from rusting ironwork.

A visit to the looted national museum in a three-storey barn-like building, where Liberia's first parliament sat in the nineteenth century, turned perilous when I ventured upstairs. Years of decay, caused by rain flooding through holes in the roof, meant the floorboards flaked to nothing under my footfall, just a few puny crossbeams saved me from plummeting to the ground. I turned on tiptoes, held my breath, as if that would somehow make me lighter, and scurried back downstairs. War had cursed Monrovia for years but its impact spiked in the wet season of 2003 with every schoolyard mobbed by terrified refugees fleeing the rebel advance, checkpoints manned – if that can be the right word – by jittery child soldiers not yet in their teens, and occasional detonations from mortars fired across a frontline just a short walk from the city centre.

Amid all the mess, two buildings stood out because they were so conspicuously clean. Outside the first there were bulky American pick-up trucks, sinisterly pimped with tinted windows and gloss black paintjobs. In a city of arthritic-looking cars burning dirty petrol hawked in plastic bottles at the roadside, these muscle-bound gas-guzzlers stood out, as did the swagger of the pro-Taylor paramilitaries who used them. They were murderous, unaccountable thugs whose cruelty worsened the closer the anti-Taylor forces got to the city. A few years later Taylor's son, Chuckie, would earn a small place in American legal history when, as an American passport-holder, he became the first US citizen successfully tried for committing the offence of torture outside American territorial jurisdiction. The offences were committed in Monrovia as his father clung to power and Chuckie led one of several paramilitary groups.

The other smart building, freshly painted and with its own generator guaranteeing electrical power, was the headquarters of LoneStar – the only mobile phone company then functioning in Liberia. For reasons that I never quite understood, LoneStar numbers routed through Monaco so you had to dial a number in Monte Carlo to get a mobile phone to ring in Monrovia. The company, profitable and cash-rich, was owned and run by the Taylor family and its cronies. With rebels choking off Taylor's traditional sources of illicit income from diamond smuggling and illegal logging, the phone company had become his last surviving cash cow.

I was excited to be covering the endgame of Taylor's regime, so I headed to the rain-lashed Mamba Point Hotel, a rare safe haven for visitors to Monrovia during wartime, where I was charged £80-a-night for a room with unwashed, damp sheets and mosquitoes that droned like Stuka dive-bombers. Down in the gloomy hotel restaurant, after curfew began, I would pass the worst of the storms watching the plate-glass doors leading to the balcony quiver in the wind as coconut palms thrashed around outside like dervishes against a grey Atlantic backdrop.

War meant that food was scarce but when it was not safe to venture outside the hotel I would still pass the time in the un-stocked restaurant, sometimes talking to the forlorn Sierra Leonean ambassador to Liberia, the only hotel guest who was not a foreign reporter. His Excellency Patrick James Foyah had been forced to decamp to the Mamba Point Hotel when his private residence was destroyed by looters just a few days earlier.

'The strange thing,' he said, ' was my house is nowhere near the place where the rebels attacked, so it must have been Taylor's own people who did it.'

I spent a few days in what had become one of the world's most dangerous and broken cities gathering material for my main report, hoping to come up with something that would make it stand out from my rivals'. I applied for an interview with Taylor himself but was turned down. I went to see a group of women who were staging a non-violent protest against the war. Wearing white T-shirts pasted to their bodies by the rain, they stood ankle-deep in mud on open ground near the city's abandoned fish market determinedly singing anthems and chanting slogans. With the curfew strictly enforced it was only safe for them to gather at dawn but they would pass all the daylight hours, no matter the weather, solemnly protesting, desperate for an end to Liberia's cycle of war, lawlessness and decay. Even though they stood no chance against thugs like Chuckie Taylor, the triumph of hope over experience was uplifting and I thought initially about focusing my piece on them.

Then I became inspired by a sinister-looking grave I had seen in the city's main cemetery bearing the name of someone who had recently died, Elizabeth T. Nimley. The letters were scrawled in a smudgy jumble of upper and lower case by someone using black paint that had dripped. It was ghoulish, almost voodoo-like, and it made me wonder how easily the dead can rest in a place with graves like this. Perhaps this was the way to encapsulate the zombie city.

But when I eventually got my satellite phone to work in one of the breaks between electrical storms, I spoke to my editor and he told me exactly what he wanted.

'When people think of Liberia they think of drug-crazed gunmen wearing magic wigs, so that's what I want,' he said.

I made my way towards the site of a recent firefight where the corpses of dead gunmen had been left to rot on the road. Next to a skull lay a wig, bloody and knotted – just what the editor had ordered.

Wigs, often brightly coloured with crazy coiffure, were regularly worn by gunmen in Liberia, along with wedding dresses, headscarves and other bizarre accoutrements. Some said they did this because the costumes were imbued with a force field of magical powers to protect the wearer; others refined the explanation, saying it changed the identity of the wearer thereby saving him from harm; others hinted at magic too secret to share with outsiders.

These responses fitted into an underlying theme of sinister ritualism, the hallmark of the fighting in Liberia, but one that was deeply frustrating as it was so difficult to fathom. When I started to enquire further, various sources said the practice reached to the top of the regime and I even heard accusations that Taylor, like other Liberian warlords, used cannibalism – not through hunger, but to somehow harness their power by consuming their enemies' body parts. As his regime faltered, Taylor, they said, had become more and more willing to explore anything that might help defeat the rebels, including the use of ritual murder and cannibalism. It was my report on this that drew the death threat from his people.

I never saw anything in writing but the message passed via my diplomat friend was that it was too risky for me to return to Liberia while Taylor was still in power. I had no choice but to report from outside the country as rebels brought down his regime a few weeks later. Two of his predecessors as Liberian president had been murdered in office but Taylor avoided these grisly precedents by accepting a flight into exile in Nigeria in August 2003 – although, eventually, he would be tried for his role in fomenting war in nearby Sierra Leone, the first African leader ever to stand trial for war crimes.

I felt both shame and frustration at missing the denouement of his regime. As a reporter I had failed. I had made it impossible for myself to get into Liberia, missing the opportunity to cover an important historical turning point, but it was not the first time I had felt a strong sense of frustration in West Africa.

My first trip to Sierra Leone, the north-westerly neighbour of Liberia, had touched on the best and worst of life – love and death. In May 2000, I had flown to Sierra Leone to report on the sudden deployment of British troops to shore up a United Nations peace-keeping mission in danger of collapse under rebel attack. Terrible leadership, muddled communications and military incompetence meant the 9,000-strong UN force had been reduced to a state of complete chaos by disjointed gangs of ill-disciplined militiamen, mainly belonging to the Revolutionary United Front (RUF).

The civil war in Sierra Leone had been started by the RUF, a non-ideological, non-tribal armed group that had effectively been created by Taylor to plunder whatever it could. Taylor wanted to destabilise his neighbouring state and at the same time make a financial profit. The rebels started with the alluvial diamond fields out in the east of the country not far from the Liberian border but then went further, including looting rampages through Freetown, the capital city on the Atlantic Ocean over on the western edge of the country. Attacking from Liberia for the first time in 1991, the hallmarks of the RUF were to be its cruelty and durability. In spite of concerted efforts by regional peacekeepers, diplomats and even mercenaries, the RUF kept the civil war festering in Sierra Leone throughout the 1990s, with occasional spikes of bloodletting and chaos.

Just such a spike had brought about the British military deployment, when attempts to negotiate the disarmament of the RUF had collapsed and the gunmen turned violent. Hundreds of UN peacekeepers were suddenly surrounded in their bush camps upcountry by hostile gunmen. Cut off from rescue and re-supply, the peacekeepers had effectively been taken hostage while a wretched few actually fell into the hands of the rebels. They were tortured and executed.

The chaos worsened when the militiamen put on UN uniforms and stole the peacekeepers' white-painted vehicles, meaning that for a time nobody in Sierra Leone knew who to trust. Panic reached Freetown as the remaining peacekeepers melted away from the rebel advance and civilians fled in fear of a repeat of the terrible bloodshed of January 1999 when the RUF had fought their way into the city, laying waste to entire suburbs, looting property and slaughtering civilians. The UN mission headquarters was located in a hotel overlooking the most westerly beach in Freetown, the country's most westerly city, and for a short period it felt like the foreign force was going to be driven into the sea.

For me as a foreign correspondent that trip to Sierra Leone was in many ways the perfect story. It was totally unexpected, strategically significant and downright exciting. I was based in London at the time and the first I heard about Britain sending a fighting force to West Africa was early one Monday morning before I commuted by motorbike across London to the Canary Wharf headquarters of the *Telegraph*. Two hours later and I was back on the bike charging up the M40 motorway desperate to reach the Royal Air Force base at Brize Norton near Oxford. I had persuaded the British Ministry of Defence to give me the last seat on a military transport plane deployed on what commanders were calling Operation Palliser, but it was a close-run thing. The straps of my hastily packed rucksack flicked annoyingly around the edges of my visor as I huddled over the handlebars trying to ride as fast as I could. I made the flight by minutes but had backache for days.

The story dominated international news for weeks and I found myself at the centre of it all. It was my first experience of sub-Saharan Africa and I can remember the thrill when the cargo aircraft doors whirred open in the small hours of the following morning and I smelled the sweet sedgy scent of Sierra Leone for the first time, still not knowing if the capital city would fall.

When I made it to the grounds of the UN hotel headquarters in Freetown the tropical night air was made even warmer by exhaust blasts from military helicopters flying soldiers in and civilians, mostly British passport-holders, out. I joshed with a television reporter friend about who would find the first white nun fleeing to safety and was then amazed that almost the first people I saw on touchdown were four sisters of The Holy Rosary.

'We missed a helicopter flight a few minutes ago and we are not going to do that again,' Sister Celia Doyle, from County Wexford in Ireland, shouted, struggling to make herself heard above the engine roar, her wimple flapping in the downdraught from the rotor blades.

By daybreak a crowd of terrified Sierra Leoneans had gathered at the gates of the UN headquarters, crushed against the fence pleading for space on the helicopters, but within a matter of days the tipping point had passed and the city had effectively been saved. Patrols of British soldiers, led by members of the 1st Battalion of the Parachute Regiment, were spreading out from the helipad and order was being restored, first across Freetown and then beyond. The deployment was bold, decisive and effective. The UN mission had been rescued.

I had been sent with the British force as a 'pool reporter', which meant that because I had been flown in first to Freetown, my reports had to be shared with rival newspapers in Fleet Street. For a few days I was able to set the agenda, an exciting time for any journalist. I slept on a basement floor, washing in a shower using water from a stagnant swimming pool, and survived on biscuits and lukewarm Coke. But for those few heady days I ignored the hardship, thrilled instead to have privileged access to the officers and soldiers of '1 Para' as they rewrote Britain's rules for overseas deployment. For several years I had served as the *Telegraph*'s Defence Correspondent and in the 1990s I had reported how the government slowly threw off caution born of the

Cold War, sending troops first to Bosnia and then Kosovo. The Sierra Leone deployment was another important step in this evolution, the first time significant numbers of British combat troops were risked on a unilateral humanitarian mission outside Europe. And the success of the mission would eventually reach far beyond West Africa as it would contribute to the decision by the British prime minister, Tony Blair, to commit British troops to the much more controversial and costly US-led invasion of Iraq in 2003. In short, Sierra Leone gave Blair his faith in foreign military intervention.

The long-term historical value of the mission was hard for me to focus on as I charged around having the time of my journalist's life. The Paras whisked me upcountry by Chinook helicopter to report on their reconnaissance specialists, the Pathfinders. They had set up a blocking position to defend the approach to the country's main airport and their bush location was the most exposed and vulnerable of all the British force. That night – after I had flown back to Freetown – the Pathfinder position was attacked under cover of darkness by the RUF. The British soldiers had seen their attackers coming but held their fire until the last moment. Several of the men approaching the position appeared to be wearing items of UN uniform and the British soldiers did not know if they were genuine peacekeepers or rebels attempting a *ruse de guerre*. When the approaching men dived to the ground and started shooting, the Pathfinders fired back. None of the British troops was injured but at daybreak the bodies of four RUF rebels were found along with a number of UN berets.

That same day senior officers briefed me on the arrest of Foday Sankoh, the talismanic brute who had led the RUF when it established its hallmark of hacking hands and arms from innocent civilians. He had been captured in Freetown along with a witchdoctor, his personal guide to the dark arts of West African spiritualism. After nine years as one of the region's most violent bogeymen, he was spirited away by British military helicopter to a safe location pending trial for war crimes. But those seeking retribution would be denied closure as he was never actually brought to trial. His health deteriorated in prison following a stroke and he died in custody, a shambling, incontinent, confused figure barely able to say his own name.

I have good reason to remember the moment when, after a few days, my British-based newspaper colleagues eventually caught up with me in Freetown. The airport was the main headquarters of the British force and I was hanging around the concrete apron waiting to speak to one of the officers when the first civilian aircraft to arrive there in days touched down. Among the journalists disembarking from the plane was a photographer from London carrying something much more important for me than any story I wrote during that trip. It was a letter from Jane, the girl I had been seeing for just two months before I rushed to Sierra Leone.

I still have it. It is one of the pole stars of my love for her. She used two envelopes and the larger one is formally addressed to 'Tim Butcher', written in Jane's confident, fluent hand, although the black ink is smudged from my sweaty first touch that day at the airport. May is the hottest month in Sierra Leone, the sweltering finale to the dry season before it is broken by rains that last months, and I can remember the exposed concrete of the runway pulsing with heat as I tore open the smaller envelope inside, one that was marked 'T x'. I can also remember the goose bumps spreading up my arms as I read the card inside. We have been together now for ten years and have two children, all of which flows directly from what she wrote.

From that euphoric private peak, my Sierra Leone adventure sank to a grieving low when, a few days later, two colleagues, friends from my days reporting the Balkan wars of the 1990s, were killed in an RUF ambush about 40 miles east of Freetown. Kurt Schork and Miguel Gil Moreno, working for Reuters and The Associated Press respectively, were covering the advance of the Sierra Leone army as it tried to retake positions lost to the RUF rebels in the confusion before the British force arrived. We had all been probing further and further out from Freetown to report on what would later develop into the full-blown rout of the RUF. But covering the advance of an army is among a war correspondent's most dangerous tasks as static frontlines shift and small pockets of resistance can be left behind. Kurt and Miguel were driving between two towns freshly taken by the army when they fell into an ambush by RUF gunmen, who shot up the two-vehicle convoy and then vanished into the bush never to be caught.

I had known Kurt since January 1992 when, early in his career as a reporter, he lasted a full winter in Iraqi Kurdistan, something few foreign correspondents had the bottle for. And I had watched

Miguel's career as a cameraman take off in Bosnia in the mid 1990s
and then soar in Kosovo in 1999 when he produced some of the
strongest images of ethnic cleansing by Serbian security forces to
come out of that conflict. During that time in Sierra Leone many of
us had driven down unsafe roads in similarly volatile situations; Kurt
and Miguel were scarcely taking greater risks than the rest of us.

Their deaths hollowed out my first experience of Africa, sapping
my zeal to be there. The shock came in part from the unsettling
knowledge that it could have happened to me. But it also came from
the sense of hopelessness that the deaths of my two friends were, in
the wider scheme of the conflict, utterly irrelevant. Journalists love to
convince themselves they matter but an incident like this reinforced
what cynics might call the pointlessness of what reporters do.

After their deaths I came to realise that the reason those first weeks
in Sierra Leone had seemed so rewarding was that, for a short time at
least, it had seemed possible to simplify a nuanced and complex African
situation. A multi-dimensional conflict with long historical roots and
significant regional links – the RUF rebels existed only because the
Taylor regime armed, trained and paid them, and Taylor, in turn,
existed only because of backing from outside sponsors, including the
Libyan leader, Muammar Gaddafi – could be boiled down to simplistic
stories about good guys (British soldiers) and bad guys (rebels).

Numb from grief I wanted out, to be back safely with Jane, so I
made arrangements to fly out with the British paratroopers who had
been ordered home, their mission done. The last thing I saw in Sierra
Leone was the ground crew at Freetown airport struggling to stow my
friends' coffins into a light aircraft for their last journey home.

My work as a reporter would take me back to the West African war
zone four more times. Working conditions were always tough and, at
times, risky, but no matter how interesting I found the stories, I never
felt I had a genuine understanding of the region, its turbulent past and
current fault lines. I struggled to get beyond the powerful but
troubling mental images triggered by the two countries, of drug-
addled child soldiers cutting off the hands of civilians or ruthless
warlords clinging to power on the profits made from smuggling. And
as a journalist I felt guilty about oversimplifying a complex situation.

I would write about combat between government soldiers and rebel gunmen, even though in a place like Liberia such plain language did no justice to the twisted reality. How can terrified children paid in cocaine by Taylor's henchmen really be described as government soldiers? And what is rebellious about a person with a gun who is defending his village from attack? Like all reporters, I rarely strayed beyond the capital cities, Freetown and Monrovia, largely because for much of the time it was simply too dangerous. I did my best but the truth was I never had a real sense of having understood the region, and long after I left Sierra Leone and Liberia my feeling of having missed something was like a stone in my shoe, a nagging irritation that never fully went away.

Then in 2004 I made a journey through another troubled region in Africa, the Congo, along a trail blazed by the nineteenth-century chancer, Henry Morton Stanley. With Stanley's writings acting as a fixed reference point I felt better able to chart the turbulent evolution, through time, not just of the Congo but of its people, and it showed me that travelling through a region offered me the best way to gain the understanding, even the closure, that I sought. That trip became the subject of my first book, *Blood River*, and several years later I began to think in terms of another journey, this time through Sierra Leone and Liberia, a journey that would deal once and for all with the stone in my shoe.

I wanted a route that would take me through the remote back-country of both countries, an area that during recent wars had been largely too dangerous for outsiders to visit, and to bring me in contact with the people living there. These remote communities were key not only because they were forced to endure the worst of the recent violence, but also because it was among them that rebel forces had survived for so long.

I began to read as much as I could about the history of both countries, including accounts of early expeditions into the interior, and discovered that European explorers largely ignored what we now call Liberia until relatively late in the timeline of African exploration. For centuries they got no further than the shoreline, which they dubbed the Grain Coast because it was a rich source of a type of ginger spice, *aframomum melegueta*, so prized in Europe as a flavouring that it became known as the 'Grains of Paradise'.

But for hundreds of years what lay behind the coastline was passed over by foreign explorers. In 1906, Sir Harry Johnston, a British geographer, described the interior of Liberia as 'still the least known part of Africa', although the first decades of the twentieth century saw a series of expeditions inland. They were often led by doughty British gentlemen, including Sir Harry himself, a dentist called Dr Cuthbert Christy and another titled geographer, Sir Alfred Sharpe. But perhaps my favourite early Liberian explorer was an adventurous aristocratic Englishwoman, Lady Dorothy Mills, who completed an impressively arduous trek in the mid-1920s, described in her book *Through Liberia*. It is full of the effortless insouciance of the early white outsider in Africa.

'The climate of Liberia is . . . quite healthy as long as you have a well proofed and ventilated house, and do not go out in the heat of the day, and do not take a stroke of unnecessary exercise except in the very early morning maybe, or during the hour before sundown to give you zest for your cocktail and cold bath,' she wrote after being carried in a hammock for hundreds of miles through the jungle.

In spite of this occasional gaucheness, she was clearly a formidable traveller. She lost her last cigarette papers in a swamp and took to rolling her tobacco in pages torn from her notebook, making roll-ups that would burn so fast they singed her lips. When she ran out of dried biscuit, she ate foie gras with banana, and when she irreparably damaged her sun umbrella by bashing one of her hammock bearers over the head, she took to stuffing the back of her blouse with banana leaf fronds that were so large they would reach above her head to cast shade.

But the expedition that came to fascinate me was made a little later by Graham Greene. He was only thirty when he set out by ship from Liverpool on a chill January morning in 1935 for his first venture beyond Europe, one that would take him across Sierra Leone by train and truck, and then through Liberia on an epic overland trek. His account of the trip, *Journey Without Maps*, is, rather like its author, darkly multi-layered.

Mystery has always clung to the motivation for Greene's trip if only because Liberia was so rarely visited by outsiders. Speculation about a possible secret dimension to his trip arose in part because years later, during the Second World War, Greene served with MI6, Britain's foreign intelligence agency, in the same region, training in Nigeria and then deploying to Sierra Leone between 1942 and 1943. Some observers, such as the authors Michael Shelden, Paul Fussell and W. J. West, have wondered if Greene's service with MI6 extended far beyond just the wartime years. Might Greene even have been working for the British government in 1935, sent to investigate Germany's covert courting of the bankrupt government of Liberia?

Publicly, Greene always described the 1935 trip as little more than a flight of fancy, an adventure inspired by his personal belief in the magnetism of Africa, an innate connection he suggested we all have with the continent if we look deep enough inside ourselves. That may have been part of his motivation but there was also a more prosaic element – money. Although relatively successful as a writer, with one of his novels, *Stamboul Train*, already made into a film, he was living at the time in rented accommodation in Oxford with his young family and desperately wanted a break from fiction. An adventurous travel book was potentially lucrative, especially after he persuaded his publishers, William Heinemann, to pay £350 upfront to cover the trip's expenses, and the newspaper he had worked for in the 1920s, *The Times*, had given a vague – and never to be fulfilled – promise to publish articles on anything he found of interest in Sierra Leone and Liberia. But it became clear as I researched his journey that Greene did have an ulterior motive, although not as an agent of the British government.

By 1935 Sierra Leone was regarded as having been largely tamed by British colonial development so the true focus of Greene's project was Liberia, which he referred to simply as the Republic. The title, *Journey Without Maps*, gives a sense of the isolation of inland Liberia in the mid-1930s. Little meaningful mapping of the area had been done and one of the two maps he used had the word 'cannibals' plastered across the otherwise blank interior. But while it might have been remote, Liberia in the late 1920s and early 1930s also represented one of the international community's most acute foreign policy issues. The country's ruling elite, descendants mostly of freed black slaves from America who founded the country in the mid-nineteenth century, had been caught systematically selling into slavery their compatriots from the hinterland – freed slaves had become slavers.

France and Britain led the attack on Liberia over slavery although for opportunistic reasons, hoping to carve up the territory of Liberia and add it to their existing colonial assets nearby. But in the end the League of Nations, recently formed and with little experience at settling international disputes, took over the problem, convening in 1930 a commission of inquiry with three members. It sat for just a few months but the report it published in September 1930 was devastating. It found that the government of Liberia had overseen years of systemic slavery, allowing large numbers of native Liberians to be rounded up at gunpoint by government forces, loaded on to ships and taken out into the Atlantic to work on plantations on a Spanish island colony called Fernando Po.

The report created a surge of political pressure that forced the Liberian head of state, President Charles King, to resign in December 1930 – an important early victory for human rights campaigners across the world. But after the hubbub died down following his departure, new fears emerged that slavery had returned to Liberia. Years after the president's resignation, the Anti-Slavery and Aborigines Protection Society, the leading abolitionist group in London, still viewed Liberia as 'one of our most difficult and anxious problems'. What the society needed was up-to-date information, and Greene, a young writer who had already worked for several years as a journalist, would make the perfect snoop.

The papers of the Anti-Slavery and Aborigines Protection Society are today held at Rhodes House in Oxford, within walking distance of the Woodstock Road flat Greene was renting at the time of his departure for Africa. Among the bundles of carbon paper, I found clear evidence that the society was the force behind his trip. It may have been Greene who dreamed of going to Africa, but it was the society that pressured him into going first to Sierra Leone and then to Liberia.

'Our Committee is of the opinion that you would like to know that it has been arranged for Mr Graham Greene, a young author, (British subject) to visit Liberia and prepare a book upon the whole Liberian question,' Sir John Harris, the group's parliamentary secretary, wrote in a private letter to the Foreign Office in London.

'Certain members of our Committee have formed a very high

opinion of Mr. Graham Greene, and they are hoping it may be possible for the Foreign Office to give to him a simple introduction to the British Consul at Monrovia, expressing to him the hope that any assistance it may be proper to render to Mr. Graham Greene should be forthcoming.'

In another letter, this time to the Colonial Office, Sir John took credit for suggesting Greene travel through Sierra Leone en route to Liberia. He wrote, 'I have strongly urged him to see a properly governed colony before he goes to Liberia, and he is now making arrangements, at my suggestion, to visit first Sierra Leone, travel through the interior, witness the well-ordered and progressive administration on the British side of the border, then enter Liberia and travel down to Monrovia.'

Many commentators, including Norman Sherry, Greene's authorised biographer, have identified a link between Greene and the anti-slavery society but I feel they failed to reflect its significance. From the extent and tone of the documents I found, it is my view that Greene was in effect working as an agent for the anti-slavery society. As a student he had played at 'spying' on trips to Ireland and Germany but Liberia was a more serious undertaking, a full dress rehearsal for his later MI6 service. Speaking in 1931, Dr Christy, chairman of the League of Nations inquiry into Liberia's slavery allegations, said the authorities in Monrovia had deliberately banned all freelance travel upcountry by outsiders, the implication being that the government had something to hide, most likely the continued existence of slavery. Throughout Greene's books he repeatedly refers to dodging government control in Liberia, first by entering the country incognito and then by completing his journey without government minders. 'If there was anything to hide in the Republic I wanted to surprise it,' he writes.

There was tidy historical resonance in Greene's role as agent for the anti-slavery campaigners, perhaps even a sense of payback, as the Greene family fortune had partly been made from sugar estates on the Caribbean island of St Kitts, properties that relied heavily on African slave labour. If he had been born in an earlier age Greene would have been expected to follow other family members out to St Kitts to oversee the slave-dependent business. He never knew his paternal grandfather because, after sailing to the Caribbean on sugar business in the 1880s, he died there from a tropical fever.

Continuing my research at Rhodes House I discovered a tantalising reference that hinted the British government was not just aware of Greene's trip but might even have supported it. Sent by the anti-slavery society, the four-line note thanked a mandarin at the Foreign Office for offering to meet Greene. In research terms this was exciting stuff, proof of a British government link to his trip. Maybe those who had suspected Greene was sent to Liberia as a British spy were right after all.

But to establish the nature of the British government's involvement in the 1935 trip I would need to see more, starting with the official's letter, receipt of which the anti-slavery society note acknowledged. I leafed through the file of correspondence several times only to be disappointed. The original was lost.

Research is a time-consuming process with long hours of mining through valueless slag punctuated by occasional moments when nuggets of fact are discovered. Finding the note was one of those highs but then failing to find the corresponding letter was a frustrating low. Feeling deflated, I left Rhodes House with one last lead to go on. The acknowledgement note included the Foreign Office registry code for the correspondence, a 'J' followed by a sequence of ten digits. After failing to find the letter in the files of the recipient, maybe I could find it at the other end, in the files of the sender, the Foreign Office. I took a careful note of the code and drove down to the National Archives in West London, where British government documents are kept.

The archives' index room alone is the size of a concert hall, permanently crowded with researchers ranging from members of the public tracking family genealogy to highbrow academics. As a new-comer I found it a little overwhelming, not least because the first librarian I asked had no idea what the J-sequence might mean. But she passed me on to a colleague who specialised in Foreign Office matters and he was able to help. He led me across the hall between various filing cabinets and bookshelves, and navigated expertly through a number of cross-referencing indexes until I finally had in my hands the original Foreign Office file on Greene's trip. It was my own modest eureka moment.

Between stiff cardboard covers the planning for the trip was laid out in full, with original letters from Greene – one handwritten, the others typed and all bearing his distinctive symmetrical signature – as well as correspondence from the anti-slavery society. There were memos, draft letters and official telegrams prepared by the Foreign Office, authentically marked with the hieroglyphic marginalia of long-retired mandarins.

These papers proved that while Greene was not officially working for the British government, the Foreign Office knew of the trip, supported it and expected information in return. From central London the Foreign Office cabled its people in Freetown and Monrovia, ordering them to help Greene. Furthermore, it obliged Greene to provide a full debrief if he managed to complete the trip.

In his first letter to the Foreign Office, Greene mentions his uncle, Sir Graham Greene, a senior civil servant who had already informally asked acquaintances in the Foreign Office to assist his nephew. In another he spells out his planned itinerary and hints at how unhelpful it would be if the government in Liberia got to hear about his journey from the British representatives cabled in Monrovia.

> Its very good of you to take so much trouble on my behalf. I very much hope that the Liberian government being informed of my plan to go through the hinterland will not enable them to forbid the journey. I am nervous on this point as the cost of the journey is being paid by my publishers and naturally I've got to get the material.

But the note that really stands out from the file is an internal memo written by a civil servant. It was for Foreign Office eyes only, meaning Greene would never have seen it, probably a good thing given how strongly it disparages the author and his plan.

> I think you may be interested in glancing through the attached draft telegram to Monrovia and letter to Mr Graham Greene, who is shortly proceeding on a visit to Liberia.....His expenses are being paid by his publishers, and the Anti-Slavery Society are much interested in Mr Greene's plans.
>
> Mr Greene called on me the other day and I undertook that we would do everything possible to ease his path. He is a young man and unfortunately does not give the appearance of being of particularly

robust health. Quite frankly, I think he is running a considerable risk in making this journey . . . I don't imagine that Mr Greene has any experience whatsoever of the tropics. There is, however, nothing we can do to prevent him going on this journey if he is determined to do so.

The Foreign Office wrote a disclaimer to Greene saying it could accept no official responsibility for his journey although, in the typically mealy-mouthed way of government officials, the diplomat then added he would be most interested in hearing about the trip when he got back. Graham Greene handwrote a cheery response, which was sent just days before sailing:

> I don't think you need worry about my wanderings in the hinterland; I've already taken expert medical advice and am going out fully set up with hypodermic syringes, serums and the rest. I should like to come and see you when I get back.

The more I read about Greene's trip, the more convinced I became an attempt to follow his route was the challenge I was looking for in Sierra Leone and Liberia. It would give me not just a smell but a taste of the region I still found so fascinating yet unsettling. It was also intriguing on a different level. As a reader of some of his novels, those that dealt with spiritual issues often drawn from Catholicism, my view of Graham Greene was framed in terms of his literary prowess. To learn about a different more earthy side to him, that of the pioneer-adventurer, would add a richer tone to my mental image of the author.

I was curious to learn Greene had taken along a younger relative on the trip. Ten weeks before leaving London he had light-heartedly invited his twenty-seven-year-old socialite cousin, Barbara Greene, to join him and, rather to his surprise, she had said yes. There was an air of frivolity to her involvement as the invitation was made at a wedding reception that was, by their common admission, well fuelled by champagne, but she was to turn out a very wise choice of travelling companion.

I had a wealth of reading material at my disposal. *Journey Without Maps* contains plenty of helpful details about the trip, especially in the first edition, a book that is difficult to find today as, shortly after publication in 1936, it was withdrawn from sale and pulped because of a libel action. Most editions available today include changes made by Graham Greene ten years later, so, to make sure I did not miss anything, I went in search of an original. My hunt took me to a second-hand bookshop in Johannesburg where I found a first edition that had evaded the pulpers because it was shipped out to southern Africa before ending up on the shelves of Bulawayo Public Library. Barbara Greene also published a book about the trip, *Land Benighted* (later reprinted as *Too Late to Turn Back*), and as my research continued I discovered the Greenes had left a trail of letters, papers and other material connected to their journey.

Close reading showed the Greenes had made several errors in their published accounts. In Graham Greene's account he is sloppy on dates; he writes that they reached Freetown by 15 January when, in fact, they arrived on the 19th, and at the end of the book he describes making it back to Britain on a cold April morning when, in fact, the ship docked in Dover on 25 March. In their books both Greenes recorded an incorrect version of the national anthem of Liberia, muddling up the line 'we'll shout the freedom of a race benighted' with a wrong version, 'we'll shout the freedom of a land benighted'. In spite of the mistakes, I felt certain that if I could follow the same route, their observations from the 1930s would provide a strong reference point against which to chart how the region had developed.

On reaching Sierra Leone by steamship on 19 January 1935 the Greenes spent just four days in Freetown, gathering last-minute supplies and hiring staff, before a train took them 230 miles across almost the entire breadth of the country. It was then a relatively stable and well-organised British colonial protectorate and they did not dawdle, anxious to reach the real object of their adventure, Liberia. Hiring a truck for the last 40 miles, they crossed the remote eastern frontier by foot on 26 January 1935.

Supported by twenty-six porters, three servants and one chef they took on one of Africa's most remote regions, its daunting climate, terrain and tropical diseases. Liberia in the 1930s had no roads so their column proceeded entirely on foot, crossing the country along jungle trails that wormed through an almost unbroken thicket of scrub and high canopy rainforest. From the border with Sierra Leone, their route traced an eastward arc through the hilly northern region until it approached a section of land bulging into Liberia from the neigh-bouring French colonial territory. To save time they decided to cross into what is now the post-colonial country of Guinea, walking south-east for 65 miles, before re-entering Liberia and swinging south and west for the last section of the walk which led them across a relatively flat, lowland plateau all the way to the Atlantic. Conditions were harsh and after tough stretches they would rest, normally for a day or two and, on one occasion, for a full week. After walking a total distance of 350 miles they reached the Liberian coast at a place then known as Grand Bassa on 2 March 1935, five weeks after crossing the Sierra Leonean border. From there they sailed home via Monrovia.

Theirs was very much a journey of its time with runners carrying messages in cleft sticks to villages further down the trail and with the two white outsiders sitting down to three-course lunches in the middle of the jungle – bread was baked freshly each morning. Graham Greene wore a sun-helmet and they took hammocks in which they could be carried by their porters, although he appeared only to use his when he got ill. Their tent went unused as they invariably spent the nights in Liberian jungle villages or mission stations where they were given huts. These would be furnished each evening with two beds, two chairs, a table, a water filter and a tin bath, all of which had to be lugged by the bearers. Along with clothes packed into three Revelation suitcases, they had numerous crates of food containing such treats as golden syrup, tinned sausages and steak-and-kidney pudding. Progress was much lubricated by a good supply of whisky, often drunk with juice squeezed from limes found along the way.

From my perspective the route was perfect as it went through territory inaccessible to outsiders during the recent fighting. The advice of the British government and a private security firm working in post-war Liberia was that it was still too dangerous for travellers, but I took the view that I could make it safely through if I found the right local guides. I have to admit there was also an element of personal vanity involved in taking on such a risky journey. The death threat from Taylor's people still niggled, piquing my pride to think I had been scared off from going back to Liberia when his regime was collapsing. Returning would be the only way to prove to myself I was no longer spooked and it might also allow me to reframe my view of the region, one still tainted by the deaths of my two friends.

As I began my preparations I convinced myself that enough time had passed for the death threat now to be meaningless, but then I got this email from an old BBC Africa hand, which rekindled a certain degree of nervousness.

> The trip sounds fantastic . . . and dangerous, particularly given the way you are regarded in Liberia. I guess that threat died a little while ago . . . or are you still on the hit list?

Security was always going to be my biggest problem, not least because I was going to have to cross what until recently had been some of the most sensitive land borders in Africa. The spot where the Greenes entered Liberia in 1935 was the same area where RUF rebels, trained and armed by Taylor, passed the other way in the 1990s, attacking Sierra Leone. And the section that passed through Guinea raised more concerns. The rebels who eventually ousted Taylor in 2003 came mostly from Guinea and there were plausible reports that they had not disarmed but had simply slipped back across the border into the Guinean forest through which my trail would lead.

Unlike the Greenes, I had the benefit of modern maps and as I started to think about the detailed route I found several of the Liberian villages they mentioned. They appeared, as described, more or less a day's walk apart. The old narrow-gauge railway they used in Sierra Leone was long gone, though, sold for scrap in the 1970s, and I knew from direct experience the only remnants were a few engines and carriages stored in a small museum housed in a Freetown shed. The museum was set up after I had written a piece for the *Telegraph* about discovering in Freetown the remains of a carriage built for the Queen's 1961 visit to Sierra Leone. I had tracked down the engineer responsible for building the royal coach and only at the very end of the interview did the old man let slip his work had been in vain.

'The Queen never did travel on our train. They never gave us a reason why,' Mohamed Bangura explained forlornly.

A *Telegraph* reader with memories of taking the colonial-era train when it ran between Freetown and Sierra Leone's second city of Bo, wrote one of those great letters you still see in newspapers from time to time, saying she could remember how the train was so slow the children mocked it with a song to the tune of 'She'll Be Coming Round the Mountain' that went:

> The train for Bo, he no agree for go,
> The train for Bo, he no agree for go,
> The engine man dun tire,
> The engine no catch fire,
> The train for Bo, he no agree for go.

The demise of the train meant I would have to make different arrangements, using taxis, buses and minibuses, known by Sierra Leoneans – almost onomatopoeically – as poda-podas, to get to the frontier with Liberia. But while Liberia now has a modest road system, my plan was to try to follow on foot the same 350-mile trail through the jungle used by the Greenes, seeking out the same villages, even staying in the same places if possible. Graham Greene described how he was warned that the climate in Liberia was so tough outsiders would perish unless they had hammocks to be carried in, but with modern medicines and water purification gear, I thought it worth at least attempting the journey entirely on foot. There was no way I could make my trip without local help with navigation and transporting my gear so, in a figurative sense at least, I would also be 'carried' by locals.

Knowing how I thrive away from routine news reporting, Jane was as supportive as ever, although she suggested firmly that I take out hefty life insurance. This would be the first major adventure I would attempt since the births of our two children so she insisted on the gold service from the insurers. It cost a fortune but came with a solemn undertaking to pay out if I suffered death arising from a list of causes that read like a bullet-point summary of the modern history of Sierra Leone and Liberia – 'war, riot, revolution, invasion and overthrow of the legally constituted government'.

When Jane asked me if I ought to do some training I remembered the thoughts of an ocean rower I had interviewed in 1992 before he embarked on an attempt to row across the Pacific. His name was Peter Bird and we met in a pub in north London. As he drained his third pint of Guinness I asked what fitness training he had done. 'Training?' he said with a quizzical tone as he got up to go to the bar again. 'There will be plenty of time to get fit during my voyage.' His adventure in the Pacific was unsuccessful and, undeterred, he tried again four years later only to be lost at sea.

It took a year of planning but finally I reached the point where I had prepared as much as possible. I had tracked down all my old contacts – diplomats, aid workers, journalists, academics – and, through them, a host of new ones. With their help I had built up a thorough picture of what I would face crossing Sierra Leone by public transport and Liberia by foot. I got in touch with some potential local guides and made plans for dealing with emergencies.

But my plan still lacked one key component: I had no 'cousin Barbara'. I had not found anyone willing to join me in the Congo, a trip described to me before I left as suicidal. This time the journey would not be suicidal, just downright dangerous. A walk of roughly 350 miles would be tough enough in any environment, let alone the war-scarred backwoods of West Africa where food and clean water would be hard to come by, and I felt I could use a companion simply to keep me going.

Graham Greene comes across as blithely patronising towards his cousin in *Journey Without Maps*. In early editions he does not even refer to her by name, although in later versions Barbara Greene's name is slipped in once. Throughout the book she is scarcely credited with any thoughts, ideas or input to the expedition and key moments are described by Graham Greene only in the first person such as 'I came on shore . . .' and 'I arrived in . . .'. She was for the most part written out of his account of the trip.

In fact Barbara Greene basically saved his life. The Foreign Office mandarin's assessment that Graham Greene might not be strong enough to cope with West Africa haunted the latter stages of the trek as he became dangerously ill with fever. The ultimate success of the trip relied heavily on Barbara Greene's wits and stamina. I felt a more honest sense of her contribution to the trip came from a private letter Graham Greene wrote to his mother after completing the journey, in which he acknowledged Barbara Greene's spirit although he played down the gravity of his sickness.

We've had a terrific trek, much longer than the one I first thought of
. . . four weeks in all, sleeping in native huts among the rats. B. stood it
very well indeed; indeed she got used to the rats quicker than I did, &
one day I got a bit ill I was glad to have her there to look after the
carriers.

The closest I came to finding someone willing to join me was the
first person I contacted when I started planning the trip in earnest. Joe
Poraj-Wilczynski was a career soldier in the British army whom I had
met in 2000 when he was a senior British military observer within the
UN mission in Sierra Leone. Later in his career he served as British
defence attaché in Freetown and then chief of security for the UN
special court set up in the city to try those responsible for the most
serious war crimes in Sierra Leone.

Joe was super helpful, giving me frank and up-to-date advice about
the border crossings and other security concerns. He was also hugely
enthusiastic about the trip, saying he would love to come, although in
the end it did not work out as he was unable to take time off from his
latest position working as a security consultant for a mining company.
At the eleventh hour he mentioned his son, David, recently graduated
from Oxford and unsettled in a London office job. Joe said his son was
keen to join me. I sent to David one of those half-joking, half-serious
messages to the effect that I was looking for a Barbara substitute to act
as the official artist for the trip, and he replied in the same vein.

I am not sure if your message was in jest or not, but I would make a
most excellent Barbara Greene. Although my painting skills are
questionable, I can at least drink whisky and would make a good Sherpa
if nothing else. When are you off and what's the route? Are you walking
the whole way?

At first I dithered, unsure if it was a good idea to have a stranger
along. I had only his father's word that he would be strong and
determined enough to cope with what would be a genuinely arduous
trip. And, of course, there was always the risk of our not getting on.
But then I took a more ruthless approach and told myself I would test
him for the first few days. If it was not working out I would have no
compunction about dumping him. Furthermore, while he might have

been a stranger, he did bring one big plus to the project. There are few people I would trust more than Joe to resolve a security crisis in West Africa, so by having his son with me I could, from a purely selfish point of view, be sure the cavalry would come if we got into trouble.

I had found my Barbara and was just beginning to congratulate myself for being so thorough when unexpected news came through. For our trip to succeed we would have to follow the Greenes for three or four days walking through Guinea, a challenging enough prospect but one that I felt was manageable if only because Guinea was so stable, ruled by the same dictator for twenty-four years.

Shortly before we were due to leave, that sense of stability vanished. The long-standing dictator died and within hours a coup had been staged by an unknown army captain called Moussa Dadis Camara. It made an already uncertain trip even more exciting. Graham Greene would have loved it.

CHAPTER 2

Province of Freedom

UNHCR ANNOUNCEMENT

It has once again come to the attention of the United Nation High Commissioner for Refugees (UNHCR) office in Sierra Leone that certain conmen are impersonating UNHCR staff and fraudulently obtaining large sums of money from people with the pretence that they will resettle them to countries abroad.

The office want to reiterate that all its services to REFUGEES are free and that the public should beware of these conmen as they will lost their money!

The office wishes to inform the general public that it will not take responsibility for loss incurred by persons dealing with these conmen.

BEWARE OF THESE CONMEN!!!!!

UNHCR Sierra Leone
January 2009

Above: Dawn ferry across Sierra Leone River estuary approaching Freetown, January 2009
Below: Sierra Leone newspaper advert warning about fraudulent asylum providers

The bass blast from the ferry's horn bounced back from the sea fog making my chest shudder, but the other passengers on the open deck atop the MV *Great Scarcies* carried on their early-morning chatter without interruption. Listening to them was like tuning a short-wave radio, the babble of foreign sounds every so often crystallising into a familiar word. They were speaking Krio, the broken form of English with roots reaching back to eighteenth-century mariners and which is still the main language of Sierra Leone. I heard *tok* for talk, *aks* for ask and *pekin* for child – derived from piccaninny.

As the ferry slipped away from the quayside of the Tagrin terminal on the north shore of the Sierra Leone River, I could barely feel the swell of the nearby Atlantic. The river estuary provides Africa's greatest natural harbour, a freak combination of powerful tidal currents that prevent silting in a deep channel tucked behind a mountainous peninsula acting as a bulwark against the ocean's motion. When Sierra Leone's capital, Freetown, was founded it was natural that the city should be built on the estuary's southern shore, the sheltered, inland side of the forested peninsula with its plentiful supply of fresh water from mountain streams.

Leaving the dock I watched a vulture circle slow and high above Tagrin just as everything beyond the confines of the ferry was swallowed by the mist. An evangelist stood up from among the packed benches, held a Bible aloft and began to praise the Lord. He wore opaque sunglasses and as his rhetoric built his head bobbed with the slightly unnatural articulation of the unsighted.

On the car-deck every inch between the vehicles was taken up by passengers, mostly women hawkers with cotton lappa wraps pulled tight around their shoulders for warmth. At their feet were baskets heaped with produce: cairns of bananas, peanuts bundled by the handful in knotted twists of plastic, portions of fried yellow plantain freckled with tiny black seeds and tinged red by the palm oil they had been cooked in. Young men sat astride motorbikes, cheap

Chinese-made models with the excess of chrome common to second-rate machinery.

We were still close enough to the shoreline for the air to have the distinctive smell of Sierra Leone, a warm fragrance just on the pleasant compost side of rotting. I had smelled it first on my chaotic arrival here in 2000 and nine years later I had smelled it again when I flew into a much more peaceful Lungi international airport the evening before boarding the ferry. The old baggage hall, where British troops had once set up bivouacs next to the luggage carousel, had been newly painted, the walls plastered with adverts for expensive beachfront properties. One of the smartest developments offered 'boys' quarters'. It showed how little had changed for the wealthy elite of Sierra Leone since the Greenes arrived in Freetown in January 1935 for the start of their journey and went in search of servants they also referred to as 'boys'.

The topography that had blessed Freetown in the era of sail now cursed it in the era of flight, hobbling the city's development. The main airport had been built at Lungi on the flatter, northern side of the estuary, meaning that people arriving by air face a fiddly onward journey to reach the city on the southern shore. To go overland involves a drive along second-rate roads ballooning far inland to get round the vast river mouth, a journey that can easily take ten hours in the rainy season. In peacetime, Tagrin ferry terminal offers a cheap but slow option preferred by most locals – although wealthier travellers have in recent years been able to choose from speedboats, helicopters and even hovercraft, all of which are costly and sometimes spectacularly unreliable. British diplomats were recently banned from using the helicopter service after one of the aircraft burst into flames in mid-air killing all on board. The diplomats responded by buying their own motorboat for airport connections, complete with tiny flagstaff from which the High Commission's official standard flies in miniature.

The ferry had not been running during the war and I rather relished this chance to reach one of the world's great seaboard cities by boat. Like many planes, ships, vehicles and other pieces of mechanical equipment in Africa, the *Great Scarcies* arrived here very much second-hand. Laxer safety standards mean machinery often comes to Africa in its dotage and airfields and ports all around the continent are full of venerable vehicles eking out the twilight of functionality. The *Great Scarcies* used to run European holiday-makers between the Greek islands in the 1980s and 1990s before a consortium of Sierra Leonean businessmen spotted a post-war opportunity and arranged for her to venture round the top left corner of Africa before creeping south along the edge of the Atlantic all the way to Freetown.

'She's a good enough ship,' Tholley Ahmed, the bosun, told me as he stared into the offing after we got underway. The bridge had no radar so during the hour-long crossing, the skipper relied heavily on Tholley's eyesight. When I asked about the owners, Tholley glanced round at me and replied with a somewhat resigned tone, 'They're Lebanese.'

It is a quirk of West Africa that a small but powerful community of immigrants from the Levant has made it their home since the 1920s, accepting the very real risks of occasional war and unrest in exchange for access to lucrative local business. Graham Greene chose a manipulative Arab diamond smuggler as the villain of his Sierra Leone-based novel *The Heart of the Matter*, written in the late 1940s, and on my earlier visits to Freetown I learned the local Lebanese business community was stronger than any other. My work as a journalist has often taken me to Beirut where the long-serving Shia speaker of parliament, Nabih Berri, one of the key players in the muddled mosaic of modern Lebanese politics, speaks proudly of having been born in Sierra Leone.

The passengers continued to chat as Tholley scanned a horizon growing as the rising sun gathered in the mist. A local fishing boat powered by an outboard engine came into view, its low, painted wooden flanks rising to an elegant prow with a single upright figure, muffled up against the chill, at the sternpost, hand on the tiller. Known in these waters as banana boats, they pay scant attention to international frontiers, slipping up and down the coast from Sierra Leone as far round as Nigeria, more than a thousand miles to the east. I could see a white flag on a bamboo cane sticking from the prow. Coastal fishermen were among the first Africans to receive the attention of Christian missionaries and I was sure the flag carried a biblical invocation seeking protection from the perils of the sea.

Down on the car-deck there was movement. The motorbikers had begun fidgeting with their kick-start pedals and the women were standing, stretching out of their lappa cocoons. Those who had heavy loads to carry on their heads fashioned hand cloths into quoits to cushion their scalps. I looked far ahead and could see why they had stirred. Freetown was coming into view.

At first it was like a watery Japanese print as I could make out only the blurred loom of mountain ranges overlaid more and more faintly, one behind the other. But as the mist dissolved the focus sharpened to reveal under the hills a shoreline of buildings, rooftops, tower blocks and the occasional startled outline of a leafless cotton tree. The sight reminded me of Graham Greene's description of Freetown as 'an impression of heat and damp'. But it also made me think of the first European explorer to describe the area in writing, a Portuguese mariner called Pedro da Sintra, who arrived around 1462 and wrote of a 'high mountain summit which is continually enveloped in mist'.

Da Sintra must have come here during the rainy season, as he described how thunder could be heard coming perpetually from the cloud-bound massif. He called it Serra Lyoa, which can be translated as the 'Mountain of the Lioness'. As this part of Africa has always been too forested to have supported its own lion population, it is thought he meant either that the constant roaring sounded like a lion or that, to his eye, the mountain was shaped like a lion. Historians remain divided on the issue but they agree that within a hundred years or so his Serra Lyoa spelling had morphed into Sierra Leone.

The discovery of a sheltered harbour with a plentiful supply of drinking water on the otherwise hostile low-lying, disease-ridden coast of West Africa meant that by the sixteenth century Sierra Leone was already receiving plenty of visitors by ship. There were traders, initially Portuguese, and their footprint is still evident today. A white person walking into a rural village near the coast of Sierra Leone will hear the children crying out 'Oporto, Oporto', the favoured local term for white man. Later came the Dutch and then the British, some of whom stayed in the area, often on off-shore islands chosen for protection. Several began families with the local population and opened trading posts. Archaeology, linguistics and oral tradition indicate various African forest-dwelling tribes had lived in the area for hundreds of years before da Sintra arrived and it was with these long-standing tribes like the Sherbro, Bullom and Temne that trade began. It started conventionally enough with the exchange of European manufactured goods for African craftwork, but the discovery of the New World at the end of the fifteenth century and the subsequent demand for slaves to work on plantations in the Americas changed everything.

Suddenly the Sierra Leone River estuary saw the arrival of more ruthless traders, interested only in profitable human plunder. There were raiders like Sir John Hawkins, the Elizabethan sailor whose hugely profitable first slaving expedition took him in 1562 from England via Sierra Leone to the Caribbean, and later, Bartholomew Roberts, a drunken, ruthless Welshman who captured more ships than any other buccaneer during the golden age of piracy and came to Sierra Leone in the early eighteenth century to burn the official British slaving fortress to the ground. The dominant Temne chiefs showed no scruples in selling prisoners from their regular inter-tribal wars to white outsiders and soon the estuary had become a nest of pirates and slavers, earning the following colourful description in the classic work, *A General History of the Pyrates*, published in the 1720s:

> There are about 30 English men in all, Men who in some Part of their Lives, have been either privateering, bucaneering or pyrating, and still retain and love the Riots and Humours, common to that sort of life. They live very friendly with the Natives, and have many of them . . . to be their Servants; The Men are faithful, and the Women so obedient, that they are very ready to prostitute themselves to whomsoever their Masters shall command them.

The dissolute character of the region in the late eighteenth century makes the next chapter in its history quite extraordinary. In London a group of high-minded idealists, supported, it must be admitted, by opportunists and even a few racists, settled on Sierra Leone as the site for a pioneering experiment in social engineering. The streets of Britain's growing cities were then crowded with the poor, among whom a few thousand non-white faces stood out. Some were slaves brought from the Americas to Britain by plantation owners and then freed; others were lascars, sailors who had joined British crews in the East Indies and disembarked in the port of London; others were former slaves who had fought with the British on the losing side in the American War of Independence and then fled to London, fearing they would once again be enslaved if they stayed in America.

They might have had a wide range of backgrounds but with few exceptions they lived the same wretched life of penury, begging on the streets of London and Britain's other major ports. This was the era of salon politics, when hugely important decisions could be made by small groups of the great and the good meeting not in parliament or government buildings but in private houses or bars. Such a gathering created the Committee for the Relief of Black Poor in January 1786. Its original aim was to collect money and rations for destitute blacks in Britain but within a few months the committee's all-white members, meeting originally in the Bond Street home of a wealthy bookseller but later at Batson's, a coffee shop in the City of London, came up with a far more ambitious plan.

The committee would persuade poor blacks to leave Britain and go to the tropics to found a utopian community where they could eventually rule themselves, free of the control of white superiors. The abolition of slavery was then being debated by Britain's ruling elite and the idea of giving the black poor their own colony was supported keenly by some of Britain's leading abolitionists. But it also received the backing of some of Britain's most high-profile supporters of slavery, owners of sugar plantations in the West Indies, who embraced the idea of clearing London of its black poor and thereby getting rid of a potentially troublesome reservoir of hostility to slavery.

Various places were suggested as a suitable location for the experiment, including the Bahamas, but, after discussion with representatives of London's black community, Sierra Leone was chosen as the site for what was originally to be called the Land of Freedom, changed later to the Province of Freedom. In copperplate manuscript, a minute dated Wednesday 26 July 1786 recorded what was discussed by committee members meeting at Batson's Coffeehouse.

> Five of the Deputies of the Blacks . . . mentioned a Person now living in London who is a native of that country [Sierra Leone] and gives

them assurance that all the natives are fond of the English & would receive them joyfully.

The brains behind the Sierra Leone plan was an English amateur botanist and abolitionist named Henry Smeathman, who had come to know the Sierra Leone River estuary in the early 1770s through several years spent on a nearby island studying plants and developing a fixation with termites. This was a time when most of the whites based in the area were involved in slavery but while Smeathman opposed the trade he appears a cheerful fellow, not interested in making an issue out of his hosts' occupation. When in 1773 he visited Bunce Island, site of the main British slaving fortress within the Sierra Leone River estuary, his diary recorded rather pleasant games of golf. It was only a few years since golfers in Scotland had come together to form what would later become the Royal and Ancient Golf Club of St Andrews but Smeathman describes in detail how the slavers of Bunce Island passed the time in between slaving raids by playing a game he called goff.

> We amused ourselves for an hour or two in the cool of the afternoon in playing at Goff, a game only played in some particular parts of Scotland and at Blackheath. Two holes are made in the ground at about a quarter of a mile distance, and of the size of a man's hat crown . . . That party which gets their ball struck into the hole with the fewest strokes wins.

Smeathman was approached by the committee because of his experience of living in West Africa and, notwithstanding the presence of various slaving sites in and around the Sierra Leone River estuary, he was able to convince the committee the area would make a perfect site for the relocation of Britain's black population. He died before the first ships set sail.

The relocation plan was high-minded and not a little confused. It referred to 'Asiatic blacks', the lascars, as being suitable for resettlement in Africa even though they came from the Far East. It bundled them together with black people whose roots did at least reach back to Africa but to parts of the continent hundreds, sometimes thousands of miles away from Sierra Leone. And for good measure the committee included more than sixty white women in the settlement plan,

prostitutes in the eyes of some historians, lawful partners of poor
blacks in the eyes of others. The thinking of the white committee
members might have been driven by philanthropy but it betrayed a
clear conceit, the idea that non-whites and their hangers-on could
effectively be dumped in any old part of Africa.

There was little joy in the reception given to the 411 predominantly
black settlers who eventually reached the Sierra Leone River estuary in
May 1787 on three Royal Navy ships chartered by the committee
behind the Province of Freedom. At first the local Temne chief was
happy enough to accommodate the new arrivals. During his life King
Tom had seen plenty of foreign outsiders, mostly slavers and brigands,
pass through his territory and although the new group was slightly
different in that it was made up mostly of black people, he had no
qualms about signing a treaty on 11 June 1787 with their white leaders
concerning ownership of the mountain peninsula which ended:

> And I do hereby bind myself, my Heirs and Successors, to grant the
> said free Settlers a continuance of a quiet and peaceable possession of
> the Lands granted their Heirs and Successors for ever.

In exchange for ceding the peninsula in perpetuity, King Tom
received a bundle of items valued at a few pennies over £59. It
included eight muskets, a barrel of gunpowder, two dozen laced hats,
bunches of beads, a length of scarlet cloth and, in a gesture worthy of
the region's piratical history, 130 gallons of rum.

In those early days there were moments of excitement when the
pioneers made encouraging discoveries that hinted at a land of plenty.
A bushfire one day was followed by the distinctive smell of roasted
coffee. On closer inspection, the settlers found part of a hillside thick
with wild coffee plants. But various delays and problems en route had
meant the settlers arrived in the country at the worst possible time of
year, with the rainy season just beginning. No staple crops could
survive the ferocious storms, while malaria and other waterborne
diseases spiked. Within three months a third of the settlers were dead,
their immune systems ravaged by hunger and exhaustion. Several key
white officials, including the two doctors and the chaplain, who had
been specially commissioned to help set up the Province of Freedom,
did not just run away, they betrayed the whole ethos of the project by

joining the slavers on Bunce Island. Occasionally some of the black settlers – freed slaves themselves – preferred to move to Bunce Island where they could at least get food, shelter and even wages in exchange for helping with the ongoing shipment of slaves. The dreamers back in London struggled to understand how freed slaves could themselves turn into slavers.

The first Province of Freedom effectively ended in 1789 with confusion and betrayal when, after a squabble, the settlement was burned to the ground by King Jimmy, King Tom's successor, forcing the few remaining settlers to flee into the bush. But the committee back in London refused to give up, sending out a colonial agent who found only sixty-four survivors from the original 411, among them a few hardy white women described unfavourably by one observer as 'strumpets'. It was just enough to found a new settlement in an abandoned Temne village consisting of seventeen mud huts. According to local lore, the houses had been abandoned because they had been 'occupied by devils' but this did not seem to deter the agent.

What the project needed most was people, so the philanthropists sent out another tranche of black settlers in 1792, this time drawn not from the streets of London but from Nova Scotia, the rocky promontory off North America where large numbers of former black slaves from America had ended up after fighting with Britain when America won its independence. They had been forced to flee America when Britain surrendered but, instead of enjoying full freedom under the British authorities in Nova Scotia, they endured a wretched existence struggling against the bitter winters, poor soil and colonial laws that left them, in some ways, worse off than they had been as slaves. Around a thousand were happy to leave the icy, rocky shore of Nova Scotia and sail to Sierra Leone, where they gave the name Freetown to the settlement they founded. And a few years later the Nova Scotians were followed by another group of settlers, Maroons, who were slaves deported from Jamaica after rebelling against their masters.

But the development that really saved the Province of Freedom project was, ironically, something that ensured its black population would never in their lifetimes enjoy proper freedom. In 1808 the mountain peninsula guarding the Sierra Leone River estuary became a full British colony.

The original plan by the eighteenth-century philanthropists had been to create a community where black settlers would be in charge of their own destiny. Quite how they would live alongside the indigenous population was a question not really dealt with by the dreamers, but the point was that blacks would, through the munificence of British philanthropy, be free to rule themselves – a beacon to all those still trapped in slavery around the world.

That dream came to an abrupt end in 1808 when the company set up by the philanthropists to run the Province of Freedom effectively became bankrupt and the British government moved in to stake the peninsula as a colony. This heralded a boom period for black settlement in Sierra Leone as, following the work of abolitionists led by William Wilberforce, the Royal Navy moved to enforce the 1807 ban on the slave trade. Navy ships were deployed along the west coast of Africa with orders to intercept ships carrying slaves across the Atlantic and it was to the newly founded colony of Sierra Leone that these warships would come to off-load the so-called 'recaptives', Africans who had been captured once by slavers and again by the Royal Navy. No matter where these people came from they found themselves settled, in ever increasing numbers, in what had been set up as the Province of Freedom.

In 1808 the settler population of Sierra Leone was just 2,000, made up of remnants of the London settlers, the Nova Scotians and Maroons. The recaptives soon swamped this original group, with the Royal Navy delivering a total of 6,000 slaves retaken on the high seas by 1815. The influx continued at a similar pace over the next thirty years, meaning that recaptives became by far the dominant settler community in Freetown.

But the irony was that, in spite of the growing number of black settlers, colonial rule meant a small cohort of white officials, appointed by the British government in London, still ran the affairs of a much larger black population, both settlers and indigenous Africans. It meant the dream of the philanthropists was only ever half fulfilled. Yes, black settlers had been saved from slavery, but they never enjoyed full freedom. And tension between white colonials, black settlers and indigenous people would dominate every subsequent turn in the history of Sierra Leone.

*

Traces of Freetown's ancestry were visible everywhere as I made my way into the city to prepare for my journey across Sierra Leone and Liberia. After the relative cool of the early-morning crossing, I had stepped off the ferry and felt the true weight of West Africa's climate. By the time I found a taxi, an old Mercedes estate with a German number plate, I had already begun to flag. Wilting into its saggy front seat, I groped for the window handle but found only a knurled, rusty stub. Taking pity on me, the dreadlocked driver, George Decker, leaned across and slapped the flat of his hand against my window with such force that the glass pane shuddered down.

Traffic oozed like treacle along hot, narrow roads clogged with pedestrians, livestock and hawkers. Street-sellers need not worry about missing a sale as they had plenty of time to catch up with slow-moving vehicles whenever a passenger showed interest in the local newspapers, knock-off DVDs, plastic bags of chilled water or other items for sale. I could barely see through the web of cracks in our windscreen but George kept up a *sotto voce* commentary on local landmarks, almost all of which were connected to Freetown's early history.

We inched past Cline Town, one of the larger suburbs, named after Emmanuel Cline, a 'recaptive' from Nigeria who made enough money as a trader in the mid-nineteenth century to buy what was then empty land near the shoreline on the eastern approaches to the city. And we paused at what was once Cline Town's largest building, Fourah Bay College, the oldest university in colonial Africa. Founded in 1827 to train freed slaves as teachers and chaplains, it produced a stream of alumni who took their qualifications far beyond Freetown – the first cohort of modern black professionals to spread across Africa. It earned Freetown the soubriquet of 'The Athens of Africa' and a suitably grand three-storey college hall was constructed close to the shoreline. Built out of quarried blocks of laterite, the distinctively coloured pinkish stone that is common on the Freetown peninsula, in its day it would have looked at home in the grounds of any Oxbridge college. Its portico was framed by elegant cast-iron columns, Norman windows lined its flanks and its grounds were tended by a staff of gardeners. But by the time I saw it the elegance was no more. Abandoned when Fourah Bay College moved to other premises, the college building was a roofless ruin, its internal floors concertinaed into a heap of

broken masonry and its walls scorched with fires lit by squatters who
overran it during the civil war.

George drove through the city centre where the main artery, Siaka
Stevens Street, passes under the spreading boughs of the Cotton
Tree. Such trees are common across West Africa but this huge
specimen in the heart of Freetown commands a special position in the
history of the country, protected as a national monument. It was
under this tree, in 1792, that a service of thanksgiving was held by the
first group of freed slaves arriving from Nova Scotia, as they sought
God's blessing for their new life in Africa. They used it as a centre-
point when they laid out Freetown's original grid of streets leading
down a gentle slope to the shoreline of the Sierra Leone River estuary,
a grid that remains largely unchanged today. As we drove by I looked
up and saw thousands of large bats, each the size of a rat, hanging from
its branches in furry, twitching bunches, unmoved by the street noise
below.

War and decay meant Freetown was not a city that wore its age
well. There were several tired-looking tower blocks in the city centre,
many with their own generators noisily providing a private electricity
supply for businesses wealthy enough to afford them, separated by
streets crowded with hawkers and tatty with rubbish. Statues erected
to Sierra Leone's post-colonial leaders, the ones who guided her
through independence in 1961, were in dire need of attention. Noses
had fallen off, lettering had faded and ceremonial fountains had dried
up. One of Freetown's oldest buildings, St George's, the Anglican
cathedral built of red laterite which Graham Greene described as
dominating the city centre, is now dwarfed by hulking 1960s
structures hung with rusting air-conditioner units, paint flaking from
the walls.

I later visited the cathedral and found the guest book. It had lost its
spine and its pages were grubbily dog-eared, but despite being almost
fifty years old it was still not full. The first signature was 'Elizabeth
R', dated in the Queen's hand 'November 26 1961', and the second
was 'Philip', the Duke of Edinburgh, marking the royal visit just after
independence.

As we continued to drive west we began to pass some of Freetown's
older shingle houses, built in nineteenth-century settler style with
walls made of overlapping lengths of roughly hewn timber. The

passage of years and ravages of rainy seasons meant the square-cut wooden frames had settled higgledy-piggledy, giving them a naive, pre-modern look, as if they were fairytale houses a child might picture in a magic forest.

In the early years, settlers who were thought by British officials to come from the same parts of Africa were grouped together, setting up their own satellite villages some distance from the town centre and its cotton-tree hub. Slaves from the Congo, almost 2,000 miles south-east of Sierra Leone, set up Congotown, and Yoruba tribesmen from Nigeria set up Aku Town. These names survive today, although the chaotic growth of the city means the communities have long been absorbed into a single, unbroken sprawl.

Originally laid out for a population of a few thousand, the city is now home to more than a million people. As the only large city in Sierra Leone it has traditionally been the main economic magnet for people living *up-line*, the Krio term for the provinces derived from the days when the railway was the main artery between city and country. When the civil war began in 1991 the city was further inundated, this time by terrified refugees, and although the war officially ended in 2002, Freetown still has the feel of a city overwhelmed. Each year shanties reach higher up the flanks of the mountains behind the city, where once-thick forests have been thinned for firewood to such an extent that in recent years people have been killed by rocks sluiced off the deforested hillsides during the rainy season.

I stayed in the relatively smart suburb of Murraytown with an aid worker friend employed by Oxfam GB, a British charity with a long history of involvement in Sierra Leone. She explained how Murraytown had been chosen for the Oxfam base specifically because the official residence of Sierra Leone's deputy president was also there, resulting in a greater likelihood of the suburb having mains electricity. That might have been true but during my visit there was not a single day without a power cut.

I saw the deputy president, or, rather, the deputy president's motorcade, while I was there. Turning on to the road outside our house was a new 4 × 4 jeep with tinted windows, led and followed by military-looking vehicles carrying uniformed men and with blue lights flashing and sirens howling. The convoy did not even slow as it manoeuvred past a large crowd of women and children gathered around a standpipe spewing water onto the road. Murraytown might be one of Freetown's better areas but, long after the war, its residents still have to queue by the roadside to fetch water by the bucketful.

I had hoped to see significant improvements in Freetown since my first visit. It was seven years since the then president, Ahmed Tejan Kabbah, had famously declared an end to the conflict by announcing in Krio '*da war don don* [the war is finished]' and in those years hundreds of millions of pounds had been provided in bilateral donations and foreign aid, mostly from Britain. But the truth is that Freetown remains a creaking, crowded, chaotic mess, with families washing in polluted streams in the city centre as basic municipal infrastructure fails to cope. Some modest repair work had been carried out on buildings damaged during the war but in the face of a growing, impoverished population the work seemed like tokenism.

Despite the squalor, it is possible for members of the Sierra Leonean elite – along with NGO workers, diplomats and well-paid expatriates – to live well. These are the people who could realistically consider buying the villas with 'boys' quarters' I had seen advertised back at the airport. But for the vast majority of Sierra Leone's population this sort of lifestyle is unimaginable. The lack of local production means that shops, still mostly owned by Lebanese immigrants, are stocked with expensively imported goods. Members of the elite retreat with their shopping to houses with high security walls, where the only way to guarantee power is to arrange for your own generator and the only way to ensure regular water is to arrange for your own plastic reservoir tanks. Since 2000 the main cosmetic change I noticed was that the outsides of these large perimeter walls were covered with adverts not for beer or milk powder as before, but for the many local mobile phone companies which had boomed since the war. Instead of printed billboards many of the ads were skilfully hand-painted by locals. Using the template of a page torn from a glossy magazine carrying the advert, the artists would stand in the sunshine meticulously magnifying each image onto the cement walls.

Along many of the main arteries in Freetown I saw clumps of signposts marking the headquarters of aid groups, ranging from the leviathans of the UN, with their multi-billion-pound annual turnovers, to tiny faith-based, private organisations. But there was still scant evidence that the efforts of the aid groups were truly bringing the country on. During my visit a ripple of exasperation passed through the foreign aid community when a survey of all public hospitals in Sierra Leone found only one working X-ray machine serving a country of roughly six million people. And a few weeks later the government had to issue a public statement when survivors of an oil pipeline explosion were taken to Connaught Hospital, one of the largest public health centres in Freetown, only to be told the pharmacy had not a single painkiller or antibiotic.

I got my own sense of Freetown's developmental problems on my way to meet John, a senior official responsible for some of the best-funded humanitarian programmes in one of the world's most aid-dependent countries. I could not spot a single new road built in Freetown since the war and yet the number of vehicles had ballooned. I saw new-looking jeeps, owned almost always by aid groups or Lebanese businessmen, but the vast majority of the extra vehicles on the roads were not new at all. They were beaten-up jalopies shipped to Sierra Leone from northern Europe to see out the end of their days as taxis. Many still had white national-identification discs with black letters – B for Belgique, F for France, D for Deutschland – and plenty had ski racks on their roofs, something that even the enterprising cabbies of Freetown had not worked out a use for. Most had had their bodywork customised with painted messages addressing Jesus or Allah depending on the faith of their new owner. 'Blood of Christ' was my favourite.

The lack of new roads combined with the surge in car numbers could mean only one thing: traffic-jam hell. Rather than fold myself into a slow-moving, oven-hot poda-poda, I started out on foot for John's office, turning towards the sea at Congo Cross and walking down past King Tom, a promontory still named for the Temne chief who signed the treaty creating the Province of Freedom more than 200 years ago. The Greenes visited this area when they passed through Freetown in 1935 and Graham Greene was impressed by the simplicity and elegance of the native huts among the palm trees. Seventy years later and those huts had multiplied into a vast shanty town where the normally sweet scent of Sierra Leone was spoiled by foul-smelling smoke from fires lit on a massive open tip and stagnant water in a river so clogged with sewage and rubbish it seemed to have stopped flowing altogether. The only apparent movement in the riverbed came from a large pig, swilling through the stinking gloop.

'The truth is that in spite of all these years of work Sierra Leone still scores lowest on almost all the major development indicators – infant mortality, maternal death in childbirth, life expectancy. By many standards Sierra Leone is the poorest country on earth, even though it receives so much help. It feels like a stone being rolled along the riverbed, too heavy to ever float upwards,' John explained over a cup of tea. His office fridge was not working so we used powdered milk.

'After all the money and all the years, does that depress you?' I asked. 'Do those dismal performance indicators not sap your enthusiasm for the job?'

John paused. His headquarters were located high up on one of the Freetown peninsula's hill ranges with impressive views towards the Atlantic. For a moment he looked out to sea.

'Strangely, it doesn't. The greatest achievement of these past few years has been peace. Those indicators tell you nothing about the fact that one of the worst wars in Africa's history, one the cruellest, one of the nastiest, was brought to an end. Christ, during the war do you think it was even possible to gather meaningful data? There have been two presidential elections since the war ended, peaceful elections that is. And in one of those elections the president not only lost, he handed over power without a single gunshot. You have got to remember that for Sierra Leone that represents huge progress.

'The achievement of these years has been no war and to the extent that aid programmes have helped with that I think we have every reason to be proud.

'But the reality is that Sierra Leone is not out of the woods. This place is very, very fragile and the biggest threat comes from a source nobody would have predicted a few years ago – Colombia and its cocaine barons.'

In July 2008 the extent of Sierra Leone's involvement in international drug smuggling was revealed when a twin-engine Cessna 441 Conquest made an unexpected landing at Lungi airport. The crew asked the tower for permission to land saying they were low on fuel, which was true as they had just flown all the way across the Atlantic from an airstrip in Venezuela close to its border with Colombia. What they failed to mention was that on board they had 703.5 kg of refined cocaine packed in Bible-sized blocks. And what the tower failed to mention in return was that the Sierra Leonean police were on to them. The first the crew knew that something was amiss was when the airport fire tender drove towards them erratically as they taxied. It made the three crew members panic, shutting off the engines, jumping to the ground and trying to escape on foot. They were chased down by policemen while officers hiding on the fire engine secured the plane and its contraband. The Sierra Leone security forces then moved to round up the reception committee, smugglers who had gathered at Lungi waiting for the plane to arrive, and their accomplices on the other side of the estuary in Freetown.

There was a series of chases as jeeps driven by smugglers roared away from the airport but the potholed roads of Sierra Leone are not made for quick getaways and several of the smugglers dumped their vehicles. One bright police officer gave the order that any non-black person found travelling by poda-poda in the north of the country should be arrested and over the next few days all the gang members were picked up.

After a four-month-long trial, one of the longest in Sierra Leone's criminal justice history, fifteen people were convicted of drugs-related offences. Three of the convicted, American passport-holders, were of sufficient value to the US authorities to be deported to New York to face fresh drug-dealing charges. Back in Freetown, the cocaine, which had been kept as evidence in the trial under the supervision of British soldiers from an army training team, was disposed of by burning in a ceremonial bonfire. The authorities insisted all 703.5 kg went up in smoke.

While the Sierra Leonean authorities can be congratulated for the way in which they dealt with the case, the worry is that other flights might have got through. Only one other cocaine flight is known to have reached Lungi, one that landed in December 2007 before being allowed to continue so that the authorities in Britain could track its onward smuggling route. It is likely there have been other flights the authorities never knew about. There is no real demand for cocaine in Sierra Leone and the smugglers are only interested in the country, along with others in West Africa, as transit points to move their product north into Europe. Their assumption is that weak, corruptible governments in the region can be bought off.

The scale of the threat that drug smuggling poses to Sierra Leone was spelled out in uncharacteristically direct language by Ban Ki-moon, the UN Secretary-General, speaking after the plane seizure. He described cocaine trafficking as 'the biggest single threat to Sierra Leone'.

John added his opinion about the scale of the threat: 'Don't forget that the war in Sierra Leone went on for ten years or so, killing tens of thousands of people, largely because rebels could get a hold of a few million dollars from diamonds way out in the east of the country. The sums of money the drug barons can offer are many times bigger and that can buy you a hell of a lot of rebels.'

I headed back to my NGO house with its high security walls, private generator and kitchen where breakfast cereal had to be stored in Tupperware boxes to deter cockroaches. I struggled not to let John's portentous analysis get me down. I was keen for a more positive vision of Freetown and for that I would have to go and speak to a blind man.

To get to Professor Eldred Jones's house I did what I had been strongly advised against. I rode pillion on a motorbike taxi. Known as 'okadas', they buzz through the catatonic Freetown traffic, providing an effective if hazardous means of transport. My driver came from the fearless school of okada riders, nipping through gaps I never thought he would get through. Several times I closed my eyes, squeezed in my thighs to make our outline as narrow as possible and prayed. I was about to embark on a long trek through the African bush and I would need my kneecaps in working order.

It took some time but I eventually relaxed enough to reopen my eyes. We passed lines of schoolchildren wearing uniforms lifted straight from the 1950s, girls in felt hats and stiffly pleated skirts, boys well into their teens squeezed into short trousers. Quite how their families kept the uniforms so immaculate when living in the derelict shanties of modern Freetown was beyond me. At Congo Cross, a notorious choke point for vehicles, a policeman on traffic duty waved his arms energetically at the stationary traffic. His black beret, blue tunic and creased serge trousers seemed to come straight from the era of National Service in Britain. He looked like an extra in an amateur drama society production.

As the road began to climb a hill the bike slowed, its engine racing against my body weight and the steep incline. Near a bridge over a mountain stream I saw a sign that said *nor pis yah*. As so often with Krio I had to speak the words out loud before I could work out what they meant. A group of women and children did not seem to be paying the sign much attention as they carried out their ablutions in the watercourse. This stream was close to the catchment of King Jimmy brook, once a source of fresh water so sweet it brought eighteenth-century sailors here from across the seas. The stream still flows today, indeed there is a market named after the King Jimmy stream down on the city waterfront, but today it is a disease-ridden open sewer and the once sandy beach is one great vermin-infested mat of discarded rubbish, rhythmically rucked by the estuary surf.

The road continued to climb, passing abandoned Second World War emplacements where naval guns had once been installed to cover the approaches to Freetown harbour. As a British colony, Sierra Leone had played a modest part in the defeat of Germany. With U-boats menacing re-supply convoys to and from America, allied ships would cling to the African coastline and creep all the way from Britain down to the Sierra Leone River estuary, where the Freetown harbour provided an excellent location to gather convoys in preparation for the trans-Atlantic run. And with the Mediterranean blocked to allied shipping, freighters heading to the Indian Ocean were obliged to take the longer route all the way around Africa, often putting in to Freetown. The harbour got so busy that the older generation from Freetown remember it at times as a solid, grey mass of military shipping.

During the war a military hospital and barracks had been built above the gun emplacement, further up the flank of Mount Aureol, a site chosen deliberately to lift convalescent patients above the ill humours of the city centre. It commanded wonderful views over the estuary and the peninsula, and when the war eventually ended the old wards were converted into halls of residence for Fourah Bay College's new campus. Up until the civil war began in 1991 the college had done well, gaining university status after forming a link with Durham

University in Britain. Leo Blair, whose son Tony was to become British prime minister, worked as an academic at Durham and he came out to Freetown to serve as an exam invigilator several times in the 1960s.

I had been introduced to Prof. Jones during my reporting trips to Sierra Leone, learning to value his erudite and authoritative perspective. When I arrived at his home on a cloudless February morning in 2009, the eighty-four-year-old retired academic spoke with the same warm chuckle I remembered and he began by reminiscing about arriving with the first intake to use the new campus in the abandoned military base.

'I can remember how we slept in the old hospital wards before they were converted. There was military equipment everywhere and when they were preparing to throw away some of the old machinery from the barracks kitchens I acquired it and we have used it ever since in our garden.'

We were sitting on his lawn and he motioned his hand vaguely towards the herbaceous borders. Peering closely I could see what he was referring to. Large cauldrons on cast-iron pedestals that were once used to prepare meals for legions of British servicemen had been rust-proofed and painted before being decoratively filled with flowering plants.

The professor's house was in the village of Leicester, one of the first communities set up for 'recaptives', high up on Mount Aureol, a mile or so above the university. If his village had strong historical links, his own bloodline read like the genome of Sierra Leone's freed-slave history. His father's family were 'recaptives' from Nigeria and his mother's birth certificate described her as a 'Maroon, Liberated African'. Born in 1925, he had been brought up during Freetown's golden age when, still under British colonial rule, it was establishing itself as a city many compared to Athens.

'I was born in a nursing home down on Sackville Street at a time when it was normal for all people in Freetown, black and white, to have access to maternity care. Of course it was not all easy back then. My mother had ten children but only four of us survived to adulthood,' Prof. Jones explained as we sat in the shade of a tree. His wife of fifty-six years, Marjorie, clucked round him constantly, making sure he was not in the direct sunshine and that our water glasses were full. He continued in the declamatory style of someone well used to lecturing.

'I went to a grammar school where I was taught by African teachers. And I married Marjorie, whose father was a trained barrister from Sierra Leone who had been recruited to work in another West African country, Gambia. Back then Freetown was the source of professionals who were the pick of the region, taking their skills and expertise from country to country. I studied at Oxford and when I came back to Freetown in 1953 I went to Fourah Bay to teach English literature and never really left. I eventually became Principal in 1974 and served until retirement in 1985.'

I asked about the war. The breezy, hilltop location of Leicester overlooking Freetown appeared wonderful in peacetime but it must have been dangerously exposed when the rebels advanced on the city.

'We had it all here. There were child soldiers on the road outside, dragging through the dirt guns that were bigger than they were. And at one time we had Nigerian peacekeepers firing from one side and rebels firing from the other. Our neighbour's house was hit in the crossfire but we escaped unscathed. During all the years of war we only ever left for two weeks when the army, the Sierra Leone army that is, told us to move a mile or so down the hill for our own safety. When we got back some of our property had been stolen and I am pretty sure it was the army that did it.'

There was an air of optimism about Prof. Jones that you rarely find in Freetown and I found it uplifting. Outside the walls of his compound, the road was as pitted and the village as decrepit as many of Freetown's downtown shanties but inside his house was no different from a much-loved home in British suburbia, albeit with slightly more exotic plant life in the garden. The lawn was trimmed, the borders beautifully arranged and the veranda laid out for maximum enjoyment of a stunning Atlantic panorama.

'The war was a nightmare, an awful period and it made me feel we had failed as a nation, but we had such strength before that I know we will rise again. We have a history that goes back two hundred years so the nightmare period of war lasting ten years or so is not the norm, and I feel certain we will come good again. The people of Sierra Leone were all over West Africa once as teachers, lawyers and civil servants. They were in demand and they can be in demand again. Yes, there is corruption here and we see it often today but tell me a country where there is not corruption. I know what Sierra Leone has been and I have faith it can be the same again.'

Marjorie was not in complete agreement.

'Come on, darling. When did we last have power? It's been three years now, I think, and I cannot remember when we last had water. And both of our children went to live overseas.'

I left them squabbling as warmly as newly-weds. As I walked through their house I had a familiar feeling, as if I were back in the home my grandparents retired to in Kent in the 1970s. The walls were crowded with ethnic pictures and hangings – African for the Joneses, Indian for my mother's parents – and no surface was free of prized ornaments and knick-knacks. Just as with my grandparents, the whole place felt a tiny bit time-worn as, with age, they struggled to keep on top of the dusting and the maintenance.

In the office a picture on the wall caught my eye. It was a college photograph from Corpus Christi, Oxford, foxed in places by tropical damp and a little washed out in others by sunshine. The year was 1951 and at first glance the students looked very much alike in their stolid tweed jackets and collared shirts. Row after row of faces made lean by rationing looked out from under meticulous partings, many wearing horn-rimmed spectacles, a few racy individuals daring to sport a cravat. And among the ranks of pimply Adam's apples my eye was drawn to the chubby face of a young Eldred Jones.

'I was lucky to get one of the first scholarships to Oxford from Sierra Leone, studying English literature as an undergraduate for three years at Corpus from Michaelmas 1950. I had a wonderful time enjoying student life to the full. I acted in the university dramatic society – acting was one of my great loves. And then there was the cricket, another passion from my childhood here in Freetown. I loved cricket so much that when I left school I took a year out and chose a job with the government printing service because it started early but finished early giving me more time for cricket practice.'

I had studied at Oxford myself in the 1980s and, like generations of its students before and since, had felt like I had briefly taken owner-ship of the place. I had close friends at Corpus and, as a journeyman cricketer, spent many long afternoons playing at the college ground, scene of a turning point in Eldred Jones's life.

'I wore glasses at the time but for some reason I had brought the wrong pair that day. We rode our bikes down to the ground as normal. You know how you have to cross the railway to get to the ground, so we parked our bikes on the gravel and crossed the railway on the footbridge.'

I smiled at the thought of the Venn diagrams of our very different lives intersecting. Many times I had used the same footbridge as Eldred Jones to play the same game on the same pitch.

'My love was batting and that day I went for a pull shot. I am not sure if it was because I could not see properly because of the glasses but I got a top edge and the ball shattered the socket of my right eye. That was the start of my vision problems.'

His sight got steadily worse over the next three decades and by 1986 he was completely blind. I left his house with its academic theses on Shakespeare, Oxford memorabilia and cherished knick-knacks, and went outside, back into the post-war Freetown of potholed roads and decrepit slums. Perhaps it was a blessing Professor Jones could not see what had become of what had once been dreamed of as the Province of Freedom.

Later, on close reading of my first edition of *Journey Without Maps*, I found Graham Greene had actually met Prof. Jones's father during the stopover in Freetown in January 1935. The reference had been excised in later editions by Graham Greene, presumably to save space, and Prof. Jones, who had spent his career teaching English literature, had never seen an original edition so did not know of his father's encounter with one of the most illustrious English authors of the twentieth century. His father had served as a customs inspector at Freetown harbour, the most senior rank then attainable by a native employee under British colonial rules, and had spent time with Graham Greene clearing the disembarkation of the expedition's equipment. In the original text Graham Greene writes glowingly about Mr Jones, the customs inspector, describing him as one of the few 'perfectly natural Africans whom I met in Sierra Leone'. It was a feeling I echoed one generation later.

CHAPTER 3

Looking for Bruno

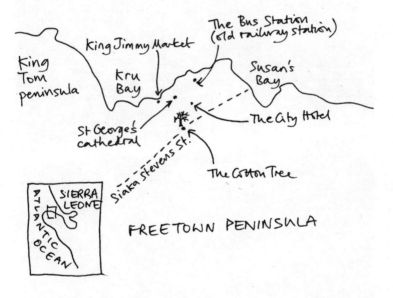

SIERRA LEONE RIVER ESTUARY

King Tom peninsula

King Jimmy Market

Kru Bay

The Bus Station (old railway station)

Susan's Bay

St George's cathedral

Siaka Stevens St.

The City Hotel

The Cotton Tree

SIERRA LEONE

ATLANTIC OCEAN

FREETOWN PENINSULA

Graham and Barbara Greene in Liverpool embarking for Africa, photographed for the *News Chronicle*, January 1935

It took over a week in Freetown to make ready for the trip. David, my travelling companion, was staying in a house his father had had built up in the hills and was spending his days breaking in new boots on training hikes through the jungle that still covers much of Freetown peninsula. We met almost every day to plan all the obvious things: what gear to take and what to discard, what we would do about clean drinking water and food, how we would get ourselves out of trouble. And we studied our maps to settle, as far as was possible, on the route the Greenes had taken. Most importantly of all, the meetings allowed us to start to get to know each other.

David is tall and thin, with the calm confidence that is common in Englishmen who, like him, have been to private school and Oxford University. At twenty-four, he was just over half my age but he appeared older than his years. His father had been based in Freetown on and off since 2000, so David had come here several times for holidays, giving him a rather different perspective from the one I had gained during my visits as a war correspondent. He was fully up to date on the city's better beach bars, newest night clubs and most competitive money-changers. When I told him how, during my years as a journalist in the Middle East, I had learned to love smoking water pipes, or narguileh, he immediately took me to a restaurant where the Lebanese owner claimed to offer the best narguileh in West Africa. As we sat down to smoke, David was greeted like a lost son by the manager and all the waitresses seemed to know him by name.

In recent years Sierra Leone has sought to reclaim its status as a tourist destination, placing great emphasis on a coastline so beautiful it once drew thousands of European visitors each year. Back in the 1970s its perfectly palm-fringed beaches were chosen as the location of a famous television advertisement for Bounty, a coconut-flavoured chocolate bar, under a slogan that promised 'The Taste of Paradise'. And since the war ended in 2002 early efforts have been made to lure tourists back, with the first guidebook dedicated solely to Sierra Leone being commissioned, and a few modest beach resorts springing up close to Freetown. But mainstream tourism in Sierra Leone is yet to take off and foreign visitors tended, like David, to be young, energetic and with some sort of connection to the country.

Surrounded by apple-scented narguileh smoke, David told me more of himself, about his years as a scholar at Sherborne, an upmarket private school in Britain, and how during the holidays he, his brother and mother would travel out to whichever exotic location his father's military career had taken him to. After school he studied theology for three years at Oxford, specialising in Islamic studies and finishing his degree in 2007 before starting a series of jobs in London.

'I chose theology because I was curious about faith and its impact on human history. It was not a vocational choice as I am not the most religious person, but trying to understand a little about Islam seemed to me a pretty important thing in the post-9/11 age. My problem is that I don't yet know what I want to do long term. I have been working in finance in London for the past few months and just about the only thing I know for certain is that I do not want to be doing that for the rest of my life.'

From the outset David displayed an admirable tact, something that immediately put my mind at rest. I can be competitive to a fault and a journey with someone who might challenge my ego-driven Alpha Male status could be a problem.

'I have been to Sierra Leone loads of times but never really gone much beyond Freetown. And I've never really done this sort of overland journey in Africa before, so if it's OK with you, I will simply fit in with whatever you arrange,' he said.

I found it touching to spot our generational differences. When it came to finances he explained he carried a small amount of cash but had printed out a list of money transfer offices in the provinces of Liberia where he planned to receive top-ups. His faith in virtual information was not one I shared. I knew the towns on the list barely existed let alone had functioning cash transfer offices. The internet has a way of homogenising the world, giving you results for online searches that look complete enough on screen but without accurate context. In many parts of the world such processing might work but not in remote West Africa. I assured David that between us we would be carrying enough dollars in cash to cover all our costs.

I could tell he was keen to get going but I urged patience. Friends of friends, who months earlier had made vague promises to provide guides, needed chasing and before we started out I wanted to make sure I had up-to-date names and details for contacts in the more remote areas. A major concern was that our journey involved three border crossings: from Sierra Leone into Liberia, from Liberia into Guinea and back into Liberia again. I spent days meeting local drivers, diplomats and aid workers asking mostly about the conditions around our first frontier crossing, but while I could find plenty of people who knew the area in general, nobody had crossed the border exactly where we needed to.

Sierra Leone has the roughly circular shape of a clockface and we needed to go from coastal Freetown, at nine o'clock, over to the far eastern edge, at three o'clock, a road journey of roughly 250 miles. In that area, the official border crossing to Liberia was near the remote Sierra Leonean settlement of Koindu, where a narrow dirt road provided, in the dry season at least, a functioning if modest artery for cross-border traffic, mostly aid convoys. But we wanted to follow the Greenes' route via the tiny and even more remote border village of Dawa, about 15 miles south of Koindu. During the war it had seen more than its fair share of action as it had been one of the busiest transit points for rebels entering Sierra Leone from Liberia, but in 2009 I could barely find a soul who had ever heard of Dawa and nobody could tell me if its nearby border crossing was open.

I was also closely watching developments in Guinea, still in flux after the coup prompted by the death on 22 December 2008 of the long-serving president, Lansana Conté. Many had assumed the presidency would pass to his son, Ousmane, a thuggish army officer notorious for ordering soldiers to open fire on opponents of his father's regime and for close links to Colombian drug smugglers using Guinea as a transit point for cocaine shipments to Europe. But Ousmane was outwitted by a cabal of junior officers who staged a coup and had him arrested. They would later parade him on national television confessing to playing a central mobster-like role in cocaine smuggling. The transfer of power to the soldiers had been bloodless but Guinea remained volatile and I was anxious to know what impact the coup might have on the remote part of the country we needed to transit.

A new and even more unexpected potential problem for our journey had also emerged: a plague of insects. Described by UN experts as 'army worms', they were in fact not worms but caterpillars, tiny, voracious little brutes reported to have appeared by the million in Lofa County, the northern district of Liberia we would soon be heading through. What made them particularly worrying for me was that medical specialists warned their faeces made streams, rivers and other water sources highly dangerous for humans. The Liberian government was taking the insect invasion so seriously it had announced a State of Emergency on 26 January 2009, just two days before David and I flew to Freetown. As soon as I heard the news, I headed to a pharmacy and sought advice but the owner, another member of the Lebanese business community, had never heard of army worms. I ended up simply buying yet more water purification tablets.

The days spent in the city served another very useful purpose in that they allowed me to acclimatise to West Africa, resetting my body to a mode of near continuous sweating and my mind to one of conserving effort. A power cut during my first night meant the fan in my room stopped working and within minutes I had wrestled myself awake in a fretful bundle of bedclothes. Discarding the sheets, I tried to starfish myself to sleep, spreading my limbs as far apart as they would go, but it did not work. Every contact point between skin and mattress was uncomfortably clammy and I lay awake fretting how I would cope *up-line*, where the West African hinterland enjoys none of the coastal cool of Freetown.

Slowly I began to recalibrate. Exploring town on foot I toned down my normal purposeful gait to more of a lope with longer, slower strides, as if walking through imaginary glue. And I learned to ignore the sweat drenching my shirt and to pause in every available puddle of shade. A guzzle from a water bottle would soon wash out of me so I took to nursing water, drinking more often but in tiny sips.

In spite of its squalor, Freetown offers up snatched moments of raw beauty. I would wake most mornings at dawn and take a cup of tea onto my balcony where a breeze was strong enough to move the mosquitoes on. Through light softened by smoke from nearby cooking fires and rubbish pyres, I would watch the mist lift over the coves separating Murraytown from the city centre. I was there during Harmattan, the season named after the dusty dry wind that blows outward from the void of the Sahara, making the leaves of cotton trees fall so their spreading branches look like fingers stretched out on terrified hands. One morning I watched a banana boat creep across an otherwise motionless bay raising an arrowhead of ripple and thought how little had changed since the days when rum-swilling pirates rowed the same inlet two hundred and fifty years before. I was rarely alone for my morning vigil. A vulture with feathery shoulders as bulky as a padded-up gridiron player would often watch me from its roost high on a palm tree. Its hooked beak would be silhouetted against the morning sky as its scaly neck cranked its head suspiciously from side to side, never quite taking its eye off me. When Graham Greene passed through Freetown in January 1935 he described counting seven vultures at one time from his downtown hotel window.

The Greenes hired three 'boys' in Freetown for the trip – one cook and a servant each – so I went in search of their descendants, asking an old journalist friend, Kelvin Lewis, to publish an appeal in the *Awoko* newspaper he edited. One morning I went to its offices in one of the frayed tower blocks off Siaka Stevens Street in the centre of town, to see if he had made any progress. Like newspaper offices the world over it was a muddle of old and new, with untidy piles of back copies on sub-editors' desks precariously frozen in mid-slither, under a web of power cables giving life to blinking internet modems, laptops and mobile phones.

'I am sorry but we have had no response to the request. I guess all of the relatives of Mr Greene's people are long gone.' Kelvin was shaking his head but I was distracted by the front-page picture of that day's edition. It showed a motionless lorry, axle-deep in muddy ruts, next to a story about how the road to Kailahun, the main town in the far east of Sierra Leone, was a national disgrace and how the government had pledged millions of pounds for its repair. Driving to Kailahun was the first part of the trip I was about to undertake.

During our ten-day stopover in Freetown I took several walks along Lumley Beach, the long stretch of sand on the westernmost edge of Freetown, going over the final details of the journey in my mind. It was along this beach in 2000 that I jogged with Phil Ashby, a British major from the Royal Marines who had just pulled off an amazing escape from RUF rebels. While serving as a UN military observer his upcountry compound had been surrounded by hostile gunmen and, fearing that rescue was unlikely, Maj. Ashby had slipped over the perimeter wall under cover of darkness with three other observers to escape on foot, a feat that earned him the Queen's Gallantry Medal. I met him after he made it safely back to Freetown but the thing that stuck in my mind were his comments about how enervating the climate and terrain were upcountry, and how, after one day, his march had left him disorientated with exhaustion. The poor man had become so tired that when he collapsed asleep in the bush he accidentally nudged the power switch on his satellite phone, running down the battery. And after returning home to Britain he lost the use of his legs, paralysed when his spinal cord was infected by a mystery virus probably picked up during his footslog through the jungle.

One of my beach walks took me to Lumley's golf course where I was interested to see what had changed since my last visit during the war. Back then, with rebels threatening the city, I had written a piece for the *Telegraph* about the bullet-holes in the roof of the empty clubhouse, the marauding monkeys waiting to pinch balls on the eighth fairway and the lack of an eighteenth – laid out between tidal mudflats and thick bush, the course only had space for seventeen holes. All this gave it a slightly fantastic, surreal air, as if it were a setting used in Julian Barnes's book *A History of the World in 10½ Chapters*, where a heavenly golf course turns into hell as a golf lover practises so much over eternity he can boringly hit a hole-in-one every time.

On this visit the clubhouse terrace was packed, the car park full. There were jeeps with diplomatic plates and others with the initials of aid groups stencilled on the side. In the shade of a tree I got talking to one of the club pros and he told me that the eighteenth hole was still missing and the monkeys still a menace. But when I tried to enter the clubhouse to check on the bullet-holes he barred my way and said: 'Members only, sir, members only.'

For Freetown's moneyed elite, such as senior government officials, foreign aid workers and well-connected businessmen, the city can be more than comfortable. Restaurants offer stunning seafood – I saw shellfish offered up as prawns that elsewhere round the world would be described as lobsters – and on the weekends the display of powerboats and jet skis along some of the beaches would not shame Saint-Tropez. A sushi restaurant had opened recently and every so often on the clogged roads of Freetown I would see high-end, luxury vehicles such as Hummers. For the vast bulk of the population, of course, this world is utterly unreachable and people are forced to struggle along in desperate poverty with little realistic hope of development – the stone being rolled along the riverbed, to borrow the analogy of my NGO friend John.

But I find there is also something unremittingly seedy about Freetown that reaches beyond the poverty and the squalor, the disease and the decay. Corruption seems to corrode all levels of life, from the boardrooms of the few functioning businesses in the city where backhanders have to be paid for contracts, to taxi customers on roads leading into the city where police, supposedly employed to fight corruption, set up illegal checkpoints demanding tolls.

The government of Sierra Leone goes through the motions of fighting corruption. Posters greet visitors at Lungi airport warning against illegal use of foreign currency and billboards stand next to some main roads with public service announcements urging all patriotic Sierra Leoneans to play their part in the fight against corruption. Indeed the Anglican cathedral that Graham Greene describes as such a landmark in 1935 Freetown is today overshadowed by a large office block snug next door that houses the country's Anti-Corruption Commission.

But the truth is corruption has become a way of life in a state as failed as Sierra Leone. Schools inflate the number of teachers on their staff roll to con the government into paying additional salaries that can then be stolen. Spot checks have to be carried out by government inspectors who arrive unannounced at schools to count how many teachers are actually on duty. A major post-war project to rehabilitate a rich iron ore mine at Lunsar involved the laying of a new railway track that would carry the ore to the coast. But no sooner had the new track and cabling been laid than it was stolen, taken to Freetown and loaded into containers for shipment overseas as scrap. The scale of the theft was so large it needed officials at the docks to be in on the scam. And when the plane carrying cocaine was seized at Lungi in 2008, the Minister of Transportation and Aviation lost his job on suspicion of involvement in the smuggling operation.

One of the most heartbreaking stories I heard came from a foreign professional whose company had tendered for a post-war government contract in Sierra Leone, a multi-million-dollar scheme to help in the humanitarian sector. When he told me what happened I thought about the billboards that picture senior government officials earnestly telling the poor and the needy of Sierra Leone to help in the fight against corruption.

When the final round of the tendering process came, each competitor was invited one-by-one into a boardroom in one of the tattered tower blocks in the centre of Freetown within walking distance of the Anti-Corruption Commission. There they faced a panel of senior government figures who asked them one final question before deciding the contract: 'How much are you going to give us in cash to be given the deal?' The most generous bribe won.

Similar stories were legion, with aid money being diverted and government spending not going where it should, jeopardising any hope of meaningful post-war economic development. In a country like Sierra Leone corruption feels like sand in an engine. No individual grain is going to do much harm but taken together over a long time the grains grind the engine to a halt.

Down on Lumley Beach the systemic poverty of Freetown was evident in the large number of prostitutes, pimps, pickpockets and chancers. During one of my walks there I recognised a man who had been on my flight from London. We had struck up a conversation at Heathrow airport and I remembered his rather vague account of why he was coming to Sierra Leone. Something about setting up a trading company, I had written in my notes. He was white and on the elderly side of middle-age with hair the colour of aubergine from clumsy self-dyeing. I had the setting sun behind me so he could not see me as I watched him lying on the edge of the beach up against a grassy bank, leering inappropriately at a Sierra Leonean girl in her late teens, plucking at the strap of her bikini top. It was a scene Graham Greene, the diviner of all things seedy, might have enjoyed.

If there is one central characteristic to Greeneland, the landscape created by Graham Greene through his writing, it is seediness and when the author reached Sierra Leone he found plenty of material to work with. *Journey Without Maps* was his first published work of non-fiction, but it reveals an interest in seediness as keen as in any of his novels. He describes the physical and moral 'shabbiness' of colonial

Freetown, a city infested by vultures with 'horrible tiny undeveloped heads' and framed by forested slopes of mountains that were 'a dull uninteresting green'. He mocks the twee etiquette of colonialism which was racist without being brave enough to admit it, preventing whites from going to the only cinema in town as it was frequented by blacks, and from associating publicly with members of the Lebanese business community. He writes that Freetown in 1935 had only two venues for a white man to 'do a pub crawl': the bar of the Grand Hotel, where the Greenes stayed for their four nights in Freetown, and the City Hotel. Both venues, he writes disparagingly, were full of whites pathetically trying to recreate England in Africa.

It was Graham Greene's description in the first edition of *Journey Without Maps* of a riotous Freetown evening with a drunken, time-serving colonist he named as 'Pa Oakley' that almost cost him his career as an author. After the book was released in 1936, a letter was received by the publishers, Heinemann, threatening a libel action on behalf of Sierra Leone's medical services director, a Yorkshireman called Philip Douglas Oakley. Graham Greene later wrote he did not know such a person existed but the similarity of name meant both he and Heinemann were dangerously exposed. In the company's archive I found a previously unpublished letter from Charles Evans, chairman of Heinemann, to Graham Greene hinting at the potentially dire financial consequences of the libel action.

> He [the company lawyer] seems to have good hopes of being able to settle the matter for a not too ruinous sum. Let us hope that he may. Did I tell you that the insurance company gave us a week's notice to cancel our policy and took us back only on condition that we paid double the premium and bore ourselves the first third of any costs or damages in forthcoming cases.

A hefty libel bill could have blighted Graham Greene's writing career before it had really started, but the two sides eventually reached an agreement that was not too 'ruinous' and the book was withdrawn from sale. It would be republished more than ten years later with all references to 'Pa Oakley' removed.

The Grand has long gone but I took with me to Freetown a photograph of Graham Greene outside the City Hotel. In *Journey*

Without Maps he describes its bar as the most lively in town, '. . . crowded and noisy because there's a billiard table; people are rather more dashing, get a little drunk and tell indecent stories; but not if there's a woman present'. In the photograph Graham Greene, hands in pockets, feet in sandals, leans on the stone balustrade at the bottom of a flight of steps leading up to a veranda shaded by a floor above supported on pale stone columns.

The hotel ceased functioning during the war and was gutted by fire in 2000 but I wanted to see if the façade was still there and maybe have my own souvenir photograph taken leaning on the same balustrade. I was four days too late. A gang of men was just completing the demolition of the building. Without cranes or power tools they had proceeded in the most basic way possible, knocking it down stone by stone with sledgehammers. In spite of the hard labour and dry-season heat, the foreman, in a floppy tweed cap that made him look like a 1920s American golfer, had not a drop of sweat on him as he clambered down from the mound of masonry to speak to me. In the wreckage I spotted one of the distinctively shaped capitals that topped the columns behind Graham Greene in the picture.

I tracked down the old owner's grandson, Victor Ferrari, a mixed-race Sierra Leonean who spoke perfect English and rolled his 'r's with the faintest of Krio lilts when he explained what happened.

'We had to knock it down. The government started making announcements by radio that all abandoned buildings in the city centre must be replaced so I arranged for the demolition. It is sad because it is part of my family history but times must change.'

Later, over drinks and a longer conversation at the Ferrari family home, Victor brought the hotel bar back to life for me with a collection of old photographs. There was no power so we had to sit outside in the twilight as he told how his grandfather, Freddie, an Italian-Swiss from Lugano, arrived in Freetown as a child in the 1920s before taking over the City Hotel and running it for decades. Victor, now thirty, had grown up there, its bar his childhood playroom. The pictures were taken from the 1950s onwards, some time after Graham Greene first visited, showing customers – all white men – enjoying a drink. Fashion changes were obvious, with the men in the older pictures wearing collared shirts and ties, their hats hanging behind them on hooks, while in the more recent snapshots there were T-shirts and sunglasses. But the bar appeared just as crowded as in Graham Greene's description, with bottles of iced beer set up on the bar's curved counter, the faces of the customers sweaty with a mix of alcohol-infused conviviality and climate-induced torpor.

Graham Greene had met Freddie, describing him in a 1968 newspaper article on Sierra Leone as the ' kindly sad Swiss landlord'. Victor recounted stories of granddad Freddie's passion for Sierra Leone and how he would travel across the entire country on hunting and fishing trips, falling in love with a local woman and starting a family. Later in life he was involved in diamond dealing and took to keeping a gun behind the bar to protect the safe in his office. At the age of seventy-seven Freddie fell over on the hotel stairs breaking his arm so badly he had to go hospital. He died a few months later in 1993.

The decline of the Ferrari family's fortunes illustrates a reversal of the flow that originally brought freed slaves from Britain to Sierra Leone. Like thousands of others fleeing its recent chaos, now the grandson of one of the country's most established hoteliers lives in London.

The exodus of those fleeing poverty and post-war chaos in Sierra Leone today is one of the country's most serious problems. I saw a half-page advert in a newspaper warning people not to be taken in by criminals pretending to work for the UN and offering Sierra Leoneans the chance to resettle overseas in exchange for money. 'Beware of these Conmen!!!!!' was the message of the advert.

Many risk everything by taking to open boats from the African coast hoping to make landfall in Europe, a hazardous exercise that can end in mass drowning or death from dehydration. Other would-be emigrants are more sly. In 2002 most Sierra Leonean athletes attending the Commonwealth Games in Manchester did a bunk and sought a new life in Britain. Four years later, exactly the same thing happened at the games in Melbourne. But the case that touched me most was that of three young Sierra Leonean men who worked at the Freetown railway museum set up after the war by a British army officer and train enthusiast. Steve Davies worked alongside the young men for over a year as they painstakingly restored antique rolling stock and refurbished a tatty old railway-yard shed into a museum. As a thank-you, he arranged visas for all three to visit Britain's National Railway Museum in York. Two of them used their visas to abscond.

Graham Greene normally saw virtue in seediness, but in Freetown his compass switched, describing with a pejorative edge the 'seedy civilisation' planted in West Africa by British colonials and contrasting it with the purity of all things African.

> Everything ugly in Freetown was European: the stores, the churches, the Government offices, the two hotels; if there was anything beautiful in the place it was native: the little stalls of the fruit-sellers which went up after dark at the street corners, lit by candles; the native women rolling home magnificently from church on a Sunday morning . . .

The book's criticism of colonial Sierra Leone is so strong that Graham Greene later felt obliged to offer an apology. *Journey Without Maps* was written after spending only a few days in Freetown, but during his year-long wartime service in Freetown with MI6 he learned a greater affection for the city. Writing in 1946 he referred to *Journey Without Maps*, saying, 'I can look back now with a certain regret at the hard words I used about Freetown . . .'

It was based on his time as a spy in Freetown that Graham Greene wrote *The Heart of the Matter*, an account of an adulterous police officer in wartime British colonial Africa tortured by guilt at his infidelity and blackmailed by a diamond smuggler. By the time the book came out in 1948 Graham Greene was enjoying success not just in publishing but in cinema, and a film of *The Heart of the Matter* was released in 1953. Filmed on location in Freetown, it has Trevor Howard playing the lead, stalking purposefully around the grid of streets centred on the Cotton Tree, rattan cane tucked under police-uniformed arm. The film has a wonderfully authentic West African air, with Howard's permanent, tell-tale slick of sweat in the coin-sized dip where his collarbones meet.

The film is the closest I can get to the Freetown Graham and Barbara Greene would have experienced. The streets were swept, kerbstones painted and buildings well-maintained and yet the author still saw shabbiness and seediness, not just moral but physical. I can only guess at what he would make of Freetown today, with its systemic post-war corruption, flat-lining economy and beachfront swarmed by prostitutes.

Critical though he was of small-minded British colonists, he saved his most acid criticism for the Krios, the freed slaves of Freetown and their descendants, who fell between the two worlds of native black African and colonial white outsider. Some of his criticism veered towards the racist.

> The men were less assured; those of them who were Creoles [Krios] had been educated to understand how they had been swindled, how they had been given the worst of two worlds . . . It would be so much more amusing if it was all untrue, a fictitious skit on English methods of colonisation. But one cannot continue long to find their painful attempt at playing the white man funny; it is rather like the chimpanzee's tea-party, the joke is all on one side.

It feels to me a clumsy remark that suggested Graham Greene bought in to one of the conceits of colonialism, the thought that black men could not rule themselves and that any attempt to do as their colonial overlords did represented folly. It felt a disservice to people like Professor Eldred Jones who, as a young educated Freetown man in the 1940s and 1950s, used to go to a dining society that met regularly in the City Hotel with a strict black-tie dress code. It seemed unfair to sneer so sharply at him simply for 'playing the white man'.

The Greenes passed through Freetown at the height of the colonial project when self-rule by the native population was so far into the future as to be unthinkable, but this was not the reason why Graham Greene disparaged Sierra Leone's colonialism so sharply. He criticised it precisely because it sought to recreate in Africa something he had come to distrust, even despise. Graham Greene saw Europe in the 1930s as a place of economic depression, political extremism and dubious morality, so colonials were to be loathed for aspiring to copy the civilisation achieved by, for example, Britain.

I was passing through almost fifty years after independence and my gloomy overview was similarly coloured by the context from which I viewed Sierra Leone. After independence in 1961, political infighting gave way to corruption, then dictatorship and finally war, crippling Sierra Leone's development. High expectations at independence that things would get better for the native population were not met. As I got to know Freetown's rhythms I kept thinking about Hong Kong and historical parallels between the two places – both wonderful natural harbours on the edge of a continent, both claimed as colonies by Britain in the nineteenth century and both developed along roughly similar lines by white outsiders. But while Hong Kong grew into a hugely wealthy entrepôt for silk and other products, Freetown didn't. The presence nearby of valuable natural resources, most notably diamonds and iron ore, served to hinder, not help, the country. In contrast to Hong Kong, trade in Sierra Leone did not beget trade, it begat rivalry, stagnation and ultimately war. As my journey progressed I would try to find out more about why this might be.

The beauty I found in Freetown was all natural – seascapes, forested mountains, dawn calm – and the ugliness manmade – squalid markets, broken-down buildings, beachfront hustlers. In Hong Kong it was the synthetic that made it a wonder, its steepling, neon-trimmed night skyline, its foreshore impossibly crowded with build-ing developments. Freetown had the air of a black-and-white-movie starlet, once beautiful with the world at her feet but who failed to make the leap to the modern era, condemned to grow ever older and uglier with nothing but memories of what might have been.

There was one more visit I needed to make before setting off and it involved chimpanzees, animals that once lived in large numbers in West Africa but which have seen their population dwindle through friction with humans. On one of my previous trips to Freetown I had written a light-hearted story about chimps, focusing on an individual male called Bruno who had become a symbol of the civil war's cruelty. But since I last saw Bruno, he had been involved in a sinister and intriguing incident.

To reach the Tacugama Chimpanzee Sanctuary you have to take the high road, east out of Freetown. You climb up past Wilberforce Barracks, named for William Wilberforce, the anti-slavery cam-paigner, and through Hill Station, a settlement built above the heat of the city for white colonials in the early twentieth century. Some of the original houses remain with their distinctive cast-iron stilts raising them high off the ground to avoid ant and rat infestation. Hill Station used to be served by its own narrow-gauge railway but it was abandoned in 1929 and only the route of the track remains, now a tarmac-topped road, and the grassy outline of the old terminus with its original Hill Station sign. During his time as a spy, Graham Greene would take late afternoon walks up the old railway line, describing how the roseate stone of the track glowed warmly in the sunset.

The first time I went in search of the chimpanzee centre I remember having great problems finding it. After Hill Station, the road crests a rise, narrows and begins to wind downhill through thickening rainforest. For a long time I struggled to explain to my taxi driver what I was looking for, carefully repeating the words several times – 'the site of the chimpanzee rehabilitation centre'. At first he looked baffled before his eyes suddenly sparkled and he exclaimed in Krio *'da ples weh day men da baboons'* – the place where they mend the baboons. Laughing loudly, he needed only a few minutes to find the turn off the narrow road for the steep drive up through the forest that leads to Tacugama.

David joined me this time after I arranged an interview with the founder, Bala Amarasekaran, a well-meaning accountant who set up the centre when he could no longer cope with having an adolescent chimpanzee in his home. Bala had arrived in Freetown as a teenager in 1978 when his parents moved from Sri Lanka and after completing his professional training he set up home, married and began working. He had told the story countless times of meeting the infant Bruno, an orphaned chimp whose parents had been shot and eaten by hunters, but the emotion in his voice was still there when he went through it once more for us.

'We were driving through a village out in the provinces near the town of Magburaka in 1989 when we spotted this baby chimpanzee outside a hut, tied to a post by a piece of string. I could see he was dehydrated and in a bad way. I had never thought of taking on a chimpanzee before but there was something about this tiny animal that made a connection, so I offered to take him. At first the "owner" refused but when I offered thirty dollars he changed his mind.

'We did not know if he would even survive that first night with us. To be honest we did not know what we were doing, as my wife and I had never done anything like this before. We bought a baby's bottle and started to bottle-feed him with milk, that's all we could think of. The day we got him home was the day Frank Bruno, the British boxer, fought Mike Tyson. Bruno was the underdog in the fight so that's what we would call this little underdog – we would call him Bruno.'

They might have made it up as they went along but whatever they were doing clearly worked. Bruno thrived. Within a few months he was bouncing around the Amarasekaran family home wreaking unintentional havoc. When word got around that Bala had given Bruno a home, they were approached by a Scotsman who was about to move back home. He had had a chimpanzee in Freetown as a pet for years but could not take it with him so he begged them to look after it. Others soon came forward with chimps recovered from the slums of Freetown and villages outside, and by the early 1990s Bala had eight chimpanzees living on his property.

'We built cages for them in the garden but of course they needed exercise so we used to let them out. Sure there was a lot of damage from things getting broken and it was chaos at times, but for the most part we could cope because they were young, apart from one older female who had been kept by a group of soldiers who fed her valium to keep her under control. The poor thing had developed all sorts of mental and behavioural problems. At sunset we would all go for a walk around the area we lived in, Smart Town, and that must have been some sight. Every so often one or two ran away but they all came back eventually, and we got used to our neighbours knocking on our door to say one of our chimpanzees had stolen eggs or ripped up some tin roofing or got up to some other mischief. We used to pay out all the time.'

As his downtown menagerie grew too large, Bala put together a plan to try to return the animals to the wild. He persuaded the Sierra Leone government to sign up to a joint programme and in 1995 Tacugama was created, helped by seed money from the European Union.

'Then all we had was a hundred acres of rainforest up here in the mountains. There was nothing here, no road, no infrastructure, no buildings. We had to come up with the money and the manpower for all of that, but slowly and steadily the project took shape. We cut the road, we built rooms for the chimpanzees, we created a quarantine section for new arrivals and then we built fenced-in compounds out in the forest where the chimpanzees could learn to be chimpanzees again.'

More chimps kept arriving but from the beginning Bruno had established himself as the Alpha Male, the dominant leader of the community. It was around then that I wrote my *Telegraph* piece on Bruno.

I can remember how the Tacugama guide warned me not to get too close to the fence around the enclosure. It was sound advice because when we got to the viewing site a large rock, about the size of a brick, came hurtling out of the thicket at head height and hit the wire netting, punching it outwards to within a few inches of my nose. Amid a loud chorus of chimpanzee screams and barks I could almost hear a 'boing' sound as the fence sprang back into shape, flinging the rock backwards into the bush.

Speaking in 2009 Bala explained Bruno's behaviour: 'A lot of people thought Bruno was aggressive but they missed the point. He had the character and the personality to establish himself as the Alpha Male and as such it was his primary job to protect the others. We had shelling here during the war, several times the area was bombed by jets and three times rebels came through here driving me and the staff away, looting our property and stealing everything, even the medicines for the chimpanzees. Bruno and the others learned strangers must be treated with suspicion so by throwing a rock he was simply telling you, a stranger, to back off.'

Under Sierra Leonean law it had been illegal since 1972 to kill or capture chimpanzees, but it was only after the war that serious efforts could be made to enforce the law. As rural communities learned more about the legal protection enjoyed by chimps, so more animals were handed over, pushing the population at Tacugama past eighty. The chimpanzees were split into new family groups under different Alpha Males, more rooms were built, new enclosures were set up behind electric fences where the animals could spend their days and more research was carried out by primatologists who came from all over the world. None of this research, however, prepared Bala and his colleagues for what happened early on Sunday 23 April 2006.

Bruno was by then the leader of a thirty-one-strong group of chimpanzees who lived together in the same accommodation block. The animals had been given breakfast and, as normal, allowed out into their forest enclosure, which is connected to their room by a 15-foot-long caged tunnel with two lockable doors, one where the tunnel is connected to the room and the other where the tunnel is connected to the enclosure. After the animals had all moved into the enclosure, a member of staff double-locked the door by the fence using a metal padlock and, for added security, a wooden block shaped perfectly to fit into the groove where the door slid to open. With the block in situ the door could not be moved even if the padlock was not in place.

Following routine, the staff member crawled through the tunnel to clean it. The animals had dispersed into the bush and he noticed nothing out of the ordinary as he finished in the tunnel and turned back to start work in the accommodation block. He did not do anything he had not done before but with hindsight he made two crucial errors – leaving open both the tunnel door, where it joins the accommodation block, and the main door, the one used by humans to access the accommodation block. Clearing up a night's mess from thirty-one chimpanzees is a serious task that takes at least an hour and it was in this window of time that Bruno's group found a way through the locked door where the tunnel joins the fence.

First the animals smashed the padlock. This was not easy as it hung awkwardly for them to reach, behind iron struts and wiring. Somehow they managed to get at it and crack it open with rocks. They then faced the second security measure, the wooden block – and this is where Bala and his colleagues were truly amazed. The chimpanzees had fashioned pointed sticks with which to fish the piece of timber out of its blocking position. They had broken off branches from trees in the enclosure and then sharpened their ends before using them to reach through the wire fence and free the block. After the incident, sixteen sharpened sticks in a range of sizes were found near the door. Bala is certain the tools were prepared in advance as there was not enough time to make them spontaneously.

The first the cleaner knew of the breakout was when he heard chimpanzees screaming behind him in the accommodation block. He turned to see two very excited and therefore very dangerous adult chimps. Not surprisingly the man ran, raising the alarm. The standard protocol at Tacugama in a breakout is for all the staff to first make themselves safe and then worry about the animals. With the cleaner fleeing, all thirty-one members of Bruno's group made their way through the tunnel and the accommodation block, out into the open.

Bala was not there that morning so control of the incident fell to his senior staff member, Moses Kappia, one of the longest-serving guides. Moses recalled the initial chaos as the chimpanzees celebrated their freedom by crashing around the treetops, climbing on the roofs of the buildings and screeching as if to wake the dead. But after the initial furore the animals began to calm down while staff members made sure all the humans were accounted for.

'You have to remember they had never been out of their accommodation blocks before so they were in unfamiliar territory. In a situation like this chimpanzees tend to stick to what they know so there was a high chance they would stay together and not leave,' Bala explained.

The staff members are trained in the use of blowpipes with darts that can put a chimpanzee to sleep, but with thirty-one out at once they simply could not cope. Since opening in 1995 Tacugama had only ever had a single breakout and that involved just one animal.

Moses meanwhile was growing anxious about getting a message down to the village at the bottom of the road to stop people coming up to the camp and running into the escaped chimpanzees. He waited for a quiet moment, slipped outside and set off down the steep road towards the village. He thought he had got away with it but then he glanced over his shoulder to see Bruno running after him. Remembering his training, Moses ripped off his clothes and shoes as he ran and dropped them on the dirt road, giving Bruno cause to pause and sniff them. It bought him enough time to get away but instead of sticking to the road, Moses, now fully naked, took a short cut through the forest towards the village. On that decision a man's life turned.

Driving up the forest road at exactly that moment came a taxi. In it was a Sierra Leonean driver, Issa Kanu, three Americans who had been working as contractors building a new US Embassy in Freetown and their local contact, Melvin Mammah. By taking the short cut, Moses missed the car as it drove up the track.

The exact details of what happened next are a bit unclear but what is certain is that Bruno appeared in front of the taxi, forcing it to stop. Melvin told me the occupants did not know anything was wrong at this point and the Americans started taking photographs until Bruno grabbed the bumper of the car, an old Peugeut 305 estate, and started heaving the vehicle up and down. The driver tried to reverse but got lodged up against a boulder and it was at that moment Melvin knew they were in trouble.

'I was sitting in the middle of the back seat and I shouted for everyone to wind up their windows and drop their latches,' he remembered. 'The chimp came round to the left side of the car and I started to push the American who was next to me into the boot over the back seat so he was out of the way but the chimpanzee then broke through the window and grabbed my left arm. We had a tug of war – he was trying to pull me out and I was pulling like crazy the other way. We were not going anywhere so he calmly bit my left thumb straight off.

'I can remember his black teeth and my first thought was about tetanus. He chewed it a bit and spat it out and then bit off my left forefinger. I was pulling all the time, punching him in the face with my other hand as he pulled the other way. His strength was amazing. I could do nothing about it. When he bit the forefinger off his teeth got a hold of my middle finger too, pulling it out so it was left hanging by just a bit of skin. There was blood everywhere. I could see it coming out of me every time my heart pumped but the animal would not let go.' Melvin lit a cigarette as he recounted the story, using his right hand to light the lighter and pincering the cigarette between the two remaining fingers on his left.

The driver then got into gear and shot forward but only as far as a gate across the road near a reservoir which he smashed through before the car got stuck again. In the confusion, the car had to be abandoned. As Melvin struggled to get away, Bruno grabbed him by the right leg and bit into his ankle. One of the Americans, Gary Brown, stopped, grabbed a heavy branch and came back for Melvin.

'Gary was shouting, "Get Off Him, Mother Fucker!" time after time and hitting him with the branch until the animal stopped and walked away. I don't know what would have happened if Gary had not helped me.'

The Americans stayed with Melvin but the driver had fled on foot. Instead of continuing straight down the road he turned up the short but steep final drive to the main entrance of Tacugama. He must have thought this was the quickest route to safety but instead he ran into a large and panicked group of escaped chimpanzees.

The sanctuary staff said they did not see what happened but they heard screaming for a minute or so. And then silence. When they recovered the driver's body, lying on the forest floor just a few feet outside the main entrance building at Tacugama, his genitals, face and several fingers had been bitten off. There have been cases before where captive chimpanzees have badly mauled adult humans, others where children have been killed. But the death of Issa Kanu is the first recorded incident of a man being killed by chimpanzees.

It was three years since the incident but getting Bala to talk about it was not easy. The Tacugama sanctuary has been his world since he set it up in 1995 and the loss of life clearly grieved him. But the value of the project was too great for him to let it be closed down after one freak event.

'We are pretty certain Bruno was not at the killing as he was down near the car and the exact animals responsible remain unknown,' he explained. 'It was a mob attack and an attack that makes sense in terms of the situation, because the animals were scared and confused, and wary of strangers. I am sure that in some countries, even America, the authorities would have simply ordered all the chimpanzees shot on sight but we are lucky here in Sierra Leone to have a government that took a more considered view.'

Bala organised a sweep of the local forest by trained guides. They took with them armed members of the Special Security Division, an elite unit from the Sierra Leone police, deployed to protect the guides. Within a short time twenty-seven of the escapees were recovered. Three years after the incident four are still out there, roaming somewhere on the forested mountain peninsula behind Freetown. Bruno is one of them.

'From time to time we get reports of sightings and we go out immediately to see what we can find but the time between sightings is getting longer and longer. The last one came when a soldier was jogging along a track near a shooting range way over on the other side of the peninsula. He suddenly became aware stones were being thrown at him so he turned round and saw a chimpanzee. Stone-throwing is not natural chimpanzee behaviour so we knew it must have been our guys. But by the time we got there the animals had vanished.'

While Bala was clearly sad at losing contact with Bruno, an animal whose life he had saved and whom he had known intimately for more than fifteen years, I also detected a slight sense of contentment. Since setting up Tacugama Bala had worked hard towards rehabilitating chimpanzees, giving them back a life in the wild. He had had to contend with civil war and weak government, and struggle against entrenched African attitudes that saw chimpanzees as a food source. It had all meant it was not possible to release a single animal until the day Bruno and his group freed themselves.

After driving back to Freetown I got the news I had been waiting for. An aid worker friend had finally tracked down the name and contact details of a guide in Liberia willing to try to locate the border crossing near Dawa and rendezvous with us there. My excitement at the news was sharpened by the exasperation I felt at Freetown's failure to make more progress since the war ended in 2002. Perhaps out in the hinterland of the country I might find more meaningful development.

David and I agreed on an early departure the next day but not before we had one last planning session. We met at one of my favourite places in the city, the old lighthouse built among the gun-metal grey rocks of Cape Sierra, where the Freetown peninsula reaches furthest into the Atlantic. The light went out years ago but a member of the local port authority still mans the look-out deck next to the lighthouse's stubby tower, armed with a pair of binoculars and a walkie-talkie, announcing the arrival of any ship that comes into view.

What I love most about the promontory is its clutch of bulky baobab trees, Jurassic-looking things with roots as thick as boa constrictors locked on for dear life to boulders wet with spray from Atlantic rollers. To my eye they are so unmistakably African they made a worthy starting post for our African journey.

The bark of a baobab is grey and as tough as elephant hide, but as we approached late that afternoon, the lowering sun picked out initials and dates carved into the tree by visitors over the ages, now twisted and distorted by years of growth. I would love to be able to say we found 'GG 1935' but it was not to be. Instead, I had to make do with the thought that these baobabs, long-time sentinels over the entrance to Freetown harbour, would have been here when the ship that brought Barbara and Graham Greene dropped anchor.

I turned to leave but not before taking a lungful of brackish sea air. If all went to plan, the next time we would smell the Atlantic would be on the other side of Liberia.

CHAPTER 4

No Provocation to Anger

Freetown Bus Station
(the Old Railway Station)

Nonsense.

German newspaper cartoon depicting Barbara Greene as a beauty queen with her own handwritten assessment alongside. Caption: 'As earlier reported, Miss Barbara Green, an Englishwoman who has won several beauty pageants, has recently set out on an expedition to darkest Africa.'

The unlit streets were deserted as we made our way by jeep to the main bus station for the dawn departure of the daily service to Bo, Sierra Leone's second city, which lies roughly halfway across the country, about 150 miles by road from Freetown. Crowded during daylight hours, at night the centre of the capital surrendered to silence and shadows because of the threat of crime. The only movement I could sense when we parked came from bats, large, ungainly shapes flickering above a decrepit skyline of rusty rooftops and non-functioning power lines.

The Sierra Leone Road Transport Corporation had taken over Freetown's old railway station as its bus terminus, meaning our journey would start exactly where the Greenes had begun theirs. Barbara Greene had felt horribly self-conscious as she walked the short distance downhill from the Grand Hotel to the station because she was wearing a rather revealing pair of hiking shorts. She had had them made during the stopover in Freetown to go with a pair of knee-length riding boots purchased at the last moment before leaving England. As she waited in the early-morning half-light for their luggage to be delivered to the platform, the shorts started to feel 'very brief and unbecoming'. Throughout her writing she emerges as painfully self-deprecating, describing herself as physically 'tall and hefty' and by nature 'stolid'. I have found only a few photographs of her on the trip and felt she rather did herself down. One was taken on the ship heading to Africa and it shows her as not much shorter than her tall cousin, her warm face framed by dark wavy hair worn tight on the scalp like the 1930s cartoon character Betty Boop. A British newspaper, the *News Chronicle*, described her as 'tall, dark and beautiful' when it reported her departure for Africa, while a German newspaper printed two cartoons that caricatured her as an English beauty queen about to take on the jungle. On the page of the family album where the cartoons have been kept, Barbara Greene wrote 'Nonsense'.

On reaching the station, the Greenes found the three staff taken on in Freetown – Amedoo to look after Graham Greene, Laminah for

Barbara Greene and Souri, the cook – were already there, fidgeting around growing piles of baggage, making sure nothing went astray before the party finally boarded the train for Bo. For Graham Greene, still only thirty years old and travelling for the first time in Africa, pushing through the throng of onlookers at the station was like going through a door into a world of new experiences. He writes that from that moment 'everything was strange'.

The building of the railway in the 1890s had been a major moment in the development of Sierra Leone. For almost a hundred years the colony had consisted only of the Freetown peninsula but, during the Scramble for Africa at the end of the nineteenth century, Britain moved to stake a much larger piece of territory, declaring the Sierra Leone hinterland a British protectorate in 1896. Central to its development was the rail network, as it allowed troops to be deployed swiftly to disputed border regions, deterring territorial claims from the neighbouring French colony of Guinea. Over time it also allowed the dispersal of district commissioners, administrators, missionaries, traders, prospectors and all other camp followers of Empire. With the discovery of diamonds and iron ore still a long way in the future, the economy of the protectorate grew only slowly on the back of modest cash crops like palm kernels – the gunmetal-grey nut at the centre of the fleshy red palm fruit which can be milled to produce oil. And what little economic growth there was in the protectorate at the start of the twentieth century depended completely on the train as the principal means to move agricultural produce down to Freetown for export.

When Britain unilaterally staked the protectorate it began levying fees from natives and the 'hut tax', as it became known, soon became a source of friction. The British argued the fees were due in payment for the benefits of British protection, although the benefits of this protection were debatable. In remote, rural Sierra Leone there was little evidence of the colonial power providing any meaningful improvement in quality of life. For years the 'hut tax' sparked skirmishes and conflict, with British soldiers routinely dispatched to trouble spots when protests turned violent.

During the Second World War, RAF warplanes, broken down into component parts, were carried along the railway line as far as its terminus at Pendembu, out in the east of the country. The roughly

230 miles spanned by the Sierra Leone railway was crucial for these aircraft as it brought the battlefields of North Africa within their range. After being reassembled on an airstrip cleared from the bush at Pendembu, the warplanes would fill their fuel tanks and head out over the Sahara to reinforce British troops fighting the German Afrika Korps.

But the problem with the train was always its size. The train in Sierra Leone was of a particularly narrow gauge – only 2ft 6in wide – limiting considerably the loads it could carry. It might have served its purpose in the late 1890s but by the time road transport developed in the twentieth century the Sierra Leone railway could not keep up. It limped on for a few years, loyal staff struggling to keep the old rolling stock in working order, but eventually it was scrapped for economic reasons in the early 1970s. The tiny, almost toy-town, character of the train was described by Graham Greene:

> Even the railway journey was strange. It was a small-gauge line; and the train nosed its way up-country with incredible slowness (it took two days to go two hundred odd miles) . . . I have never been so hot and so damp; if we pulled down the blinds in the small dusty compartment we shut out all the air; if we raised them, the sun scorched the wicker, the wooden floor, drenched hands and knees in sweat . . . the train rattled and reeled forward at fifteen miles an hour.

With dawn still some way off I walked into the station. The tracks were long gone but the original cast-iron pillars were still in place. By the light of my torch I found an old foundry stamp bearing the name 'A. Handyside', a once famous company from Derby that produced ironwork for Britain at the swaggering zenith of its imperial age. In the late nineteenth century, bridges and buildings made by Handyside were shipped all over the world, to the 'pink bits' of Britain's empire, and some of the firm's most notable structures still grace central London: the Albert Bridge spanning the Thames, and the roof of the original exhibition hall at Olympia.

My torch caused a stir at floor level so I looked more closely. Dozens of people, many of them cripples, were sleeping on the filthy ground. Among the squalor there was something very intimate about the scene – the arm of one man lying nonchalantly across the bare chest of another, one person's cardboard mat being shared with a neighbour.

A man moved. His upper body was huge, as muscled as a body-builder's, but his legs were a withered parody of health. His face reeled away from the light and for a second I saw a look of shame as he lay prostrate before, unknotting himself from the other sleeping figures, he dragged his torso upright, using his old wheelchair for support, and finally heaved himself into the seat with a grunt. The chair creaked under his bulk, its bare wheel rims scrunching on the gritty floor, the rubber tyres long since stripped away. After manually arranging his legs and tucking away his cardboard sleeping mat, he looked up and I noticed the shame had gone, replaced by defiance. He moved the wheels forward, skilfully nudging past those still sleeping, and headed down towards the other end of the old platform.

Stations the world over are hangouts for vagrants and drifters. Tucked away from busy platforms and ticket halls you commonly find human flotsam washed up in dark corners and basements. But what made Freetown station different was that the entire place was a doss house. No matter its tatty state of repair, the fact it had walls and a roof made it valuable in a post-war city overrun by the homeless and penniless. There was a tang of urine in the air and a fragrant echo of marijuana smoke as daybreak approached and slowly the place came to life. Against the back wall, a hawker opened his stall, hoping to catch the early-morning bus passenger trade, and turned on a disc player that boomed out 'Sympathy for the Devil' by the Rolling Stones.

He sold packets of batteries, biscuits and plastic sachets that looked like the fruit ice-pops I used to suck as a child. But these ones contained alcohol, double shots of samizdat gin, whisky or vodka, 12 pence each. I had seen them before, during the war, when I ventured out of Freetown and came across a position held by troops belonging to the Sierra Leone army, many of whom were just boys. Empty sachets littered the jungle floor among the dead leaves, their job of numbing senses and blurring memories done.

Outside it was growing lighter and I could see the minaret of a large, newly-built mosque growing sharper against the sky. Sierra Leone is one of Africa's great meeting points between Islam, spreading down across the Sahara from the Muslim Maghreb, and

Christianity, seeping inland after arriving on the coast with European missionaries, but, in an example to the rest of the world, the rivalry between the two faiths here has rarely caused friction. I met several people in Sierra Leone named Mohamed who had converted to Christianity easily enough, and Christian girls who married Muslims. In the nine years since my first visit, Islam had clearly made gains, with a visible increase in the number of large mosques functioning in the city, many of them funded by Iran. Links between Shia Iran and the Shia members of Sierra Leone's Lebanese community meant the green, red and white flag of the Islamic Republic could be seen stencilled on noticeboards next to mosque building sites across the city, proudly announcing the source of the money for the construction.

Back inside the station I walked across to where the tracks used to lead out for the journey across the country and I spotted the man in the wheelchair once more. He was in a group of other wheelchair-bound people loading up buckets with small plastic bags of water chilled overnight in a haphazard collection of rusty chest freezers. A power cable from somewhere outside brought the electricity needed to make them work so the water bags froze at night before being sold as refreshments the following day on the city's street corners. After filling his bucket to the brim, the man placed it on his lap and began to wheel himself slowly out of the station and up the slope in the direction of the Cotton Tree for a long day's hawking.

A young man who had been sleeping on a raised bench suddenly woke, cursing. There then began one of those blathering tramp rows where drunken men shout incoherently over each other until their attention wanders and they eventually shut up. I looked at the wall where someone had daubed a list of what amounted to ordinances and fines designed to keep order in the doss house. 'No swearing', the graffiti decreed, 'no fighting', 'no jamba [marijuana]' and 'no provocation to anger'.

The bus for Bo left two minutes ahead of time with a former army truck driver, Sammy Conteh, at the wheel. He was neatly dressed with a pair of large-lensed sunglasses balanced on his forehead in readiness for daybreak, and he had the air of quiet competence I associate with regimental sergeant majors. A crowd had gathered around the door of the bus when Sammy first arrived, backing the coach skilfully between the Handyside columns. The bus was modern and in good condition, a stark contrast to the station, and it was painted in the green livery of the national bus company. Foreigners, often aid workers, use the bus from time to time so David and I were given no special attention as the departure time approached. The fare to Bo was 15,000 Leones (about £3), a price that was unaffordably expensive for most of the population. For long-distance transport they would instead be forced to rely on cheaper, less reliable and more dangerous local taxis and poda-poda minibuses. So the crowd was made up mostly of hawkers and hustlers hoping to earn some Leones carrying luggage or delivering snacks to the travellers wealthy enough to afford seats. In the jostling crowd voices were raised, but the noise grew more out of boisterousness than anger. A transport company employee made sense of the chaos, checking tickets, efficiently allocating numbered seats and loading our luggage into the belly of the bus, 35 pence per item. Amid the hubbub Sammy stayed calm.

'I drove for the army for thirty years,' he told me after setting off, his vivid eyes flicking robotically between right and left side mirrors. He said he was fifty-five but he could have passed for twenty years younger. 'There's not a road in this country I do not know. I have been along them all. And during the war I was ambushed so many times I lost count.'

Dawn had not yet fully broken and the city roads were still free of traffic so we made good time. We stopped for no apparent reason towards the edge of the city while Sammy went off to speak to someone, so I jumped down from the bus and bought some fried plantain from a child street seller for breakfast. It was delicious; crisp and dry, not spoiled by too much oil.

David was quiet. We were two relative strangers about to embark on a long shared journey and I sensed he wanted to avoid unnecessary chatter. He returned the copy of Barbara Greene's account of the trip that I had lent him and we talked briefly about the excitement the Greenes must have felt when they left the city for a journey that represented a genuine adventure into the unknown. My feeling was also one of excitement but sharpened with nervousness born of my experiences during the war. I might have had better maps and a fuller library of reading material than the Greenes had enjoyed, but the bloody turmoil in both Sierra Leone and Liberia meant this also felt to me like a journey into the unknown.

The eastern approaches to the city were now passing outside the bus window, perhaps the most fought-over part of Freetown. Gunmen and soldiers had run riot here several times during the war, but the worst attack, one that is still remembered with horror by the locals who lived through it, came in January 1999 when RUF militiamen overran this area.

Coming from the Sierra Leonean hinterland, the rebels reached the eastern district of the city first and it was here, after fighting in the bush for years, that they vented their drug-fuelled hatred of the capital, its leaders and its people. Civilians were dragged out onto the streets where some were decapitated, others disembowelled and some burned to death, while all symbols of modernity and of law and order – police cars, council offices, shops even – were deliberately destroyed in a twister of vandalistic brutality. Over the eleven years that the war raged, it established a reputation as one of the world's cruellest, but the events of January 1999 represented for many its nadir. Sitting in my comfortable, numbered bus seat, I saw evidence of the attacks spooling past my window like a film reel, with burnt-out buildings, one after the other, punctuated by other pieces of destroyed infrastructure. It was ten years since the attack but only now was the city's eastern district police headquarters being rebuilt, the building and nearby clock-tower landmark splinted with bamboo scaffolding.

Somewhere out there to my right was a mass grave that dated from long before the war, from the corrosive, creeping decline of Sierra Leone in the 1970s when attempts to entrench the rule of law started to fail. The civil war did not spring out of nothing but from years of steadily worsening corruption and autocracy that created the conditions where anarchic, lawless armed groups like the RUF could exist. When dealing with complex African conflicts observers often seek refuge in categorisation, eager to put them in boxes marked tribal or ideological, mercantile or religious, references that outsiders feel they can understand. During the Cold War, African rebel groups were tagged communist or capitalist no matter their actual ideology because it tidied the analysis of tricky conflict situations.

But the truth about the RUF gunmen was that they defied neat labels. In Sierra Leone, journalists like me were guilty of striving to

oversimplify the war, looking always to frame it in terms of government troops versus rebels. We tended to overlook the complex,
systemic regression that had taken a country with a capital city once
viewed as 'The Athens of Africa' and turned it into arguably the
world's poorest country. The regression did not lend itself to easy
analysis. Sierra Leone has no iconic figure, no Nelson Mandela nor
Patrice Lumumba, and no great symbolic turning point, no
Sharpeville Massacre nor Wind of Change speech. Indeed, one of the
country's one-time heroes of the independence era, Siaka Stevens,
whose name is still borne by the main street in Freetown leading to the
Cotton Tree, blurred two separate identities as he was revered by
some as a democrat loved by the people and decried by others as a
murderous plunderer. For those who like tidy categorisation, Sierra
Leone is a problem.

Its post-independence decay is captured beautifully in a book called
The Devil that Danced on the Water, published in 2002 by a half-
Scottish, half-Sierra Leonean writer, Aminatta Forna. The author
describes her search for the truth about a single episode at the heart of
this opaque and often-overlooked period of the country's history, the
arrest and execution of her father, Mohamed Forna. After the colonial
period when Krios, the freed slaves, had prospered, Mohamed was
part of an upwardly mobile generation of indigenous Sierra Leoneans,
born and educated in the provinces, who saw independence as the
arrival of a new age when their turn to thrive had finally come. For
me, the book fills in much that is missing about recent Sierra Leonean
history, describing the potential of the immediate post-independence
years, a time of optimism and hope when families could live normal
lives, saving money to send children to school, earning qualifications
to get meaningful jobs with genuine career paths, dreaming of self-
betterment and development.

Forna was one of the first from the provinces to qualify as a doctor,
bringing modern medicine to rural Sierra Leone, something that had
been done only modestly under British colonial rule. His work earned
him a wide following and within a few years he was persuaded to move
into politics alongside Stevens, then in his democratic, man-of-the-
people phase. Forna rose to the position of finance minister, but his
intolerance of corruption meant he fell out with the increasingly
greedy Stevens clique. He was arrested repeatedly before being

detained for the last time in 1974 on trumped-up treason charges and hanged the following year. His daughter's elegant account of the destruction of her family's life allowed me to picture the catastrophic void created in Sierra Leone by this period of political decay, when law and order collapsed and the pillars of society that I take for granted in a functioning state, such as the availability of fair-minded police or economic stability or unbiased journalism, crumbled away. These were the elements that created the vacuum in which the horrific civil war could develop.

As we drove out of Freetown I thought about his daughter's long search and how it finally led here, to a once-empty piece of scrubland on the eastern edge of the city where Forna's corpse had been brought following his execution. Under cover of darkness government soldiers had tipped the body into a mass grave and then, in a final act of cruelty, disfigured it with acid.

The sprawling muddle of Freetown has blurred the city limits but eventually the shanties disappeared and the bus picked up speed in open country heading towards the rising sun. Overhead, a flock of cattle egrets kept up with us for a few moments, flying east in formation, high enough for their white wings and yellow bills to dazzle in direct sunlight while we were still in shadow. A few moments later and the African sun reached us too, Sammy lowered his dark glasses into position, passengers fussed with curtains for shade.

After crossing a low ridgeline known as the Occra Hills, the road, refurbished by an Italian company which patched over the potholes left from the war years, swept down into the flatlands of central Sierra Leone, an almost unbroken expanse of low forest with an even skyline broken only by the raggedy heads of palm trees. Parched by the fierce dry-season heat, the bush was surprisingly barren in appearance, the mango trees fruitless, the verdant lustre of the vegetation washed pale, waiting for the rains to come. Traffic was sparse, with pedestrians – heavily laden with loads balanced on heads or strapped to backs – out-numbering vehicles. Sierra Leone is one of Africa's smaller countries, less than 250 miles across at its widest point, covering roughly the same area as Scotland, and in the dry season it is possible to drive across it in one day. But in spite of its modest size man has made only a modest impact on its forest.

Cultivated fields of rice or cassava are rare and only occasionally would I see villages clinging to the roadway like clumps of mussels to an anchor line, a few mud huts clustered in the dirt between the tarmac strip and the green expanse of the bush. For most the highway represents a way of escape, a means to leave the poverty of the countryside and head to the capital city and even beyond. It means the settlements along the road have a left-behind air, simple buildings that are neither cherished nor developed but used as way stations for a desperate journey away from the countryside. An aid worker told me that a policy of taking graduates from the rural areas and training them as teachers in Freetown had to be stopped because few of them ever returned home. The city might be crowded and squalid but it still offers greater opportunities than life *up-line*.

The country's main highway had been built along the route of the old railway track and several towns we passed through were old stations that retained their colonial-era names. In Hastings and Waterloo it was possible to still see old infrastructure that had served the rolling stock. The station sign for Waterloo stood right next to today's road and in Hastings I spotted the sort of water tower I associate with Western movies, a large funnel-shaped structure with a swinging arm outlet at the bottom that was used to refill steam locomotive boilers. As we drove the modern road in open country, it was possible occasionally to glimpse traces of the railway in the distance, with abandoned box-girder bridges still spanning gorges, metalwork rusty and concrete foundations blackened with age.

The landscape of central Sierra Leone is mostly flat, blanketed by low forest, an outlook Graham Greene found deeply uninspiring. Just as he disparaged the small-minded white expatriates of Freetown and their Krio underlings, he scorned an African environment made bland, as he saw it, by British colonialism.

Outside the dusty Sierra Leone countryside unrolled, like a piece of drab cloth along a draper's counter, grey and dull-green and burnt up by the dry season which was now approaching its end . . . The bush was as ragged and uninteresting as a back garden which has been allowed to run wild and in which the aspidistras from the parlour have seeded and flourished among the brown-scorched grasses and the tall wrinkled greenery.

My attitude towards this landscape could not have been more contrasting. It still made me feel edgy. The road might now appear a dull strip of tarmac but nine years earlier it had been a very different proposition. The only real route out of Freetown, it was down this road that journalists had to come to report on the fighting as RUF gunmen threatened the city. Timid reporters like me only came a few miles, never venturing beyond the Occra Hills. But Kurt Schork and Miguel Gil Moreno went further and paid for it with their lives.

After they were killed on Wednesday 24 May 2000 I was initially too overwhelmed to focus on the details. It was after sunset that day when word got back to Freetown that some journalists had been hurt, possibly killed, upcountry and I can remember the reception of the UN headquarters echoing to a howl of anguish from a BBC colleague, a woman who had already lost a journalist friend in Sierra Leone the year before. It's a clear double standard but for a long time I, a journalist who reported countless times on the suffering of people at moments of death, displacement or crisis, found it too difficult to think about what had happened to my colleagues that day. I blanked it from my mind, refusing to consider what it might mean for the life I had chosen to lead.

I had known Kurt for longer but was closer to Miguel. His eyes would sparkle when we talked about the books we shared a love for, and he had a passionate, unpredictable streak that made him a magnificent cameraman. One day in northern Bosnia he left the handbrake off in his jeep, causing it to roll down a slope and hit a farmer's prized plum tree. The Bosnian grabbed Miguel's video camera, saying he would only return it when damages had been paid. To a cameraman the loss of a camera is like the loss of a limb and I can remember Miguel getting more and more desperate, his pleading more and more pathetic and his *sotto voce* curses more and more blue, as he negotiated its safe return.

No matter my relationship with Kurt and Miguel, the key thing was that the day they died they were not doing anything particularly different from what I have done in my work countless times, driving along a road threatened by rival forces. To deal with the anxiety in these situations, I had my own private and very childlike mental procedure, telling myself on roads in Congo, Iraq, Bosnia, Kosovo, Algeria and elsewhere that if I get to the next bend all will be safe – and then the next big tree, the next landmark and so on. By breaking the journey down into little sections I would get through the danger zone, convincing myself I was in some way in control. It was nonsense, of course, just a way of dealing with fear. It was, very simply, luck that kept me alive, the same luck that abandoned Kurt and Miguel that day while at the same time protecting one of their colleagues, Yannis Behrakis, who somehow survived the ambush even though he was sitting in the same car only inches from Kurt when he was killed.

I heard about Yannis's remarkable escape at the time, but was too muddled in my mind to focus on it. It was only nine years later when our career paths brought us to the same city, Jerusalem – Yannis as chief photographer for Reuters and me as Middle East Correspondent for the *Telegraph* – that I had the chance to talk to him about what happened.

Yannis and Kurt were close colleagues and closer friends. In Sarajevo during the toughest years of the Bosnian War they developed one of the great double acts of 1990s foreign reporting, Kurt doing the words and Yannis the pictures for one of the world's most demanding news agencies, Reuters. Greek by nationality, Yannis described his own character as in many ways opposite to the non-drinking, vegetarian, former Rhodes Scholar from America, but the opposites clearly had an attraction. Greyer than I remembered him from Bosnian days, a few moments after we met up at his Jerusalem office Yannis pointed to the watch on his wrist.

'It's Kurt's,' he said. 'His girlfriend wanted me to have it.'

Yannis explained how the Sierra Leone trip was the team's first foray into Africa. At an awards ceremony in New York in April 2000, where they were honoured for their work in Kosovo the previous year, they both agreed they wanted a break from the Balkans.

'It was the Millennium, a new century, and we decided Africa was where it was at,' he said. 'We agreed that when the first big story broke in Africa, we would go. A few weeks later and the United Nations mission in Sierra Leone was going to shit so we headed to Freetown.'

I recognised perfectly his description of those chaotic, exciting days in Freetown because we had covered many of the same events. But as the city stabilised the story moved down the road to where troops loyal to the government of Sierra Leone were trying to take back territory from the RUF.

'On the Tuesday we drove as far as the town of Rogbere, which by then was in the hands of the army,' Yannis remembered. 'We met their commanders and they showed us some of the remains of UN peacekeepers killed in the town by the RUF. There were femurs lying around and some uniforms and blue helmets. It made a story and Kurt tried to get in touch with the UN command to see if they would check it out. The army commander told us that the next day they would try to take back the next town further east, Lunsar, so we told him we would be back the following morning and to expect us.

'The Wednesday began as normal. In town we bought food, cigarettes and booze because, as you know, we could need them as gifts for soldiers. There were four of us in our Mercedes, the Sierra Leonean driver, Kurt, me and Mark, the video cameraman. When we got to Rogbere late in the morning we found Miguel already there in his own little jeep, something like a Suzuki, with a Sierra Leone driver.'

Lunsar is about 10 miles due east of Rogbere, and shooting could be heard coming from its direction. The journalists discussed what to do, a scene I found horribly familiar, where bravado, joshing and fear all mix together to deliver an almost inevitable decision to push on. Yannis said the two local drivers chose not to come, so the Mercedes took the lead, with Kurt driving, Mark in the passenger seat and Yannis in the back sandwiched between two Sierra Leone army soldiers. A couple more soldiers jumped on the bonnet and one on the back bumper.

'The commanders in Rogbere knew our faces from the previous day so we had a kind of relationship. I never like to sit in the back of a car, especially in the middle seat as it is hard to shoot pictures from that position. But the guys who came with us were kind of officers and they sort of ordered me to sit there.

'The road was completely empty. I can picture it in my mind right now. It was the start of the rainy season so it was sweaty, much too hot to wear body armour or helmets. There were clouds, and the tarmac was wet with rain as we drove along. We were on alert, high alert as the shooting in the distance got louder and louder, but I remember thinking, I am going to shoot some fucking amazing pictures today.'

The two-vehicle convoy, Kurt driving up ahead, Miguel behind, stopped after a short distance at the shell of a burned UN vehicle. Yannis took some photographs. The sound of fighting intensified and so did the air of excitement as they drove on, senses heightened, eyes sweeping empty huts as they drove past an abandoned village.

'We were just about to make a right curve when suddenly I saw these guys just thirty or forty metres away standing up and shooting at us from the left side of the road. I felt the car being hit time after time, pock, pock, pock, but somehow the windscreen did not shatter. "Come on," I shouted, but instead of speeding up to get away the car just kept driving towards them, slowing steadily. It was terrible. We just kept on moving towards the shooters. It made no sense and then I saw Kurt, his face covered in blood, his foot nowhere near the brake.

'Still the bullets came. There was a whoosh and a rocket-propelled grenade went over our heads. The soldier next to me on the right was dead, with blood all over the place and the other soldier, the one to my left, just threw his gun out of the window and climbed like a mad thing over me, over the dead man and out the right window. I remember feeling so very disappointed that the soldier did not fire back. He just ran.'

Kurt had been fatally hit but what saved Mark and Yannis was the way Miguel's car then drew the fire of the ambushers. As the Mercedes glided to a halt on the left verge of the bend, Mark ran for cover among the trees while Yannis wrestled the right-hand door open and pushed out the corpse of the dead soldier.

'I must have had just a few seconds when the shooting was focused behind me but I fought my way out over the dead body. A strap on one of my two cameras caught on the door frame and I dumped it and then ran for my life across the verge and into the bush. Ten seconds, twenty seconds, I don't know how long it was but I got a little bit away from the car and hit the ground crawling into the thickest bush I could find.

'I was wearing a white T-shirt so that did not help. I started rubbing shit onto it and onto my face, leaves, dirt, anything to break up the white. The shooting was still going on so I composed myself, got control of my breathing. I remember peeing. I was proud of that, of not having peed myself during the ambush. With the shooting continuing, I kept crawling and crawling, keeping to the thick bush. My belt had pouches on it for lenses and other gear and it was catching on the bushes making a terrible noise, so I took it off and buried it under some dirt and leaves. I kept going, all the time trying not to make a sound and all the time expecting them to come look for me.

'After fifteen minutes or so all of a sudden there was no noise, no shooting. I lay still and waited, trying to bury myself in the leaves, in the wet dirt. I felt my pulse. It was seventy or eighty. I was in control and kept thinking, this is their territory and their climate – to survive I have to be smarter than them.

'Then I heard them coming through the bush. There were voices and sounds of branches being broken and I just lay there, as still as I could, as low as I could. It was the worst moment you can imagine. They were searching for me and I knew they would kill me if they found me.'

The sound of the search came within a few yards of Yannis. He held his breath. Sweat trickled down his face but he dared not stir to wipe it away.

Slowly the sounds of the search passed, cracks from breaking foliage fading into the distance, but for a long time Yannis did not budge. When he heard the whistle of birds he worried it was the gunmen communicating with each other using the bushcraft of hunters, so still he waited. For an hour or so he did not move, thinking through what had happened. He felt certain Kurt was dead but did not know what had become of Mark or Miguel. Slowly he got the confidence to creep forward, all the time listening out for the sounds of the gunmen while trying to orientate himself, to keep going in a straight line away from the ambush site and not circle back to where he had begun.

'It was then I heard firing, really heavy firing coming into the trees around me. What had happened was the army soldiers in Lunsar had heard the shooting from the ambush and were coming back along the road, back in the direction of Rogbere towards where I was. The problem was they were firing everything they had into the bush, not caring if they had a target to aim at. They had a fucking great gun, a

30-mm anti-aircraft gun and they were firing it into the trees. For me it was perhaps the most dangerous time. Branches were crashing down on top of me as bullets and shells flew over my head. I really thought a lot at that moment about dying and it went through my mind that nobody would ever find me and how bad that was and how the animals would eat my body.'

When this second wave of shooting died down, Yannis was able to think a little more clearly. He kept crawling forward and then stopping, waiting to hear if he was being followed, all the time scared that the ambushers could have set another trap. The time passed and while his mind was full of images of his friend covered in blood, he forced himself to focus on survival.

'Two or three hours had passed since the ambush and I was suddenly beginning to feel dehydrated. It was as hot as hell under the undergrowth with no breeze or air. I knew without water I would not be able to think straight, so I turned to my right and made my way back towards the road. That was the only way I could find water for sure.

'Eventually I got to the road. It was empty. There was nobody there but shell casings lay everywhere like snow on the ground. They made a tinkling sound when I stood up on the tarmac. I looked to my left, towards Lunsar and to my right, back towards Rogbere, and tried to think which way to go. I had no idea if the ambushers were still near the road but I had to get moving, had to get to water.

'I turned right. After half a mile or so I came to the cars. The Mercedes was shot to shit and there was blood everywhere but no bodies. And then Miguel's jeep was there, hit even heavier with bullet holes that made it look like a Swiss cheese and, again, no bodies. I kept going.

'I had no idea what I was walking into and it started to go through my mind that I should prepare a farewell message, something that I would leave behind in case I got killed. I am a photographer so the obvious thing was to take pictures. I had one camera still with me so I set the lens on wide, held it high up in front of me, turned it round and took pictures of myself. Maybe I would die, I thought, so maybe they would find my camera and find these last pictures.'

A few miles down the road Yannis finally reached a position held by government soldiers. The first ones touched him to see if he was a ghost, unsure how he had survived. A few yards away, under a stand of trees, was a large group of soldiers and on the ground nearby the corpses of Kurt, Miguel and four of the soldiers who had been riding with the convoy. Mark had arrived on foot a short while earlier and the two journalist survivors embraced. Yannis helped load the bodies of his friends onto the back of army trucks before their long final journeys, Kurt to Washington for cremation and Miguel to Barcelona for burial.

A few days before taking the bus out of Freetown, I had arranged a jeep for my own personal pilgrimage to the ambush site described by Yannis. The road between Rogbere and Lunsar had been resurfaced and widened so it took a bit of finding, but after a few hours and with the help of some nuns from a local convent, I found the heavily overgrown spot where a small, steel memorial cross had been erected by Miguel's mother. The heat was formidable out on the road and would have been worse under the cover of thick bush. I tried to imagine the fear, sweat and chaos of those moments back in May 2000.

'I took a long time off after it happened and of course there was a lot of questioning about the job,' Yannis had said as we finished talking. 'But you've been there yourself, you know what it is like doing this work. If you are the sort of person who is good at this job you are the sort of person who would most likely go down that road. You just have to remember the part that luck plays and that in many ways the best of us are just the luckiest of us. I got back to work on the ninth of September 2001 and two days later the twin towers came down in New York. Since then, I haven't really stopped.'

Graham Greene was not ashamed to articulate his love for danger, indeed he wrote often of coming alive through brushes with death. As I thought of what Yannis had said, I felt a connection to Graham Greene's attitude. For years I had reported from war zones and had tolerated danger precisely because of its sense of thrill, of personal release as you witness life at its most unvarnished, humans stripped of all artifice as they cope with the ultimate drama of conflict. Late in life, Graham Greene wrote how coming so close to death had stirred in him a passionate interest in living. Thinking about it now, I fear the death of Kurt and Miguel had a more permanent effect on me than I admitted at the time. In the game of chance that governs a war reporter's life, my bluff had been called and I would never again take the risks I had once blithely embraced.

A few yards from the memorial cross on the roadside, I found a rusty shell casing from the 30-mm cannon Yannis had described, the one that soldiers fired into the trees and that terrified him as much as the original rebel ambush. I picked it up and, much later, presented it to him back in Jerusalem. He thanked me quietly and emailed me a picture. It was one of the self-portraits taken when he did not know if he would live or die, an unforgettably stark image. Journalists tend to be people of swagger and self-confidence and I found it incredibly brave of him to share a moment when he was lost, scared and desperate.

CHAPTER 5

Peace Garden

War-Damaged Rail Bridge,
Sewa River

Above: Pioneering railwaymen in Sierra Leone pass Waterloo Station by pump trolley, circa 1900
Below: The author with original Sierra Leonean pump trolley, Freetown railway museum, January 2009

I dozed as the bus churned along deteriorating roads and was woken by talk of the devil. An evangelist, a young man with immaculate clothes, was standing next to the driver's seat, swaying with the motion of the vehicle, holding a Bible and declaiming forcefully on the virtues of Jesus. Islam might have been enjoying a surge in mosque construction in Freetown but out here in the provinces, Christianity was booming. From the window I could see growing numbers of roadside signs indicating Pentecostal, Adventist and Baptist churches, as well as others linked to more unorthodox denominations.

The young man at the front of the bus wore a badge that read 'Youths For Christ'. Next to him was an assistant earnestly holding up a flip-chart of images, pictures drawn on large pieces of paper, all attached at the top to a bamboo cane, which he would turn over with a flourish as the narrative developed. As I came round, the image on display showed the outline of a man and inside his chest a large heart had been drawn with two smaller, stylised figures gripping it on either side, one a winged angel, the other a horned devil.

'Jesus teaches us that during all of our life, from when we are born to when we die, our heart will be fought over by good and evil, by the side of angels and the side of devils,' the young man said in commentary, raising his voice for the final flourish. 'Jesus will help you but to be certain that good wins you must always, always turn your back on the devil.'

With that he nodded at the driver and the bus pulled over. 'Thank you all in the name of Youths For Christ,' his voice boomed, before he and his partner jumped off. As we drove away I glanced back at them standing in the roadside dust, the speaker looking about him eagerly for souls ripe for saving, his assistant more concerned with reorganising his parasol of pictures.

The bus picked up speed, curtains streaming out of windows opened against the heat, passengers groggy with torpor. Potholes started to appear, occasionally to begin with but then replicating like bacteria until the tarred highway had morphed into a dirt track broken only by rare scabs of tarmac. At the same time the roadside under-growth grew steadily more rusty, every leaf, frond and branch talced with the finest of dusts churned up from the exposed red earth of the road. We turned a corner and a scarcely airworthy vulture attending to road-kill flapped untidily out of our way. It was the only movement that I saw outside for miles.

The word devil dwelled in my mind. Throughout my research into Sierra Leone and Liberia the term kept coming up, with explorers, including the Greenes, describing the central role played by devils in tribal society. From my reading I learned these mysterious figures – humans who assumed special power through the wearing of magical masks and costumes – acted as guardians of tribal lore, straddling the mortal and spiritual worlds. One of their principal responsibilities was the organising of initiation societies, a type of graduation school for youngsters held in remote parts of the bush. So powerful were these bush societies – the male version was commonly known as Poro, while for women it was called Bundu in Sierra Leone and Sande in Liberia – that graduation was regarded more as a process of birth than coming of age.

Students were taught practical skills such as hunting but they also learned about darker arts, drawing power from the worship of ancestor spirits. For some tribes these initiation societies were as common as high schools in the developed world, with villages all over Sierra Leone and Liberia convening them whenever it had a large enough group of young people. The names differed between tribes but the tradition of initiation by masked elders dominated both countries.

Located far from parents and home comforts, these camps were places of austerity ruled by a hierarchy of specially trained bush society members under the ultimate control of devils, who would appear masked and in costume at crucial times such as circumcisions or graduation. In many communities the identity of the person behind the mask was an open secret, indeed Graham Greene joked that one should never be rude to a village blacksmith in Liberia as he was almost always the village devil.

Anthropologists have long recorded the existence of these bush societies and found clear parallels with initiation rituals followed by other tribal communities around the world as far apart as Asia and

South America, but what made me really curious was whether they
had survived into the twenty-first century. Finding out would not be
easy as initiates swear an *omertà*, a code of silence, and are warned on
pain of death never to divulge the secrets of the bush societies.

What I found so interesting about the West African devil was that
it was more nuanced than the devil as framed by Christianity. Instead
of being the epitome-of-all-evil, it was regarded by its tribal followers
as being capable both of benevolence and of cruelty. When I was a
schoolboy I remember struggling to understand a history teacher
describing early Christian communities as God-fearing. God, in my
child's mind, was a good thing, not something to be feared. I remember my teacher urging me to consider how respect for God relies
ultimately on fear of omnipotence. In a similar way, communities
from Sierra Leone and Liberia can be described as devil-fearing.

Wanting to know more, the devil talk on the bus felt like a way in
to this sensitive subject so I looked around at my fellow passengers,
hoping to ask some questions. Most were asleep but the lady directly
across the aisle from me had been listening closely to the preacher.
Haja Miniatu Konneh – she preferred 'Mini' – wore a two-piece outfit
of gown and headscarf tailored from cotton with the same brown and
yellow floral design. We got chatting and she explained how she was
going to Bo to attend the funeral of a daughter-in-law who had died
from diabetes. Aged sixty-five, she was a devout Muslim running the
Sierra Leonean branch of an American-Muslim charity, LIFE for
Relief and Development, and was clearly well-travelled and educated.
I steered the conversation round to the evangelist's sermon.

'I am a Muslim and that man was a Christian but I agree with him
totally,' she said. 'The devil is waiting to take you at every turn in your
life. Look at what happened to our country when Foday Sankoh came
here with his rebels from the RUF. Now he was someone whose soul
had been taken by the devil.'

'But is the devil you are talking about here the same as the devil
from the Bundu society?' I asked, using the local term for women's
initiation society.

Her expression changed. She gave me an empty smile and shook
her head. 'Of course not. The bush devils are not evil. They bring
good things to our society.'

I persisted. Could she explain a little more?

'I am sorry but I cannot talk about those things,' was her polite but firm reply.

We drove on in silence for a few moments. I was curious about the duality of an observant Muslim also believing in the power of tribal spiritualism, so I came back to the subject from a different direction. One of the most important issues for aid workers in post-war Sierra Leone is female circumcision or, as the current aid community vernacular calls it, female genital mutilation (FGM). FGM is a very modern term for a very ancient procedure undergone by every girl who passes through Bundu initiation. An account published in 1670 by an early Dutch visitor to Sierra Leone, Olfert Dapper, describes the procedure in some detail:

> They bring girls of 10 or 12 or over to a special secluded place in the bush . . . then they cut off their hair with a razor, and bring them on the following day to a river in the bush, where, at the appointed time, the priestess arranges the circumcision, one holds the other tight and the priestess cuts the ring of pleasure out of the private parts, which bleed very much and hurt very much. After the circumcision the priestess heals the wounds with green herbs; this lasts about 10 or 12 days.

In Sierra Leone FGM is as widespread today as it was in 1670 but the reality is not quite as benign as that described by Dapper. It is carried out in non-sterile conditions, using blades that have not been cleaned properly, meaning female circumcision claims the lives of many women and ruins the lives of many more, leaving them in permanent pain and discomfort. Some foreign aid workers, especially those with projects in the rural provinces, have been trying for years to persuade Sierra Leonean women to end the practice but so deeply entrenched is Bundu lore that attempts to change a central component such as this have been largely unsuccessful.

I wondered what, as a senior aid worker, Mini thought of FGM?

'It is a good thing. It stops girls being promiscuous and in this modern day that is a good thing,' she said, before folding her arms and turning away from me. Our conversation was at an end, a lesson for me in the difficulty of trying to break through taboos associated with local tradition.

*

It only took five hours to reach Bo by bus and, when we arrived, David and I took the same attitude to the town as the Greenes did – we moved on as fast as we could. During the colonial period, Bo had been developed as the capital of the protectorate, the tranche of inland territory staked belatedly by Britain long after the Freetown peninsula was colonised, but even at its height that development did not amount to much. There had been a sizeable government reservation in Bo, with a dozen or so bungalows and offices built to house colonial administrators, next to a small town centre which consisted mainly of trading stores, mosques, churches and schools.

Bo was their journey's first landmark and while Barbara Greene ignores the town completely in her book, one can detect a sense of gathering excitement in Graham Greene's brief description. He had been so irked by the complacent imperialism of Freetown that, out in the protectorate, he was delighted to find colonialists with what he regarded as a more genuine connection to Africa.

> The Englishmen here were of a finer, subtler type than on the coast; they were patriots in the sense that they cared for something in their country other than its externals; they couldn't build their English corner with a few tin roofs and peeling posters and drinks at the bar . . . suddenly, inexplicably, I felt happy in the rest-house, the square squat bungalow built on cement piles to keep out the white ants, as the hurricane lamps were lit and the remains of the tough, dry, tasteless coast chicken were laid out . . . I was happy; it was as if I had left something I distrusted behind.

Fought over repeatedly during the war and barely touched by meaningful post-war development, today Bo is a modest sprawl of mostly single-storey buildings built around a frame of dusty, pitted avenues of beaten dirt, spreading out from the national highway that runs across the middle of Sierra Leone. With a population of roughly 200,000 it has a few college campuses, teacher training schools and shops, but most of the buildings are low-cost houses and shanties that make scant impression on a skyline dominated by treetops. The only sign of the modern world comes with the occasional mobile phone mast peeking through the foliage. In its time-worn simplicity Bo felt no different from Freetown, although I was interested to learn the burghers of Bo had horizons that reached far beyond West Africa. After the civil war ended, a friendship link was established between Bo and, of all places, Royal Leamington Spa, a town close to my birthplace in Warwickshire. As we passed Bo it was a struggle to connect mentally its tatty streets with the spa's famous bathhouses, pump-rooms and neo-classical crescents.

After deciding to push on we waited for Sammy to drop off the other passengers before he kindly delivered us to a spot on the main highway where he told us we could find a ride further east. His advice was perfect as it was here, in a roadside shack, under an awning providing protection from the midday heat, that we found a willing driver called Michael Ngebeh. He had his head tipped back and was swallowing lager from a can.

'Sure I will give you a ride to Kenema,' he said. 'The drive costs me a lot in petrol so I always wait here and have a few drinks before I pick up passengers who will pay for the ride. If you pay me 30,000 Leones [about £6] we can go now if you want.'

'How many of those have you had?' I asked, indicating the can of Heineken in his hand.

'This is my second,' he said earnestly, before adding, with a grin, 'I think.'

We loaded our gear into his old Mercedes and set off on the 40-mile journey to Kenema, passing a large construction site on the edge of Bo with a perimeter wall bearing a sign written in large, red Chinese characters. The English translation gave the name of a corporation, owned by the Chinese government, announcing a project to build a football stadium and rehabilitate part of the main highway. This was proof of China's twenty-first-century Scramble for Africa and how it impacted even on relatively small countries such as Sierra Leone. The surging Chinese economy meant Beijing had begun investing heavily in bilateral projects all across Africa as a way to persuade local governments to grant favourable terms for the purchase of raw materials, which were then shipped to mainland China. Sierra Leone's iron ore deposits, rich in geological terms but expensive to get at because of a dilapidated infrastructure, were enough to generate interest from China. Some in Africa embrace the colossal injection of investment, saying it will allow the continent to turn its back on aid handouts from the West, but Michael was not so sure.

'I have seen these Chinese turn up with their digging equipment and their vehicles and their surveyors,' he said, draining his beer can and dropping it casually out of the car window as we drove along the ever-worsening road. 'The odd thing was they did not employ many people here in Bo. They brought their own labour force with them, their own cooks and even their own food. It's like they do not want any contact whatsoever with Africa.

'And now as the demand for iron and steel falls around the world we have already seen they have stopped working. It does not feel like an investment in Africa at all, just short-term opportunism.'

In his thirties, Michael was a teacher of economics and computer skills at a secondary school in Kenema so his analysis sounded convincing enough. Born in Bo, where he spends his weekends, he picked us up on his Sunday commute back to his workplace. He had a chumminess about him and within no time was boasting of his wife in Bo and his 'mamas', or mistresses, in Kenema. His boisterousness also extended to drinking and as we made our way to Kenema he talked enthusiastically about the virtues of 'poyo' or palm wine, an alcoholic drink created through the fermentation of sap that gathers in the flowery head of a certain variety of palm tree and which, depending on how long it has been left, can be formidably potent. To me it tastes like watery, rancid yogurt. Several times he slowed his car when he saw sellers on the roadside holding old bottles and jars filled with the white, milky substance.

'There has been an outbreak of lassa fever in Kenema in recent weeks so it is not safe to drink the poyo from there. I have to make sure I buy it out here, in the rural areas, where it is safe,' he explained.

Lassa is one of the world's deadliest diseases and not one to take chances with. It is a viral haemorrhagic fever, similar to ebola, that inflicts a slow and painful death on its victims by destroying blood vessels and causing bodily extremities to swell with excess fluid, like balloons filling with water. In extreme cases blood can gush from nostrils, eye-sockets, ears, even fingernail beds, and victims often die from drowning as their lungs fill with liquid.

What makes lassa so dangerous is that all secreted fluids can carry the virus, so family members, nurses or doctors looking after a victim can easily become contaminated. Entire families can be wiped out and the fatality rate among health workers, especially in the undeveloped world, is often terribly high. When scientists handle the virus in research facilities in the developed world they apply the highest safety standards, known as Biosafety Level 4 (BSL-4), wearing sealed suits inside special laboratories where the air is not just filtered but kept at a pressure lower than atmospheric pressure, so that if there is an accidental leak the air inside the chamber cannot readily leak out. If caught early enough – something that requires sophisticated clinical testing – lassa fever is treatable with antiviral drugs, but by the time it is identified in rural areas of Africa, for example, where testing is limited, it is often so advanced that treatment becomes a battle of fluid levels as medics try to stop the patient from bleeding out while at the same time stopping themselves from becoming infected. Kenema lies in the border area between Sierra Leone and Liberia, a region with the unfortunate distinction of being one of the world's lassa hotspots. It is most commonly spread by infected rats, through urine trails which they have the unsavoury habit of dripping everywhere as they move. Michael's mention of the disease reminded me to steer clear of rats as much as possible.

After a few false starts Michael found what he was looking for, a seller with poyo harvested from a tree that morning. He bought four pints: enough, he said, to last three days.

A few miles later we crossed a road bridge over the Sewa River, one of the longest and most important in Sierra Leone, with headwaters up in the north-eastern highlands close to the border with Guinea. Water, as insipid as tea made with skimmed milk, lazed in the midday heat between forested river banks as, initially, my attention was drawn to a damaged rail bridge a hundred yards or so downstream, one that the Greenes' train would have passed over. Michael stopped the car and when I got out the humidity, insect noise and the collapsed span brought to mind the film *The Bridge on the River Kwai*. But Michael then pointed out the way the sandy river bank was not smooth but pockmarked, as if chewed away by outsized weevils. The reason for these cavities was, in large part, the explanation for Sierra Leone's troubled modern history – diamonds.

Diamonds were first found in Sierra Leone in January 1930 by a British geologist named J. D. Pollet in the gravel of a stream close to the Sewa River. Until then, mining in West Africa had been focused largely around Mali and Ghana, with Sierra Leone viewed as geologically barren. All that changed when Pollet's survey team found not just significant numbers of gem-quality diamonds, but also indications that other deposits lay in riverbeds spread across a huge swathe of the eastern part of the country.

These sought-after gems are forged deep under the earth's crust, an anomalous molecular coming together of carbon atoms brought on by unimaginably high temperatures and pressures, a process taking millions of years. While forming they float about like superheated croutons in a molten rock soup and the only reason we, up on the earth's surface, know about them is that, every so often during the planet's four billion years of existence, the soup has burst upwards through cracks between the shifting plates in the earth's crust. These structural weaknesses allowed diamond-bearing magma to spew out in explosive eruptions that eventually cooled to leave behind carrot-shaped columns, known as pipes, of gem-rich volcanic rock reaching back down into the earth from whence they came. It was in Kimberley, a tiny community in a remote desert region of South Africa, that such a pipe was first identified in the late nineteenth century on land owned by a family called De Beers, a name still held by the world's largest diamond mining and trading company. Kimberley itself gave its name to the diamond-bearing volcanic rock and henceforth the commercial hunt for diamonds became largely the hunt for kimberlite pipes.

From a commercial mining point of view the best way to exploit diamonds is to find where gem-rich kimberlite pipes breach the earth's surface and dig down. If you secure the area, build a meaning-ful perimeter fence around the top of the pipe and bring in the necessary earth-moving and processing equipment, diamond mining can be orderly, efficient and transparent. It becomes a matter simply of digging out the kimberlite and sifting it to recover the stones.

Sierra Leone's curse is that the elements have already done much of the sifting, spreading diamonds far beyond the tops of the original pipes. Over time, the action of water, through seasonal rains and ever-changing river systems, skimmed off the heads of the country's pipes dotting the east of the country, washing away the valueless kimberlite but spreading its valuable diamonds far and wide, albeit in smaller

concentrations, within gravel along river banks and streambeds. After
Mr Pollet's discovery in 1930 it was not initially possible to locate
Sierra Leone's kimberlite pipes but this was largely academic – profits
could still be made as river gravel in many places was rich enough in
diamonds to be worth processing.

The problem was that under these conditions control of diamond
mining here has been effectively impossible. The authorities could
not bar people from all the gem-rich riverbeds as they could not fence
off the entire eastern region of the country and new arrivals did not
need expensive processing equipment because it was not necessary to
dig deep in order to strike lucky. A spade, a sieve and access to a
promising-looking stretch of riverbed was all that was needed for a
person to become a diamond miner. It has been this lack of barriers to
entry that has made Sierra Leone's diamond industry so problematic
over the years.

From the moment Pollet's discovery became known, the British
colonial authorities struggled to control Sierra Leone's diamond
industry. Smuggling was always a problem and indeed during
Graham Greene's wartime service in Sierra Leone, he was under
orders to stop unscrupulous Arab dealers smuggling stones to
Germany for use as industrial diamonds in the Nazi war effort. And
later the mostly Lebanese diamond dealers of Sierra Leone acquired
such a reputation for hardheadedness that Nicky Oppenheimer,
current head of the De Beers diamond giant, was sent here as a young
man to hone his trading skills.

But it was not smuggling that made Sierra Leone's diamond
industry so damaging. The country's poverty meant that when
diamonds were discovered they prompted a social revolution, ruining
any chance of the economy becoming sustainable. Tens of thousands
of young men left a life of poorly paid toil on farms and headed east to
the diamond fields. So significant was the loss of young men from the
agricultural sector in the 1940s and 1950s that a country which used
to make profits from the export of rice was declared bankrupt as farm
output collapsed, forcing it to rely on handouts to pay for food
imports.

It was this diamond-skewed economic mess that Sierra Leone's
new government inherited on independence from Britain in 1961, a
challenge it was incapable of dealing with. Throughout the post-

independence era diamonds were built up as the country's potential saviour, an asset that would lift the country once and for all out of poverty. But corruption, shady deals and the fact that the extensive diamond fields were still so difficult to run efficiently meant the promise of a diamond-bright future for Sierra Leone remained folly.

Diamonds were the major driver behind Sierra Leone's civil war and a significant reason it festered for so long. The relative ease with which diamonds can be recovered from river gravel meant all the RUF gunmen needed to do was drive government forces away from the east of the country in order to get access to a regular money supply. This was a period of medieval cruelty in eastern Sierra Leone, a time when villagers were forced to scrabble through riverbeds at gunpoint in the search for gems that the rebels would then smuggle across the border into Liberia and eventually on to the world's diamond-dealing markets, such as the one in Antwerp. Evidence given in recent war crimes trials described mayonnaise jars filled to the brim with rough diamonds from Sierra Leone being trafficked through Liberia. Money earned from the sales would be spent on more weapons used by the rebels to secure yet more territory and enslave yet more people to search for yet more stones. It was a self-sustaining cycle of violence. The term 'blood diamonds' feels an entirely appropriate name for gems mined, smuggled and traded to sustain the conflict.

Hollywood took on the subject convincingly with the 2006 film *Blood Diamond* starring Leonardo DiCaprio. It is a wartime story of a white diamond smuggler joining forces with a desperate black Sierra Leonean villager to snaffle a priceless stone from under the noses of rebels and mercenaries out in the country's chaotic hinterland. For me, the film captures the overwhelming but dangerous allure of diamonds, how ordinary people can be dazzled by the promise of vast wealth. It is a promise that is rarely fulfilled and often comes at a terrible price but it is a promise that is hard to resist.

After the war finished in 2002 I visited the diamond town of Koidu, which lies about 50 miles north of Kenema, right in the middle of the country's diamond fields. There I saw the pathetically simple but back-breakingly grim reality of mining. It is such an inefficient and disorganised industry that much of the digging today takes place in river gravel that has already been worked over several times, with experience telling the miners they still might find something missed by their predecessors.

So, like dogs gnawing an old bone in the hope of finding a passed-over lick of marrow, they toil away using nineteenth-century methods to find twenty-first-century stones. Without heavy equipment it takes long, sweaty days to shovel away valueless topsoil, before reaching the beds of ochre gravel where diamonds might lurk. Post-war attempts have been made to organise the industry but it has proved as difficult as ever to fence in the richest deposits and defeat artisanal miners who keep arriving in large numbers. The language they use comes from an earlier age, almost as far back as Sierra Leone's buccaneering past, as the miners speak of digging as 'tripping' and use 'fathoms' as their measure of depth. And with foul-smelling water welling up from below, they pan the gravel, spadeful by spadeful, sluicing it through a wire mesh sieve, backs bent, eyes straining at the swirl of grit and dust, hoping to catch sight of a life-changing gemstone.

As I left Koidu a teenager approached whispering secretively. Would I like to buy a stone, he mouthed, his eyes anxiously flicking around to make sure we were not overheard. Selling rough diamonds without a licence is a criminal offence in Sierra Leone, although it is a rule more honoured in the breach than the observance. Licensed buyers, mostly Lebanese, offer such low prices that diggers often look for other buyers. The boy's hand dipped into the pocket of his threadbare shorts and there, suddenly, on his palm was a marble-sized stone, pale grey in colour with the foggy texture of scratched glass. I had no idea if I was looking at a genuine rough diamond or a fragment of old car windscreen but I can remember the momentary tightening in the stomach, the dizzying rush of temptation. Dangerous things diamonds, I thought, as I forced myself to walk away.

Graham Greene's spirits rose the further away he got from Freetown but my feelings were a little different. After the passed-over decay of the capital I had hoped to find at least some evidence of progress out in the provinces, but I was disappointed. It started with the roads that got worse the more distance we covered, like narrowing blood vessels in a diseased liver getting more sclerotic and ineffective. We were hoping to make Kailahun by nightfall, a notoriously wild frontier town where the Greenes spent their last nights in Sierra Leone before trekking into Liberia, and although we were travelling in the dry season, when the roads were at their most passable, we only just made it.

As agreed, Michael dropped us in Kenema, a tatty town similar to Bo, although with more diamond dealers. Cheery to the end, he shook our hands before driving off mumbling something about 'being thirsty'. He had left us at what passed for Kenema's main bus station, an open piece of ground on the edge of town crowded with unconvincing-looking poda-podas, many with doors missing, shattered windscreens, and bodywork patched with crudely welded shards of metal. To my amateur eye a cream-coloured Mazda appeared the soundest of them all and the message stencilled in black letters above its front bumper felt somehow reassuring. It said '*if God gree*', the Krio for God willing or *Inshallah*, a message that felt like a good hedged position in a region that was part-Christian, part-Muslim.

The minibus had seats for eight passengers but the driver waited until he had squeezed in fourteen people, each paying £3 for a trip that spanned roughly a fifth of the country, before announcing he was ready to leave. The engine fired and we lurched across the dusty field but only as far as what amounted to a service station. A hand-operated pump delivered fuel from an old barrel on the ground next to what looked like a car-boot sale of old pipes, valves and gas cylinders, all vaguely attached to one another. With a single tug on a hand crank the ensemble came to hissing life like an ill-tempered viper. I had never before seen the insides of an air compressor but this alfresco arrangement worked well enough and our bald tyres were soon inflated to the driver's satisfaction.

After setting off I remembered the article I had seen in the news-paper office in Freetown, the one that described the 50-mile stretch of national highway between Kenema and Kailahun as 'deplorable'. Ruts churned up by trucks and jeeps during the last rains had been baked hard by the dry-season sun, creating an assault course that destroyed axles and gearboxes. The elephant-ear fronds of roadside banana trees were not just rusty now but deep red with dust thrown up by passing traffic, and often I saw the skeletons of vehicular road-kill, abandoned trucks and vans that had reached the end of their road in Sierra

Leone's wild east. A fellow passenger could sense my astonishment at the road surface so he leaned forward and tried to emphasise the positive: 'You think this is bad? You wait until the rains come and then the mud and the broken bridges and the fallen trees will block this road completely for weeks on end. The road might seem bad to you but it is a blessing for us that we can get through without having to walk.'

The coming of peace meant roads in the east of Sierra Leone have been opened, a clear improvement on the civil war when fighting made many of these areas unreachable. But the traffic using the roads was opportunistic and piecemeal. What chance meaningful economic development when traders had to factor the regular destruction of vehicles and season-long delays into their pricing?

The driver, a lean, elderly man wearing a flat cap, had the disconcerting habit of removing the minibus key from the ignition as we drove and spinning it by its fob looped round his little finger. David and I spent six hours wedged up together on the front passenger seat but I never worked out how the engine kept going when he did this. The appalling road surface was for him such a normal feature of life it was not even worth commenting on. Like an expert skier who can see a route down a mogul field he picked his line through the rock-hard mud, nursing his overladen Mazda forward, the whole ensemble crowned by a bulging tarpaulin-wrapped hulk of luggage lashed to the roof rack.

He had the air of a train driver keeping to a timetable, as whenever passengers joined us at a stop he would give a single warning cry before setting off. The teenager responsible for the overhead luggage was in constant danger as the driver did not wait for him to get down from the roof. Several times the poda-poda set off before he had clambered back down, meaning he had to swing gymnastically by one arm to make it safely back into the passenger compartment. He was obviously not the complaining type. There was no seat for him and he passed the six hours of the drive on his haunches.

More significant for our driver than the awful road conditions were police checkpoints. For optimists who believe official corruption has been done away with in post-war Sierra Leone, I recommend a drive along one of its main rural arteries. A rope strung across the carriageway and a uniformed figure sitting outside a mud hut nearby shows how the canker of corruption eats at the country's advancement. The police know that everyone knows they are up to no good, but for the sake of appearances the officers still go through the motions of discretion. The driver is summoned inside the hut so the size of the bribe can be arrived at out of earshot of others. The presence of two white faces in a poda-poda spells trouble for the driver as the policeman sniffs the chance of a larger fee – the assumption being that the driver will have fleeced the foreigner so it is only fair for the policeman to upwardly adjust the fleecing of the driver. Several times in Sierra Leone I felt drivers look at us cursing as they disappeared under a hut's thatch for their police shakedown.

The far east of Sierra Leone is higher than the central plateau and for the first time on our journey across the country I felt a sense of elevation as we started to climb gently over undulating hills separated by ravines and gullies, although there were still no major breaks in the bush. The country used to have large pockets of high rainforest but most of the monumental trees, such as the mahoganies and cotton trees, have been cut down by loggers and only one sizeable remnant remains – the Gola forest, straddling part of the border between Sierra Leone and Liberia. The resulting scrub that covers most of Sierra Leone is lower than rainforest but every bit as impenetrable and difficult to navigate. With the Liberian border getting closer all the time and, with it, the moment when we would have to start walking, I was reminded of how crucial it would be to find reliable local guides.

The road continued to follow the route of the old railtrack so, when we passed villages, traces of the railway were occasionally visible, an old sign here, an abandoned telegraph room there. We stopped briefly at the old terminus at Pendembu, end of the line for the Greenes in 1935 and the place where they had to board a truck for the final, bone-shaking pull to Kailahun. I remembered seeing an original map of the Sierra Leonean rail network that meticulously marked Pendembu as lying 227½ miles from Freetown, but after being badly damaged in the war the town was in many ways more primitive today than when the Greenes passed through. Few of its buildings were habitable and the central crossroads consisted of a few roadside stalls set up by hawkers selling cheap dry-goods, things that did not need expensive refrigeration – biscuits, batteries, cans of fizzy drink. A radio broadcast live coverage of an English premiership soccer game (a scoreless draw between Arsenal and Tottenham Hotspur).

During Graham Greene's service with MI6 in the 1940s he came back up here by train but found standards had already begun to slip. He thought the government guesthouse too dirty to use, so he set up camp between the rails, a scene described in one of his volumes of autobiography, *Ways of Escape*.

> One took one's 'boy', one's own supply of tinned food, one's own chair,
> one's own bed, even one's own oil-lamp to hang on a hook in the
> compartment when dark fell. The little train stopped for the night . . .
> and thence chugged laboriously uphill to Pendembu. At Pendembu
> there was a rest-house, not very well maintained by the local chief, so I
> preferred to take my evening meal on the railway line, my camp table
> set up on the track.

The sun set soon after our poda-poda left Pendembu but on we ploughed. The key-spinning driver continued at an ever-slowing pace, his one functioning headlight enough to pick his line through the ruts on slopes that grew steadily steeper. A fullish moon rose as we crested an open hilltop and for a second I could see a wide vista of West African forest in negative, the treetops outlined in watery silver under the sky's wide shadow. Evening mist then gobbled up the moon and we continued in complete darkness for several more hours.

It was in Kailahun, a district capital with a population of 25,000 people, that the Sierra Leonean civil war had its crucible, the first large town to fall to RUF rebels invading from Liberia. It would be fought over repeatedly and after the war it became the focus of tens of millions of pounds in foreign aid and development work. Peering out into the darkness I was expecting to see a large town come into sight and perhaps even to spot some new buildings. But, six hours after leaving Kenema and without fanfare, the driver suddenly stopped in the middle of an apparently empty road and announced we had reached Kailahun.

Hungry, dusty and tired we got out of the minibus and there, in the shadows, were the glowering shapes of broken buildings and vehicles. Round a corner we found light spilling from a shack onto white plastic tables under which chickens pecked enthusiastically. Just as enthusiastically, David and I took our places at the Peace Garden, Kailahun's only restaurant, and were served with large plates of rice and what the landlady called beef. The sauce was great but the meat gritty and tubular. I turned off my headtorch, thinking it best not to investigate too closely. Aid workers were the only people wealthy enough to eat at the Peace Garden, where an evening meal cost £2.50, and when I paid, the landlady routinely handed me a pro-forma receipt. 'So you can claim from your expense account,' she said.

By daylight Kailahun looked as if the waters of a tsunami had only just retreated. It was seven years since the war had finished and yet as the morning fog lifted the town felt like it was still in a state of shock. It was not just its architecture of war, the rutted roads, the ankle-high outlines of destroyed buildings, the bare-branch hovels roofed with plastic sheeting. An even stronger sense of trauma unhealed could be seen in the eyes of schoolgirls fallen to prostitution to earn money for textbooks; the menace of young men – former child soldiers – leaning idly over the handlebars of the okada motorbike taxis they had been given in exchange for laying down their arms; the desperation in the pleading of people queuing up for jobs outside aid groups' headquarters, the only source of employment in a moribund local economy.

These NGO offices were among the few buildings in town with any sense of order and there were dozens of them, built behind high perimeter walls with guards manning iron gates. Lawlessness meant that the presence of computers, generators, satellite communications and, of course, jeeps, inside the compounds made them ready targets. The concentration of aid groups' signboards in Kailahun outdid even that in Freetown. They stood in thickets, the older, rustier ones indicating that many of the groups had got here shortly after the war ended in 2002 and still had not completed their operations. Marie Stopes, the sex education group, appeared to have just arrived in town, its signage conspicuously pristine.

Kailahun is about as far from Freetown as it is possible to travel and still be inside Sierra Leone. Its position close to the country's three-way border junction with Guinea and Liberia had, in its day, been a blessing, ensuring cross-border trade and a sense of wide horizons, as outsiders passed through, bringing with them different languages, customs and faiths. There had been Mandingo traders, the wanderers of West Africa, who stood out with their flowing gowns and brightly coloured fezzes. Their Islamic zeal and desire for profit cared little for international boundaries drawn up by colonial cartographers. And there were ambitious Krio administrators from Freetown who came out to the provinces with their textbooks and college degrees, determined to drag rural Africa into the modern world. And there were white missionaries, who sought to seed Christianity in the heathen hinterland of Africa, and who worked alongside assorted colonial administrators.

This was the Kailahun the Greenes saw in 1935, a remote, colonial trading town that was undergoing development, albeit incrementally slow development. They spent two nights at the government guesthouse, drank warm beer with a jittery Scottish engineer sent all the way out here to build a bridge, and dined with a book-loving district commissioner. In the first edition of *Journey Without Maps* Graham Greene noted how pleased he was to see his worst-selling novel in the commissioner's collection, 'rotting among the others on the shelf', although the reference was removed from later editions.

The Greenes were not the only ones to use Kailahun as a jumping-off point to explore Liberia. The train-lorry combination through Sierra Leone had already been used by numerous explorers, missionaries and prospectors wanting a backdoor into Liberia. Indeed, while in Kailahun the Greenes met one of them, a young German man with a shaven head and a grubby vest, someone Greene initially suspected of being a diamond prospector. In fact, he turned out to be an academic anthropologist with years of experience in the region, familiar with the trails from Kailahun into Liberia, and he ended up guiding the Greenes safely across the border. Graham Greene describes him as having 'an aristocratic air in spite of his beachcomber's dress', while Barbara Greene writes he 'looked startlingly like the usual pictures of Jesus Christ with his carefully cut beard, softly smiling eyes and gentle face'.

The strategic location that had brought the Greenes, the German anthropologist and all the other outsiders to this small but prospering border trading town has, in more recent years, been its curse. When Charles Taylor, then a warlord seeking to take power in Liberia, set about stirring up conflict in Sierra Leone in 1991 it was through Kailahun that rebels and guns poured, with Taylor allowing his proxies to launch their grab for the nearby diamond fields. Government troops, police, teachers and civil servants all fled, and for years the town of Kailahun was the epicentre of one of the world's most brutal, chaotic conflicts.

The ghost of the Greenes' anthropologist guide looked after David and me as we were given lodging at a guesthouse run by GTZ, the German government's international development arm. It was basically a shell of a building undergoing what the caretaker rather extravagantly called 'refurbishment'. I have travelled a fair bit through Africa and found it perfectly acceptable but I was interested to see David's reaction. There was no power, the insect screens over the windows were torn and the water supply was not working – but, fortunately, he was clearly not the complaining type. By the light of his headtorch he got on with suspending his mosquito net from some nails in the ceiling above a bed and then sat down quietly to write his journal.

The overland journey had been straightforward but to follow the Greenes' route from Kailahun would be a different matter. While the region's aid traffic and commercial trade entered Liberia north of Kailahun at Koindu, we would have to head due east for about 15 miles, through a region with no marked roads, to the Sierra Leonean village of Dawa, close to the border with Liberia, and then try to cross on foot. Dawa is the village that no one back in Freetown had heard of so, after breakfast of plantain and chicken back at the Peace Garden, we headed to the Kailahun mayor for advice.

'Of course I know Dawa,' came the answer in a tone just shy of booming. Tom Nyumah clearly liked to use his voice to reinforce his authority as town mayor and chairman of Kailahun District Council. 'I am a Kailahun man, born and bred in the country, from the Kissi tribe. I know every road, village and town in the area.'

I probed a little more, wanting to know if there was a functioning border crossing at Dawa.

'Well, I have never actually been there,' he replied. 'But every-thing is at peace now so I don't think you will have any problems. There was a lot of fighting, you know, around Dawa. Those rebels hit us hard in 1991, in three places at the same time along the border, and

Dawa was one of them. We lost Kailahun quickly and it was four years before we won it back again. I hope you don't meet any trouble out there.'

He asked us about our plan to follow the Greenes' route and David and I performed a little routine we had developed, which entailed me telling the story of us following in the footsteps of a famous English author, while David provided what he called the 'visual aids', holding up the map-page from my paperback copy of *Journey Without Maps*. When I told Nyumah I hoped to write a book about our trip, his interest stirred.

'I am a soldier boy at heart, you know. Sure, I made it to the top but my boys knew I led from the front and they always stood behind me. I know all about the war and all the secrets of what went on. I even met Foday Sankoh, face to face, back in 1996 at peace talks in Abidjan. I should have killed him there and then but he said he regretted what he had started in Sierra Leone so I forgave him. I was Born Again in 1991 so I had God on my side. Don't you want to write a book about me?'

I smiled politely and said I would certainly consider his idea.

His description of making it 'to the top' was no exaggeration. In 1992 Tom Nyumah, then only twenty-two years old, was one of a junta of disgruntled young army officers who staged a coup. For four years the National Provisional Ruling Council junta ran Sierra Leone, although 'ran' hardly seems an appropriate description for the feuding, bloodletting, attempted coups, executions and political paralysis of this period. Nyumah served as defence minister and it was under his rule that the Sierra Leone army collapsed so calamitously that RUF rebels took control of the eastern half of the country and white mercenaries were brought in to defeat the rebels, paid for by the promise of diamond revenues. After other members of the junta were either killed or arrested, Nyumah slipped out of the country and spent nine years in the United States studying at university, having a family and working for an insurance company. But the fact he was back, elected to office, suggested post-war politics in Sierra Leone were not so fundamentally different from before the war.

As we were leaving his office I asked him about his family and why his five children had not come back to Sierra Leone with him.

'It's much too dangerous for them here,' he said without any sense of irony.

There was one person I met in Kailahun whom I struggle to forget. To protect her I will change her name to Bendu but I will not alter anything that she told me. Across Sierra Leone today victims of the war are so common that for me there are times when they lose definition. I met them everywhere, in shops, bus queues, bars, town centres, rehabilitation camps, but somehow the horror of what they underwent as individuals became lost in a single numbing brand of Sierra Leonean suffering. For years the dominant image of this country had been of young people with their limbs cut off, victims of the barbaric RUF practice of not killing civilians but forever marking them, by cutting off hands (long sleeves, as the attackers put it in cruel euphemism) or arms (short sleeves).

While other warring factions committed numerous atrocities, the cutting of arms was something the RUF specialised in, although there was no clear reason for them doing this. Some said it was to punish those who had taken part in elections the RUF did not approve of. To show they had cast their ballot, voters would have their hands marked with ink by election officials, so by cutting off hands, some said, the RUF stopped them ever voting again. Others said it was an RUF ploy to stop the civilians from mining diamonds for themselves, something the RUF sought to control when it overran the diamond-rich east of the country. Others said it was simply a terror tactic to intimidate the civilian population. Whatever the reason, the spectacle of otherwise healthy Sierra Leoneans with stumps for arms became a grisly national hallmark.

During the war one of the first things outsiders saw when they arrived in Freetown was a camp for amputees on the main road into town. The image dominated this country to such an extent that I know of aid groups who offered journalists online testimonies from victims along with sets of photographs so these reporters could put together graphic accounts without ever actually coming to the country.

The scars Bendu bore were not visible. When we met in Kailahun she was resting in the shade outside the single-room mud hut she called home wearing a school uniform that could have been out of Britain *circa* 1960, with a green felt hat tied with a ribbon, pleated skirt and white blouse bearing the crest of Kailahun's Methodist School. She looked much too old to be a schoolgirl but the local aid worker who introduced us, Sarah Smart, had already explained that while Bendu was probably in her early twenties nobody knew her age for sure.

'After what happened to her we all think it is best that she has the sanctuary of a school to go to,' Sarah confided.

For privacy Bendu invited me into her room before she started speaking. The beaten earth floor had been recently swept and her entire wardrobe of clothes, amounting to a single armful, was neatly folded on a handmade cane chair. On the mud wall hung a poster of the soccer player Thierry Henry wearing the strip of the Arsenal football club. Inside the room the heat was intense and the atmosphere close as she began to speak.

'I was about three when the rebels first came to Kailahun. I was with my father and my mother and they tried to run away to Guinea but my mother was shot dead with me tied to her back. You know what I mean? She had a lappa, the wraps that mothers use to tie their children to their backs. Well, my mother was dead but the bullets did not hit me. A rebel woman, the wife of a man who called himself Major, found me on my dead mother and she had pity and took me to a village. The Major was a bad man and he raped me many times. I was a child of three or four or five, I do not know exactly because I have never had a birth certificate and nobody from my family survived.

'Then some soldiers came to the rebel village and the woman who had been looking after me was killed. The Major ran away but I could not run because I was hurt from the rape. The soldiers took me to a doctor called Farida and she was kind to me. She carried me a long way through the bush and slowly I got better so I could walk and after a week we got to Makeni, where there was a hospital we called the Arab hospital. I had a pain in my stomach and liquid coming from my ear, so they took me into the hospital and gave me an operation that means I cannot have babies for myself.

'Then the rebels came again and attacked the hospital and Dr Farida was killed. The rebels took me once more and I became one of the wives of Issa Sesay. He took me for sex whenever he wanted to. He took me every night. When Makeni was attacked by the government the rebels gave me a gun and we ran into the bush shooting. We got back together to Kailahun and Sesay was there and I was still his wife. I don't know how long it was I was like this but it lasted for years.

'When the war finished I earned money by having sex with men. It was the only way I could survive but the UN gave me money to go to school. They gave me 300,000 Leones [about £60] and now I am going to school here. The Methodist School is the oldest school in the town, you know. Today we marched to mark its fiftieth anniversary.'

The name Sesay jumped out from my notes. He was one of the main figures within the RUF, a sort of Himmler to Foday Sankoh's Hitler. Both were detained at the end of the war but Sankoh died in custody, leaving Sesay the most senior RUF leader ever tried for war crimes in Sierra Leone. He was eventually convicted at the special war crimes tribunal created in Freetown on sixteen separate charges and jailed for fifty-two years. The indictment list includes many horrors, such as extermination, murder and terrorism, but he was also convicted of rape and sexual slavery. I had read some of the court testimony but found it strangely unmoving, a world away from the chaotic reality of bush villages where the rebels had committed their atrocities. Bendu gave that testimony a life the lawyers never could.

She was a broken human being. Physically she had suffered horrendous internal injuries from the sexual abuse. Sarah explained how doctors had only just saved her life when they operated on her during the war. And, emotionally, she was wrecked. The only power she had ever had during her life was sexual so she was left feeling this was her only attribute. It was an easy step for her to lapse into prostitution.

Even after all that had happened to Bendu during the war, the local community in Kailahun had still forced her, against her will, to be initiated into the Bundu bush society. This had involved her being taken under cover of darkness from her hut, and kept out in the forest for two weeks culminating in circumcision.

'They cut my clitoris,' Bendu told me flatly.

From the chorus of suffering that at times deafened me in Sierra Leone, Bendu's voice stood out. For me she symbolised the entire country: a young girl whose life was cursed by a combination of outsiders fomenting war and locals imposing traditional discipline.

The moment to take on Liberia was approaching. We found a driver who claimed to know the bush tracks to Dawa, and Sarah said she would provide us with a jeep, but I was having problems with the route on the other side of the border in Lofa County, the northern region of Liberia. The Greenes drove from Kailahun towards the frontier and then, with the help of their German guide, managed to trek all the way to the Liberian village of Bolahun on the first day, where they were given sanctuary at a mission station run by the Order of the Holy Cross, a community of Anglican monks from America. The Greenes had warned the Father Superior of their arrival by sending a messenger ahead with a letter in a cleft stick. When I emailed the order's headquarters in New York about relaying a message to Bolahun, I was told links with the mission had been cut in the early 1980s. One of the senior monks wrote back:

> The facilities were turned over to the local church and then the ravages of the Civil War took a great toll. Unfortunately, I do not have any way of contacting Bolahun . . . I'm sorry I can't be of much help in this. Blessings and safety in your travels. Go with God.

I had built up a database of contacts in Lofa County but by the time I got to Kailahun the only person answering his phone was a man called Moses Kallie, a field officer with an aid group named Samaritan's Purse. The mobile phone network is intermittent in Liberia so our connection was not good. When I explained I wanted to walk from the border Moses asked me several times to repeat myself.

'But why would you want to walk when we have motorbike tracks and jeep roads through the bush?' he bellowed back.

It took a while for the sceptical tone to disappear from his voice but Moses eventually agreed to meet us at the border. Part of the mission at Bolahun, he said, still existed and he promised he would go there on our behalf and ask if it would be possible for us to stay. The fact that I had someone on the Liberian side of the border willing to help represented progress, so after agreeing a border rendezvous for the following morning I headed back to our Kailahun guesthouse to help David with our final preparations.

As I went to bed I received the following text message:

Mr Butcher will you please text me your diet for the 2 or 3 days or nights that you will be here at Bolahun. We are waiting.

Who needs cleft sticks in the age of the mobile phone?

The only surviving photograph of Barbara Greene in Liberia. Wearing the Freetown-made shorts that were to incense her cousin, she joins the bearer column

CHAPTER 6

Falloe's *Stick*

St. Mary's Church, BoTahun
Completed in 1924

Above: Graham Greene on foot near Sierra Leone's eastern border, January 1935
Below: The author, similarly, February 2009

The next morning we found Mother Nature had placed markers close to the border between Sierra Leone and Liberia. As we bounced along a twisting jeep track, approaching the frontier, a pair of huge rock mounds came into view, standing proud from the otherwise low horizon, African versions of Ayers Rock rising not from the red Australian desert but from the wide jungle wastes of Sierra Leone. It had felt as if there was nothing but unbroken forest stretching all the way across the country from Freetown, so there was something a little sinister about these looming outcrops where no plant life could grow. They look like toxic fossils, scarabs of humungous Jurassic beetles. Revered by the local Kissi tribesmen as magical twins called Ginah and Joh, they radiated heat and a trace of menace from their dark flanks as we crept past on the last few miles of our journey by vehicle.

Dawa was muffled by late-morning heat when we finally arrived. A tiny nothing of a place, it consisted of a few thatched huts opening on to some bare ground, where matching sets of scuff marks in the soil and vertical bamboo poles betrayed occasional use as a football pitch. I could see people resting in the shade of mud walls watching us but nobody seemed to stir as the jeep turned and parked. The driver killed the engine and fearing a long wait I glanced at David but his attention was already focused on some movement in the distance.

Two figures, improbably dressed in thick coats and woolly hats, were walking towards us. For a second I thought they might be border officials but before I had time to think through what that might mean, one of them spoke and I recognised the voice from my mobile-phone calls over the past few days.

'I am Moses Kallie. Please can you tell me who is Mr Tim?'

We introduced ourselves and Moses explained that his companion, Johnson Boie, had agreed to act as our overland guide to Bolahun. We all shook hands before Moses took quiet control of the situation.

'I have a motorbike which I left on the Liberian side of the border and then walked across to find you. You are late. It will take about eight hours of walking so you must get started.'

Our jeep drove us the last half mile or so to a border crossing that consisted of a bamboo cane arm lowered over a jungle track. On the Sierra Leonean side we saw no officials but on the Liberian side there was a thatched hut, Moses' parked motorbike and an attendant gaggle of people in rags staring at it. I smiled when I saw the bike. Five years earlier when I had crossed the Congo it was exactly this model – a Yamaha AG – that had got me safely through the badlands of north Katanga. It was even painted with the same livery of red and black.

From beneath the low-slung doorway of the hut a tall, thin man emerged, unfolding himself like a mantis. I braced myself. When the Greenes passed here they had to spend long hours negotiating customs dues and import permits for almost everything they brought with them, from the water filter to tins of golden syrup. The only item the officials missed was the one thing they would have cared about most – a pistol. To speed up the whole process Graham Greene had agreed to pay a hugely inflated figure and then set off on foot, only to be pursued several days later by Liberian officials demanding yet more fees.

Our experience could not have been more different. The truth is that in the 1930s this was a meaningful border crossing regularly used by missionaries, prospectors, adventurers and scientists, so the authorities had good reason to park customs officials here. By 2009 this cross-border flow had dwindled to nothing so there was only one semi-detached official without passport-stamping equipment or customs mandate. He did not even have a piece of paper on which to write our names.

We had another advantage over the Greenes in that our border guard was not entirely with it. It might have been palm wine or some other form of alcohol or maybe jamba, but his eyes were swimming and he seemed to have lost the power of speech. I asked if he wanted to check our visas, stamp our passports or go through our health certificates; he just grinned lopsidedly and remained silent.

Even during the earliest stages of planning the trip I had been concerned about our luggage and between us David and I had stripped it down to the lightest possible load – two rucksacks and two daypacks between us. In spite of the reduction, the loads were still unfeasibly heavy for the terrain and climate. We would have to get help. The Greenes had used twenty-six bearers to carry their possessions but, to begin with at least, we would make do with Moses' motorbike to carry our rucksacks. While he took responsibility for packing, I approached Johnson to discuss the first day's route to Bolahun.

Awkwardly deferential to begin with, Johnson listened patiently while I explained we wanted not just to walk but to take forest tracks. In 1935 there had been no roads in the Liberian hinterland so the Greenes had had no alternative. But since the 1950s the interior of Liberia has been, to some extent, tamed by a network of roads and bridges. And the large UN peacekeeping force which has been in Liberia since the war ended in 2003 still spends much effort looking after that network, repairing years of neglect and wet-season damage. Johnson looked curious and asked why on earth we would not use jeeps and bikes like the few aid workers he had ever seen in the area. I explained, in brief, our interest in following the Greenes' journey from 1935 and how important it was for us to keep to their exact route, starting with their first overnight stop in Bolahun. After listening closely, he asked to see my map, speaking a very polite form of English learned at a mission school.

'Here we are at the border,' he said, using a twig as a pointer. 'And here is Bolahun east and a little bit south of us. I was thinking of taking you along this road marked here, which goes in a big curve to the north. That way, we can always hitch a lift or find a motorbike if you change your mind. But, if you really want, I know a way direct through the forest. It's been years since I went that way but if you like we can try.'

I told him that was exactly what we wanted.

The moment to start had come. Moses said he would be a while yet strapping down our packs, so I shook his hand, thanked him for his help and promised to see him that night at whatever remained of the old mission house in Bolahun. Johnson and David strode off in the lead and I fiddled around with my camera to capture the moment. This was my first time back in Liberia since the death threat put on me in the dog days of Taylor's regime so I felt just a tiny bit jumpy. I glanced back at the border official for the last time, worried he might have sobered up enough to take a closer interest in us. I had no reason to worry. He had flopped down on a wooden stool as limply as the

Lone Star flag of Liberia hanging motionless on the bamboo flagstaff above him.

The flag of the independent state of Liberia has been flying since 1847 when the country was founded by freed slaves and their descendants returning to Africa to escape racism in the United States of America. Just as Sierra Leone was created by British groups urging former slaves to go 'back to Africa', so Liberia was created by their American counterparts. But in spite of similarities in the two African countries' early histories there remains one major difference – Britain would eventually stake Sierra Leone as a colony while early foreign settlers in Liberia would have to survive without the embrace of any overarching colonial power. This allowed Liberia to develop its own form of black rule more than a century before the rest of the continent.

For a long time history painted the Liberian project in the glowing vernacular of philanthropy. Guilt over America's troubled dependence on slavery was, it was argued, partly assuaged by a process of generously giving freed slaves the chance of new life in their traditional African homeland. Some of the religious supporters of the project phrased it even in terms of persecuted former slaves being born again into a life of liberty, comfort and plenty.

This was mostly bunkum. The main group behind the shipping of the former slaves, the American Society for Colonizing the Free People of Color of the United States (known more commonly as the American Colonization Society), was run entirely by white men with a range of agendas. There were a few altruistic souls genuinely committed to finding a better life for slaves, but many of the society's members actively supported slavery and saw the 'back to Africa' project as a way not to undercut American slavery but to reinforce it. In the early nineteenth century, America was home to over two million black slaves but there was also a growing cohort, numbering perhaps as many as half a million, of so-called 'freemen', former slaves living mainly in the northern states who had, in some way or other, secured their freedom. White slave-owners saw them as a threat and so they supported keenly the 'back to Africa' project as a way to get rid of them, to ethnically cleanse America of freed blacks. James Monroe, the American president in whose honour the Liberian capital,

Monrovia, would be named, described freed black slaves walking the streets of America as 'a class of very dangerous people'.

So the purity of America's 'back to Africa' project was tarnished from the outset by double standards and opportunism. Bitter divisions opened up in the coloured community in America, with those willing to go back to Africa criticised as lackeys by those who stayed behind. The dispute got so bad the American Colonization Society was even accused of kidnapping former slaves and shipping them overseas to be imprisoned in Africa against their will. Many freed slaves argued they had as much right to live in America as whites and to get on the ships back across the Atlantic was an act of betrayal that undermined the much more important overall struggle against slavery. Controversy festered for years so the number of freed slaves willing to take part in the Liberia venture was never that large, and the American Colonization Society only ever managed to relocate to Liberia a small fraction of the number sent to Sierra Leone.

The first ships set sail from the United States in the 1820s. They had no clear idea where exactly they were aiming so they simply followed the earlier British returnees and made it up as they went along. Making landfall on the coast of Sierra Leone, by then already established as a British colony, they let the northerly winds inch them around the African shoreline southwards. There were some false starts on islands belonging to Sierra Leone but eventually they reached the Grain Coast and found what they were looking for, local African chiefs willing to hand over pockets of land. Over the next twenty years a series of piecemeal settlements was created, dotted along a 200-mile-long stretch of virgin coastline.

Life was as tough for these early American settlers as for the British pioneers thirty years earlier in Freetown. Decimated by disease, hunger and clashes with hostile tribes, some of the settlements dwindled, some died out, and others bickered among themselves over precedence. According to one count, within twenty years of the arrival of the first immigrants almost half had already perished.

By 1847 the whole American project had reached crisis point. At the identical moment in Sierra Leone's history Britain had come in as the colonial power, mopping up the remnants of the settler communities that had been sent there and declaring it a British colony. But the government in Washington had no such territorial interest in

Africa, so the few thousand surviving freed slaves in their separate communities clinging to the Grain Coast took a brave and ambitious decision: they would unite, sever official links with the American Colonization Society and go it alone as a sovereign nation to be known as Liberia.

At a special convention in Monrovia, a Declaration of Independence and a Constitution were formally agreed on 26 July 1847, using language borrowed directly from the American versions, although with some crucial differences. In the Liberian declaration, the former slaves described how they had been so ill-treated in the United States that they were forced to come to Africa as 'asylum from our deep degradation'. And in the constitution, the American order was inverted as whites were explicitly forbidden from ever becoming citizens in Liberia. Article V Section 13 said 'none but persons of color shall be admitted to citizenship in this republic'. The clause's language was later hardened, restricting citizenship to 'persons who are Negroes or of Negro descent'.

Monrovia was declared the new nation's capital and nominal inland borders were assigned, although it would be years before any government official actually battled through the jungle to stake the frontier. The whole project was predicated on the granting of freedom to previously oppressed outsiders, an ideal enshrined in the national motto, 'The Love of Liberty Brought Us Here'.

Life was not easy for the infant republic. Surrounded on all sides by acquisitive colonists – the British in Sierra Leone and the French in both Guinea and the Ivory Coast – it was an achievement even to make it through to the twentieth century. In an almost permanent state of bankruptcy, the young state limped along, surviving on occasional remittances from the American Colonization Society and a series of expensive bank loans. In many ways it was saved because it had nothing worth invading for – no meaningful diamond fields or gold deposits had been found – so the imperial powers let it be. The shortage of funds meant, however, economic, social and educational development stalled in Monrovia and never even began in the rest of the country. For decades, the country was formally recognised only by a few nations such as Britain, which supplied an old gunboat from the Royal Navy as the sole ship in the Liberian navy. America's internal divisions over race meant that for years it refused officially to acknowledge the new country in case that led to a black Liberian diplomat having to be formally received in Washington.

But the most active fault-line that runs through Liberia's history is not so much its rivalry with foreign powers as its rivalry between the small cohort of black outsiders, mainly freed American slaves, who assumed power over the country, and the much larger number of native Liberians, who effectively became their vassals, a tension that echoed that in Sierra Leone between the Krios and the indigenous tribes. With their American education, Christian faith and English language, the settlers in Liberia were as different from the animist hunter-gatherers and subsistence farmers of the jungle as any white occupying colonial power arriving in Africa. To distinguish them from native Africans these ex-slaves' descendants became known as 'Americo-Liberians', although the natives later came to call all black outsiders 'Congos', an echo from the huge number of Africans taken into slavery from homelands around the mouth of the Congo River. In turn, native Liberians would be referred to pejoratively as 'country people'.

The image of Liberia projected around the world was one of a democratic nation run by Africans for Africans. For years the country was known as The Black Republic, even The Negro Republic, precisely because it was not run by whites, a stark exception following the colonial land-grab of the Scramble for Africa. But the reality was that tension simmered for decades between Americo-Liberians and country people, erupting first in the 1890s when fighters from southern, coastal tribes, such as the Kru and Grebo, rose against the Liberian government, and then in an almost endless cycle of clashes upcountry when administrators sent from Monrovia arrived to levy taxes. For the first time the government raised an army, known as the Frontier Force, comprising tribal soldiers from the 'developed' coastal towns led by officers drawn exclusively from the Americo-Liberian community. Their deployment inland was often as bloody and ruthless as campaigns by occupying white colonial forces elsewhere in the continent.

Tension reached crisis point in the late 1920s when the government of Liberia, a country with a founding charter explicitly condemning the slave trade as 'that curse of curses', allowed large numbers of its people to be sold into slavery. The motive remains disputed. Some argued it was a way for a broke country to make money, others said it was the best way of getting rid of troublemakers from the tribal hinterland. Defenders of the Americo-Liberian elite suggested that the authorities were simply continuing a long-standing tradition whereby tribesmen effectively 'belonged' to village elders who could do with them whatever they wanted.

In the end, the League of Nations inquiry found that the Liberian government had shipped its countrymen overseas 'under conditions of criminal compulsion scarcely distinguishable from slave raiding and slave trading'. There can be no greater metamorphosis for a state founded by former slaves inspired by the 'Love of Liberty' than for it to start selling its own people into slavery.

The resulting scandal was one of the great international crises of the early 1930s and the issue festered on for so long that it provided grounds for the anti-slavery society in London to send Graham Greene on his journey through Liberia in 1935. Tension between the two communities would simmer in Liberia long after the Greenes passed through, although the Americo-Liberian elite skilfully contained the issue for decades. Elections were held, but through shameless gerrymandering and vote-rigging the party of the settler elite, the True Whig Party, monopolised power for a hundred years, its leaders deporting themselves like nineteenth-century Congressmen in Washington, with a dress code of morning coats and top hats – utterly inappropriate for the West African climate – that lasted deep into the 1970s, and a peculiarly strong attachment to freemasonry – one of the most prominent buildings in Monrovia is the national masonic temple. With a weak and undeveloped economy, the party's leaders looked overseas for help, forging close links with the United States, first during the Second World War, when Liberia signed a defence agreement to allow America to develop the airport at Roberts Field, and then during the Cold War, when Liberia provided Washington with a like-minded, capitalist bulwark against the Soviet Union's allies in post-colonial Africa.

Backed by America, economic growth in Liberia was weak but just strong enough to keep the settler elite in power, although tension with the indigenous population never went away. Modest progress towards integration was made, especially in the 1970s, but the gap between the two communities continued to such an extent that an American academic, R. Earle Anderson, could publish a book in the 1950s called *Liberia – America's African Friend* in which his support of the Americo-Liberian elite led him to begin a chapter:

> For every member of the ruling class in Liberia there are a hundred or more tribal people. They are the country's greatest problem.

It would be a problem that would finally explode in 1980 and launch the sleepy but stable nation of Liberia on a path of civil war and ethnic violence.

The track from the border could not have been more perfect. Framed on both sides by elephant grass and overhung in places by palm fronds, it was shaded, comfortable under foot and easy to follow. Ecstatic to have started the trek, I was initially able to ignore the heat and humidity as Johnson, still wearing a thick body warmer and woolly hat, set a gentle strolling pace. David knew by heart Graham Greene's description of this same moment of departure in 1935 – 'snow in London, the fierce noon sun on the clearing, yellow fever in Freetown'. I smiled. The night before I had called my parents in Britain by satellite phone to hear a seasonal February snowfall had wrought travel chaos across the United Kingdom.

That first day's walking has stayed with me in minute detail. I still reconstruct it in my mind when struggling for sleep, so reassuringly complete was its span. It took us from the Sierra Leone frontier for 14 miles into the forested hills of Lofa County, the northernmost region of Liberia, past clutches of thatched huts, home to subsistence-farming communities surviving on rice grown in clearings hacked from the jungle. For the few moments it took to walk through a village we would touch on a lifestyle barely changed from that which the Greenes witnessed. There were modern T-shirts and the occasional Chinese-made plastic bucket, but the cardinal features of 1935 were the same in 2009 – communities winnowing rice for the evening meal, gathering fuel for the fire, drawing water from a stream or well, resting in the shade from the force of the sun.

We met countless groups of villagers whose curiosity at the sight of white travellers was always tempered by polite discretion. We saw no

trading posts or roadside stalls but the locals invariably offered what
they could, water most often and, on one welcome occasion when my
internal battery was beginning to dip, bananas. The trail took us
through grasslands so high the fronds arched over the footpath to plait
a tunnel roof. One of the few surviving photographs of Graham
Greene at the start of his trek shows him wearing a topi, walking
through head-high elephant grass. David took a matching photograph
of me, although on my head I had my lucky hat, a floppy thing much
bleached by the African sun. The path meandered under huge trees as
tall as skyscrapers, remnants of the once complete rainforest that
covered this region before the advent of industrial logging, and
through thickets where each trunk wore its own bulky outfit of ivy,
creeper and other secondary vegetation. In places, candyfloss wisps of
fibre from the in-season cotton trees drifted across a track that
rollercoastered its way up and down through gullies made by the
headwaters of Liberia's principal rivers.

What made that day so important for me was that, after a year of
hard planning and expectation, I could enjoy the traveller's sense of
release. I let go of bus timetables, phone connections, emails about
security and fretful links to the wider world, instead committing
myself to a calmer rhythm, that of rural West Africa where days were
shaped by how far you could reasonably walk and where you might
stop to find food, water and shelter.

My sensory receptors were primed and I can still taste the bitter
heartburn that came from biting into a kola nut. Villagers
traditionally offer kola nuts to visitors and I was given my first by an
old man in one of the first communities we reached, Kpongoma
Wayan. It was about the size of a healthy conker with flesh the
purplish tinge of a radish. I could only manage a few chews before I
spat out the woody, chalky pulp, noisily hawking up gobbets of
acid saliva. Bearer parties in the early twentieth century subsisted
on kola nuts, chewing them by the hour in part to suppress appetite.
Mandingo traders would travel miles through these forests buying
up kola nuts and transporting them north towards the desert
communities on the edge of the Sahara where they were prized as a
delicacy. And the smell of forest decomposition also stays with me. I
can remember perfectly the stomach-turning stench of rotting
matter when I stepped on something damp in the forest, blue and

black butterflies exploding upwards from where they had been feeding.

Johnson grew in confidence noticeably that first day. He was thirty-six years old with the face of a much younger man, fresh and at first glance, perhaps, a little gullible. But he soon showed that in these remote backwoods he was anything but a fool. Since the end of the war in 2003, he had spent years working as a 'tracing officer' for aid groups, using remote trails like the ones we were on to reconnect people separated by war. Lofa County had seen many atrocities and every village community had, at one time or other, been forced to flee into either Sierra Leone or Guinea. The social fragmentation was deep, with family members losing sight of each other in the chaos before washing up in distant refugee camps where many lived for years unaware if their kinfolk had survived. It was the job of people like Johnson to help those returning refugees find their missing family members.

'My family and I fled to Sierra Leone when the fighting got bad and my home village of Yassadu was burned to the ground in 1991,' he explained. 'It was Taylor's people who did it, led by a man known as J P, and for years we could not go home but I got to know these forest trails well and how to survive.'

He laughed properly for the first time when I said I wanted to find a walking stick. David had brought one of those telescopic metal things that looks like something a skier would use, with a moulded plastic handle and fancy lockable flanges, but I was happy to make do with a wooden stave from the forest. All I wanted was something solid, straight and strong. Within an hour David found a good-looking specimen and threw it across to me. It reached to my shoulder, was slightly tapered and had a good feel. I began to use it immediately, enjoying its balance as I swung it forward and struck the ground every second step.

'That is an old man's stick,' laughed Johnson. 'We call a man who uses a stick like that *falloe*. It means an old man who cannot walk very well. You want to walk across Liberia and you need a stick like that! How are you ever going to do that? Oh *falloe*, what is going to happen to us?'

If anything, David was coping better than me with the pace and the terrain. Excited at having crossed the border, we both made the rather basic mistake of setting off too fast but it was David who was sensible enough to suggest slowing down.

'We must remember the Greenes' column of porters and cooks and hammocks would never have gone this fast. Let's just keep going slow and steady and Bolahun will get here soon enough,' he said.

As well as finding our route, Johnson also helped decode the forest. Many of the accounts of the Liberian interior written by foreigners, including the Greenes, describe the closed green world of the forest in unfavourable terms. Barbara Greene describes at length how boring she soon found the bush trails and Graham Greene writes that the novelty of the forest trail wore off quickly to be replaced by choking claustrophobia.

Johnson was able to leaven the experience for me. Throughout the day he kept up a commentary, naming streams and explaining how they went on to form the country's major rivers, describing the different types of terrain we crossed and telling me the names and characteristics of trees and which animals liked to eat their fruit. At one moment he pointed out mammoth seed pods hanging from ivy strung through the branches of a large tree. The pods were brown, leathery and as long as a sword's sheath, with eight or so egg-sized seeds rattling loose inside individual compartments. I recognised them immediately from a shop I knew in Johannesburg which specialised in Africana and sold them individually – and expensively – as 'pygmy rattles'. Jane had bought me one and for years it has sat in my office on a stand, a larger-than-life souvenir of a larger-than-life continent.

'The jungle elephants love eating these things,' Johnson said. 'They'll knock down an entire tree just to get at them.'

Through Johnson I came to understand the centrality of the palm tree to rural Liberia. With their omnipresent rag-doll heads, palms seemed to play the role of a weed, cluttering up almost every patch of forest one looked at, but Johnson explained the inestimable social value of the oil produced by their fruit.

'Almost everything that is cooked is cooked using palm oil,' he said. 'Every house has a bottle of oil in it somewhere. I cannot even imagine what life would be like without it.'

As a child, he said, he had been light and lithe enough to shimmy up palm tree trunks to cut down the dark fruit, bundled together in tight clutches. An account of West African life in the 1940s by an old European forester had taught me the colour 'carmine' for the fruit's red-so-bruised-and-dark-it-is-almost-black. After harvesting, they would be crushed, heated and processed to produce oil from their flesh. The oil has a reddish-orange colour that gives it a feeling of warmth, as if it has a radioactive power of its own. The processing is not finished there, however, as the kernels can be crushed to produce another type of oil, this time fine and colourless.

'Look at me now,' Johnson patted his stomach extravagantly. 'I am too old and fat to harvest palm fruit any more. It is a young person's job.'

When we got to a hillside where the grass had been burned away he explained what had happened.

'This is because of the bush-cow, the animal you might know as a buffalo. They live here wild in the bush but they are very dangerous. When the grass grows so high it can hide them, it is burned away by the locals. You don't play around with bush-cows and if you bump into them they will attack first and then run away. They are serious animals and if you hunt them then make sure you kill them first time because if you don't they will come after you.'

During my research I had come across several portentous mentions by Big White Hunters of encounters with Liberian buffalo. It is said these animals look at you with the eyes of someone who is owed money. Fortunately, the closest we came was some dried-out droppings that looked like fossils.

Johnson also opened my eyes to what is meant by farming in rural Liberia. At one point during the first day we came to a section of forest which he called, rather grandly, a field. To me it looked like a place where a cyclone had struck. Half-felled trees lay skewed at drunken angles, fouled by a web of ivy and undergrowth that trapped them in mid-fall, and the ground was uneven and cluttered with huge rocks the size of cars.

'The fact that these trees have come down means the light can get through, which means you can grow rice here,' he explained. 'Look over there and you will see strings of coloured paper that the farmers hang out to try to scare away the birds and stop them eating their rice.'

I began to look more closely and then I saw mountain rice shoots growing here and there in disorganised clumps, strands of shiny tinsel tied to nearby stumps. The process of growing rice, known locally as 'cutting farm', is beyond back-breaking and the wastage prodigious but, in spite of attempts by aid workers to introduce other staples, rice remains king of food here. The people of rural Liberia are trapped, forced in their hunt for a staple foodstuff to use their energies in 'fields' like this. So tough was this matrix of survival that I began to understand why this area was in many ways no more developed than in 1935 when the Greenes passed through. What chance development if all your energy is used on simply surviving?

That first day's walk lasted more than seven hours. As the miles passed, my feet felt increasingly sore, so I began putting pressure on the outside of my left foot to relieve what felt like a huge blister sloshing around near my big toe. I could not have cared less. The mere fact we were on foot, heading overland through Lofa County, more than made up for any discomfort. I was so thrilled I ignored the sweat drenching every fibre of my clothes from my sunhat to my socks and the first traces of chafing between my legs.

As my tiredness grew my senses became a little confused and at one point I had to check with David if I was seeing things. We had paused in a village midway through the afternoon, slinking out of the direct sun into the shade next to a mud hut wall, and Johnson was talking to the chief, asking politely if the trail east to Bolahun was open.

A crowd of children had gathered in the dust to look at us. Suddenly from around the corner lurched a hulking giant of a man wearing rags clumsily sewn together as bunting. The seams all had tufts of uneven stitching and his ungainly gait was caused by his hands being bound tightly to his sides, a huge piece of wood, the size of a railway sleeper, hanging from a strap tied around his waist. It was so cumbersome it took all his strength to lug it forwards through the dirt. His eyes flickered unnaturally and when he opened his mouth the only sound that came out was a groan, muffled by a huge kola nut wedged between his teeth like a gum-shield.

'Have we just met our Harlequin?' I asked David, referring to the mysterious figure encountered by Joseph Conrad's Marlow far up the Congo River.

'Not sure quite who or what that was but it feels like time we left,' came the reply.

A few hours later we came across some teenage boys on the track holding on to what was very obviously a dead rat.

'It is a possum,' said the tallest of the group. 'We are going to eat it and when these little ones grow up we are going to eat them as well.' In his hand he held three squirming, sightless baby rats. I thought about lassa fever and its main vector – rats.

With the sun beginning to dip, Johnson announced Bolahun was getting near. He was getting increasingly excited and I asked him if he had been to Bolahun before.

'Been here before? I was at school in Bolahun for twelve years in the 1970s and 1980s. It's like my second home but I have not been back for a year or so. I cannot wait to see everyone again,' he said with a broad smile. He had already told me his home village, Yassadu, was at least a day's walk north of Bolahun and I was curious how he came to attend a school so far away.

'I was born in 1972 and back then the people from the school would walk all around the region stopping at villages and asking if the local chiefs would allow them to select students. If the chief agreed, they would gather the children from the village together and ask a few questions. If you could answer the questions they would offer you a place at the school. The day they came to my village I must have been about six or seven but I was able to answer their questions.

'It was strange at first to leave my family and walk all the way to Bolahun for schooling. I come from a poor family of farmers and we did not have money to pay the fees so I used to spend the weekends there and some of the holidays, working at the school to make up for the fees. But the teachers were the best in all of Lofa County and it was the only way I could get an education.

'I really liked it, you know. It was the best of times,' he said as we walked into the soft light of sunset.

I had tried to ration my water during the day but the heat and the effort of the trek meant by now I was down to the last licks. We were as grubby, footsore and hungry as the original Episcopalian monks from the Order of the Holy Cross when they reached here, having themselves also walked from Sierra Leone to found the mission in 1922. The story goes that once they crossed the border they approached the first village chief they met to ask permission to build a Christian mission house but were refused because the local bush

societies, the Poro and Sande, were too powerful. So the monks just
kept on going until eventually, near Bolahun, they found a chief who
was not so cowed by the power of African tradition.

  Graham Greene describes dumping his gear outside the mission
house and collapsing exhausted on a seat to wait for the white priests
to finish Benediction. Those monks had long gone by the time we
arrived but their local successors, still struggling to keep alight the
flame of Christianity deep in this African jungle, welcomed us warmly
and fetched fresh water from a well. They watched in scarcely hidden
astonishment as both David and I calmly drank pint after pint after
pint and did not budge for at least an hour from the wooden bench
they offered us. Neither of us had truly appreciated just how draining
it could be to hike for seven hours along Liberian jungle tracks. Seeing
our exhaustion, our hosts arranged for food and offered us a sparse but
functional guest room with two beds, where Moses had already
delivered our rucksacks. Barbara Greene writes that on reaching
Bolahun she was so tired she was asleep within two minutes of lying
down on her hard campbed. Ignoring the sound of scurrying rats, I
think I probably beat her.

Day broke slowly over the mission's forested hills. The morning mist
lay so thick that it seemed to muffle the bell summoning novitiates to
prayer, defying the effort of the sun to break through. I was up early,
keen to get my bearings around the old mission station, buckling my
sandals gingerly so as not to anger my blisters. I had been so exhausted
the night before that I had barely been able to make sense of the layout
of the place, so I left David sleeping under his mosquito net and
stepped outside.

  The first thing I noticed was the silence. It was not the cloistered
quiet of a religious order but more the silence of something broken.
The buildings appeared solid enough but when I looked again I saw
just how decayed they were. The corrugated-iron roof of the main
mission house was not just rusty, it was distressed. Panel-beaten flat
by seasonal rainstorms, the rusty iron sheets clung lamely to the roof
beams. The lights had gone out at Bolahun a long time ago so when I
walked inside I peered into the darkness to see daylight leeching
through a web of holes overhead. As my eyes got used to the gloom I

noticed I was surrounded by books. This was the old library but the books were in an advanced state of decay. I picked one up, *A Pilgrimage to the Holy Land* published in 1927, but when I opened the covers its message of faith was lost, the pages crumbling to damp, dusty flakes.

Back outside, I walked to the edge of a slope and looked out through a screen of palms as the mission campus came into focus through the lifting mist. There were some old school buildings, burnt out during the war and not yet rebuilt and, in the distance, a stand of trees around the original church, St Mary's, started in 1923 and completed the following year, with every nail, tool and roof panel painstakingly carried here by porters from Sierra Leone. Graham Greene called it a 'little ugly tin-roofed church' and it was surprisingly well preserved. Concrete piles lifted it a few feet off the ground to save it from termite attack but a falling tree had taken a large swipe out of the tin roof and knocked down part of a side wall.

It was hard to imagine that a ceremony held at this church was reported on the front page of *The New York Times*, making the city, in the words of a columnist, 'stop in its busy stride to read the romantic story of an old man's adventure'. The ceremony was the funeral of Father Sturges Allen, one of the pioneering missionaries from the Order of the Holy Cross, who defied medical advice by coming out to Liberia late in life to help found the mission at Bolahun. Local experts said he would not last six months but he survived for six years before passing away at the age of seventy-eight on 26 March 1929.

After some searching I found the old man's headstone. It was badly overgrown and took several minutes to clear, but after tugging away the tendrils of some ground ivy, the white marble block came into view. I thought of the planning and effort that the stone represented. Someone in the mission would have had to order the stone from overseas and then arrange for it to be brought through the jungle, most likely by bearer party along a similar route to that which we had taken from Sierra Leone. And someone had taken the trouble to engrave on the stone a stylised book with the epitaph 'The Lord is My Shepherd', as well as the date when Father Allen took his vows of poverty, chastity and obedience in 1888, only the second monk to join the order.

I asked around Bolahun but could find nobody who had ever heard of the old man. It gave me a sense of time-worn neglect that made me think of the Philip Larkin poem, 'An Arundel Tomb'. Of all the material drilled into me by my English O-level teacher, a passage that has stayed with me touches on the fleeting power of memorials:

> Such faithfulness in effigy
> Was just a detail friends would see:
> A sculptor's sweet commissioned grace
> Thrown off in helping to prolong
> The Latin names around the base.

The Greenes stayed in Bolahun for a week. The first day's walk had taken it out of them so they needed to rest, and Amedoo, the servant hired in Freetown to look after Graham Greene, had already fallen ill. He was treated at the mission hospital, which was run by a German doctor who hung a portrait of Adolf Hitler on the wall of his house. In the mid 1930s loyalty to Nazism was to be expected by representatives of Germany deployed around the world, even in as remote a back-water as Bolahun.

The week-long sojourn was useful for the Greenes, as it allowed them to hire bearers willing to take them all the way to the coast on the other side of Liberia, hundreds of miles away to the south and east. It was a canny thing to do and added to my changing view of Graham Greene. Readers often take ownership of authors through their work, forming clear ideas of the characteristics of the writer. Through the Graham Greene novels I had read, the image that grew in my mind's eye was of a sophisticate who was most comfortable dealing with rarefied issues of human morality and spiritual belief. But as I followed him through West Africa, that picture grew in different, unexpected dimensions.

Throughout *Journey Without Maps*, Graham Greene seeks to present himself as an amateur traveller, a hapless *ingénu* even, blundering about the African bush, but I was learning this was not entirely accurate. It was no modest undertaking to trek through this inhospitable terrain and climate, and his insistence on forming a team of porters in Bolahun for the entire journey marked him out as wiser than other professional explorers who took on this region, experts such as Sir Alfred Sharpe. They wasted time, money and energy travelling through Liberia because they hired a fresh set of bearers each morning for that day's walking. This would invariably involve talks with village leaders in the local palaver hut, where the community gathered for discussions, to arrange terms, something that would drag on and on. 'Palaver', a word that has come to mean time-wasting bother, comes from West Africa.

Graham Greene showed further nous when he bought from the Bolahun missionaries a pair of lightweight hammocks that could be carried by two porters, to supplement the single four-man version he had brought from Britain. The first day's walk clearly made him reconsider how tough the trek was likely to be. And during their stay they made time to relax and enjoy the hospitality of the missionaries. Graham Greene writes the fathers were well supplied with hampers shipped all the way from Fortnum & Mason in London to Freetown, and then onwards by train and bearer party.

The mission might have officially closed down in the 1980s but the old visitors' logbooks were taken back to the New York headquarters of the Order of the Holy Cross where they still survive. With the help of the order's archivist, Father Adam McCoy, I tracked down the page covering the Greenes' visit. Typed in clunky and occasionally eccentrically aligned letters it logged the movements of all the missionaries and their visitors. On Saturday 26 January 1935 it recorded, 'Mr Graham Greene and his cousin, Miss Greene (who are touring Liberia to write a book), arrived about 7 p.m.' On Sunday 3 February 1935 it simply said, 'Greenes left for Zorzor.' In between these bookends to their visit there were references to Father Joseph Parsell playing tennis with Barbara Greene and the Greenes hosting the fathers to tea on the eve of their departure.

I watched as the mission's morning rituals, religious and practical, were observed by a team of staff led by Frank Foday, who styled himself as the Caretaker Brother. After leading a dawn prayer in one of the gloomy rooms, Brother Frank was now busying himself re-stoking the previous night's fire to heat up some rice for breakfast. Cooking was done on a scrap of grass at the back of the mission house and I looked on as he went through a routine of drawing water from a well, sloshing out the dirty pans and bowls, and blowing life back into the fire's grey embers.

'We try our best, and with blessings of God we survive,' he said with a voice as light as the morning breeze now stirring some banana trees close by.

'It was me who sent you that message the other day, Brother Tim, the message about the food. We have no signal here for the mobile phone but there is a hill nearby where you can sometimes get a signal, so when Brother Moses came asking about you staying I went there and sent the message. I hope you were comfortable last night.'

I thanked him and told him everything had been fine. The effort of the first day's walking had been prodigious but a bucket bath and a good night's sleep had me feeling at least partially restored.

He continued: 'I am forty now and my father was one of the first students ever to be taught by the fathers here at Bolahun. I have lived here all my life. The war was a difficult time and many of the things we were working on, like the hospital and the leper colony, were abandoned but today there is hope again. The war is over and perhaps we can get back to where we were before the war.'

He had a warm face framed by disfiguring growths like slabs of melted chocolate that clung to both cheeks. He could see I was curious so he offered a brief explanation. 'I was shaving one day and somehow they got infected. It was years ago now so I have just got used to it.'

Johnson came bustling round the corner, greeting Brother Frank warmly. He had spent the night with old school friends nearby and was keen to know what our plans were. The first day's walking had been tough so it made sense to rest in Bolahun at least a day before heading onwards and, following the example of Graham Greene, I asked Johnson if he would be willing to join David and me for at least the next few days of the trip. I had been impressed by how he dealt with the first day and felt he would make a reliable and useful companion.

His work as a tracing officer had ended long ago and ever since he had been without employment. It took him a second to agree so, after a brief discussion about pay, we shook hands and I asked him about our most pressing current problem, which was how we would move our rucksacks. Moses was busy with his aid work and would not be available so I asked Johnson if he could think of any local person with a motorbike who could be hired as our luggage courier. He said he would make enquiries and disappeared back down the hill towards the village.

Over breakfast of unsalted rice and the remains of last night's chicken, Brother Frank gave me a potted account of what had happened at Bolahun during the war.

'You know we have been attacked so many times that I cannot quite remember which came first. The order in New York cut links when the first fighting began down in Monrovia around 1980 but I remember one of the white missionaries, Father Joseph, stayed on for a few years before the fighting got really bad. There were some terrible times, like when rebels came through here and we hid in the roof of the library. From up there we could see them take away the women who used to cook for us. We never saw the women again.

'But the truth is the mission here at Bolahun is well respected in the community. Its school used to be the best school in the region so there are many people who remember it and value it so the rebels knew there would be trouble if they destroyed everything. It was as if they were scared of something if they tried to fight the work of God. I honestly believe that God was protecting us. The rebels knew they were against the work of God. Let me show you something.'

He led me to the entrance of the mission house and showed me the old sign that used to say 'Holy Cross Episcopal Mission'. The word Holy had been deliberately scoured out.

'You see, they knew there was something godly, something blessed about this place. They seemed to be happy to rub out the word Holy as if that would be enough to defeat God but of course it was not. God lives on here in the work we do.'

'So what is there left for you to do?' I asked.

'The work of God is never done. Through scripture, education and love we do his work and there is still much to do.'

After breakfast, David and I were taken for a tour of the campus. I started to feel a bit dizzy with thirst, in spite of drinking a huge amount of well-water, a sort of delayed shock from the efforts of the previous day's walking. The tour was only a short distance but I remember sweating prodigiously, as if my internal cooling system was having trouble recalibrating, pumping out pints of unnecessary sweat.

Among all the decay the saddest sight was the convent where a small community of nuns from Malvern had once lived. Barbara Greene describes them as the 'greatest, most human and most lovable teachers of Christianity that it is possible to imagine'. Set away from the main body of the mission station, the attackers had not spared their building, looting everything, defecating in the old chapel and vandalising what they could not carry away with them. On a wall was a message scrawled in black ash signed by 'Colonel One EYE' that said, 'First man BC. I do not be afraid. My boys and I was here. We will be back at Blood Wasting.'

As we walked back to the mission house Brother Frank said there was to be a football match that afternoon between the school team from Bolahun and another from the nearby village of Tailahun. He asked if I would accept the honour of starting the match with the first kick.

'We do not get many visitors here any more and it would be good for the children to see that outsiders are still interested in our work,' he said.

Kick-off was scheduled for the relative cool of late afternoon so I spent the middle of the day resting and trying to get sugar back into my bloodstream. In the absence of any Fortnum & Mason goodies, I made do by gorging on a series of pineapples Johnson bought in the village at a market stall. Since the government's State of Emergency over the plague of army worms poisoning water sources in northern Liberia, David and I had been on our guard about dirty water, but nobody in Bolahun had ever heard of these worms. The mission's well and a filtration pump brought by David meant we had, for the time being at least, no problems with lack of drinking water.

As kick-off approached Johnson came back up to the mission house with some news.

'I have found an old friend who has a motorbike and will be happy to help us carry our luggages,' he said solemnly. (We would go on to spend weeks together but, in spite of my polite urgings, Johnson doggedly stuck to the word 'luggages'.)

I thanked him and confirmed the biker would, like Johnson, come with us for at least a few days, perhaps even to the border with Guinea over on the far side of Lofa County. Then, almost as an afterthought, Johnson said something that really got my attention.

'And the devil is ready to dance for you after the game if you want.'

A crowd of a few hundred drawn from people living in nearby villages had gathered at the pitch near St Mary's. I kicked the ball onto the threadbare grass and the game began, but the crowd seemed more interested in a young madman who howled and screeched his way through the game, charging up and down the far touchline and hurling himself into the elephant grass that surrounded the pitch amid hoots of amusement from onlookers. He wore an Arsenal shirt.

Thoughts of an imminent encounter with a Liberian devil distracted me from the game. I chatted to a number of people in the crowd but as the match reached its end I was happy to see Johnson trying to catch my eye.

'It is time we went. The devil will be dancing soon and you do not want to keep him waiting,' he urged.

As full time blew on a 2–1 defeat for the home team, David and I followed Johnson down onto the dirt road that runs through Bolahun and began to walk north out of town.

'I have been told the devil will come somewhere along this road and there will be people with him making music. We must just walk until we meet them.'

We walked slowly and in silence. Twilight was approaching and with it a looming sense of menace. All of the buildings fronting the road bore damage from war and neglect. On one wall some wartime graffiti remained, announcing in large black letters the onetime presence of 'young col Black Gina' and promising 'No Die, No Rest, Blood Sprots in Lofa'.

After sundown the jungle has the effect of hurrying on the arrival of darkness with the tree cover making the shadows seem inkier and faster at massing. It was just at the point when I was struggling to see into the distance that the sound of the devil dance reached us. First, I heard drums and rattles, then voices chanting a chorus. Out of the gloom came a small group of people, huddled together as if for safety, and in front of them a swirling, shaking blur.

Cloaked in raffia, the devil was capped by an ancient-looking headpiece carved from a single piece of jet-black wood. There was a shrunken, human-like head with carp lips and oversized ears on an extended, twisted alien neck sticking out high from the baseplate of the headpiece. It was difficult to tell quite how large the being was below. One moment it crouched motionless, close to the ground, the head no higher than my waist and the grass tresses of its coat hanging limply, and then, with an explosion of dust and screeching, it span and shook, the mask now above my head, the raffia startled with energy.

The musicians followed the performance closely. As the devil slowed and shrank so their music faded, but when he started to spin and gyrate, so their chanting and drumming grew in throbbing, repetitive turns. All eyes were focused on the performance of the costumed figure as the dust rose and the darkness gathered.

As well as the devil's musical entourage there was another attendant, a young man who fussed over the raffia coating, combing it flat in between spins to make sure nothing of what was underneath could be seen. Everyone in Liberia knows that under every devil costume is the body of a man but quite what has happened to that body when taking on the costume, what spiritual power has been assumed, remains an important and powerful mystery. The young man I saw flattening the raffia tendrils was simply protecting the spiritual illusion, doing something that the Greenes had also seen in Bolahun when they saw their first dancing devil. Graham Greene's description would have worked perfectly for what I saw seventy-four years later:

> The devil's interpreter squatted beside him carrying a brush with which, when the devil moved, he kept his skirts carefully smoothed down lest a foot or arm should show.

The energy of the dance was powerful and the setting amidst the darkness and war damage had a hint of menace but I was struck by the lack of threat in the devil's display. A few young children stared wide-eyed at his dance but on the faces of the adults there were smiles and looks of mild amusement. A dancing performance by the devil such as this was, above all, an entertainment. The devil was playing the role more of minstrel than magician, an entertainer rather than an enchanter. It was a very different performance from that when the same devil appears at initiation schools in the forest.

After his routine, when the devil had disappeared into the night, the musicians gathered round me expectantly and Johnson whispered something about me offering to pay. I proffered a bundle of grubby Liberian dollar notes and the comber, the young man responsible for keeping the raffia costume in order, clasped both his hands round mine and thanked me solemnly. His hands were cold.

As we walked back through the unlit hovels of Bolahun, I listened closely to Johnson's thoughts.

'You see the devil plays an important role in all our village societies here in Liberia. Sometimes he can be bad but most times he is a person who entertains us, who helps us at important times like funerals and village ceremonies, with dances such as the one you have just seen.

'The devil you saw dancing here is the good devil. I only hope you never meet the bad devil.'

Bolahun felt like a barometer for attempts to develop rural Liberia. Founded in a rush of Christian zeal in the 1920s, the remnants of its buildings are an archaeological record of the country's troubled history. There was the original church of St Mary's, the one seen by the Greenes. Constructed by Father Sturges and his fellow missionaries, it was relatively modest but still standing, albeit battered by climate and time. The hospital where the Nazi doctor had worked was the next to be built, but had fallen into ruin as the money ran out in the late 1930s. Then in the 1950s a newer, larger St Mary's had been consecrated with new money sloshing into Liberia in the post-war boom years when the local rubber industry was taking off, and this was followed by the construction of new schoolrooms in the 1970s.

But conflict and chaos had ultimately prevailed over the missionary project. The school had limped on for some years after the foreign missionaries from the Order of the Holy Cross pulled out but the government had proved too corrupt and ineffective to run it properly. The decay was compounded when the war began, with various waves of rebels sweeping through Bolahun, plundering, looting and killing, and since the war attempts to reinvigorate the school had stalled. The strongest sense I got was of the power of African tradition prevailing over imported Christianity. The missionaries might have gone but the devil danced on.

I walked back up to the mission house in the darkness and found Brother Frank and a few other novitiates gathered in a room. It was lit by a single feeble bulb drawing power from an old solar battery and they were sitting in silence reading scripture. Brother Frank still dreamed of a better Christian future but I could not help thinking of a comment made by Father Joseph in an interview shortly before he died when he hinted at how little impact the work of the mission had truly had on life in this part of rural Liberia. Father Joseph had arrived at Bolahun in 1934 – he was the one who played tennis with Barbara Greene the following year – and he lasted fifty-four years at this remote outstation but this was his assessment of the impact of the missionaries: 'They think things are accomplished here, but they are not.'

CHAPTER 7

Message in a Bottle

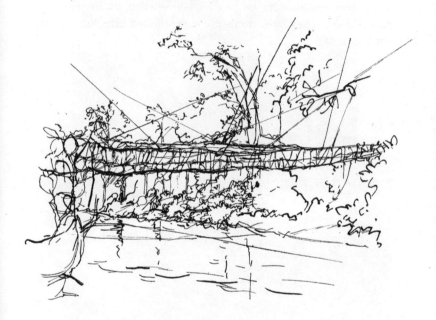

Monkey Bridge, Mé River
Guinea

Above: Masked Liberian devil rests during a dance, as photographed by the Greenes, February 1935
Below: Dancing devil in Liberia, as photographed by the author, March 2010

Dawn mist hid the mission buildings when we left Bolahun just as it had for the Greenes. Brother Frank insisted on saying a few words of blessing before we set out, so David, Johnson and I gathered solemnly, eyes lowered, in the murky half-light as he opened his service book and read us 'Prayer Before a Journey'. His delivery was monotone but these lines stood out:

> The Lord shall preserve you from all evil;
> It is he who shall keep you safe.

By the time they left here, the Greenes' entourage had grown to twenty-six bearers and four servants. As well as the two valets and one cook hired in Freetown, the Greenes took on another personal attendant at Bolahun, an irrepressible teenager called Mark who acted, in the words of Graham Greene, as 'interpreter, jester and gossip'. The Greenes sat outside the mission house at the top of the hill eating a leisurely breakfast of freshly baked rolls and watched as their slow-moving column set off, snaked slowly down the slope and disappeared into the gloom.

Johnson's local contact with a motorbike had turned up promptly, a very sober even sombre individual. After agreeing terms, he shook my hand and introduced himself formally as 'Mr Omaru'.

'And your first name?' I asked chattily. He made as if he had not heard me, walked off and set about loading the two rucksacks on his bike.

Brother Frank joined us for the first half mile or so as we walked past houses branded by war. As well as the sinister graffiti there were bullet-holes and, in the mucky roadside gutter, the occasional spent shell casing. When I pointed them out Brother Frank shrugged his shoulders, unable to remember from which of the many armed attacks on Bolahun they came. Once he was happy we were heading in the right direction, he wished us well one final time, shook our hands warmly and turned for home.

Ahead stretched a jungle trail reaching all the way across Liberia to the Atlantic coast, a route I knew only from the writings of Graham and Barbara Greene. I had no idea if the villages they described, or the forest trails in between, still existed. For a few moments I was taken back to my first true travel experience when, at the age of seventeen, I was sent across the world to spend a year in New Zealand. After arriving I remember looking at a calendar and crying. The year ahead, spread across the columns and pages, reached way beyond the limits of my teenage experience. I had never spent more than a few weeks away from home and yet there, in front of me, stretched twelve long months in four even longer, upside-down austral seasons. I remember recovering my composure after a few moments and resolving to take each day as it came. The months could look after themselves.

The same thought went through my mind as Johnson cut away decisively from the jeep track and led David and me onto a forest trail gorgeously cool with dew. The beauty of a trek is that every step taken is progress in itself so I simply put aside all macro worries about how we might keep to the Greenes' route, whether we would be able to follow them across the border into post-coup Guinea, how we would explain to the Liberian border authorities the lack of entry stamps in our passports, how we would cross back into Liberia, what to do about army worms and a whole matrix of security worries drawn from Liberia's systemic lawlessness.

Instead, I focused on dealing with the immediate concerns of keeping one foot landing safely in front of the other and finding the track to Kpangbalamai, a small jungle village the Greenes described reaching after a seven hour-walk almost due east from Bolahun. In all my research I had not been able to establish if the village had survived the conflict that had ravaged Liberia for so long.

Liberia's slide into chaos began in 1980 when more than a hundred years of control by the Americo-Liberian elite came to a bloody end. Riots the previous year over price rises for rice had shaken the country's image of sleepy stability but few would have forecast the brutality with which native Liberians, country people, took power for the first time.

Under cover of darkness early on Saturday 12 April seventeen soldiers staged a coup. Senior positions in the armed forces remained the exclusive preserve of Americo-Liberians so the plotters, all country people, were privates or non-commissioned officers. They struck, simultaneously, at strategic targets around Monrovia but the key was neutralising the head of state, President William Tolbert. This was achieved in spectacularly bloody fashion. A small gang, led by a twenty-eight-year-old master sergeant called Samuel Doe, stormed the Executive Mansion – a 1960s tower block overlooking the Atlantic beachfront in central Monrovia – and found the president there asleep. He was killed still wearing his pyjamas, shot in the head several times, then disembowelled.

The coup sparked a ferocious cycle of killing, looting and score settling. Thirteen members of Tolbert's cabinet were dragged down to the beach in front of a howling mob and executed on the sand. Firing squad feels too dignified a description for what happened as drunken soldiers, egged on by the crowd, emptied magazine after magazine into already lifeless corpses. Elsewhere decades of resentment by country people spilled out into attacks on wealthy Americo-Liberians. A book published in 2008, *The House at Sugar Beach*, by American journalist Helene Cooper, captures powerfully both the affluent dominance of the Americo-Liberian elite in the 1970s and the moment it came shuddering to a halt. Cooper describes how her own mother sacrificed herself by persuading marauding soldiers to rape her and not her daughters. Like many Americo-Liberians, Cooper left on the first available flight for a new life overseas.

Any hope that the coup would lead to more enlightened government in Liberia vanished promptly as the plotters fell out with each other. Their claim of having taken power in the name of all downtrodden country people rang hollow as they unleashed inter-tribal violence on a scale never seen before in Liberia. Doe, a member of the small Krahn ethnic group from the south of the country, outfoxed his rivals to secure the presidency, and then used the power of the position to launch bloody purges of his enemies, often members of the much larger Mano and Gio tribes whose traditional home is Nimba County in the centre of Liberia. Many people from Nimba County remember the 1980s as a period of creeping civil war. The tension between country people and Americo-Liberians had effectively been used as a cover for a power grab by a small gang of ruthless, corrupt thugs who set about settling ethnic scores. Low-level tribal friction had long been a feature of life in rural Liberia but only under Doe did it reach the level of national crisis.

In the ten years of Doe's chaotic rule the already weak state of Liberia began to fail. His end was inevitable but the tipping point only came after an invasion on Christmas Eve 1989 led by a former friend, turned enemy. Charles Taylor had mixed ancestry – a mother who was an indigenous Liberian from the Gola ethnic group, and a father descended from foreign settlers – but he carefully exploited the hatred of Doe in Nimba County. It was Nimba County that his rebel force first invaded from neighbouring Ivory Coast and, although he started with only a few dozen armed supporters, within weeks he had recruited thousands of Mano and Gio gunmen looking to settle scores with President Doe.

After months of fighting, during which Taylor's force split into warring factions, Doe was captured by rebels in Monrovia on Sunday 9 September 1990. Stripped to his underpants and bleeding from gunshot wounds in his lower legs, he was tortured by his captors. Among other abuses they sliced off his ears, a grisly display of African regime change that was caught on video. The cameraman missed the finale, the moment when Doe actually died, but by the following morning his corpse was being paraded in a wheelbarrow through the streets of Monrovia by jubilant gunmen. Doe had often used sorcery as a source of power throughout his rule and his killers made a point of displaying his body to convince the public that he had not magically escaped.

Once again, any hopes of a better future for Liberia emerging from its president's demise were ill-founded. Taylor's forces were not strong enough to secure the entire country so fighting dragged on for years between Doe loyalists, Taylor's troops, regional peacekeepers, mainly from Nigeria, and a shifting cast of rival rebel groups. It was a war of notoriously anarchic brutality as unaccountable, feral gunmen on all sides killed and plundered, and national institutions collapsed so badly that in many places the state effectively ceased to function. The darker side of African spiritualism was prominent in the conflict, with fetish-worshipping gunmen ritually eating their enemies' body parts in the belief that it would make them stronger in battle. Child soldiers, sometimes traumatised by the murder of their parents, swarmed through the country acting out a nightmarish vision of *Lord of the Flies* armed with Kalashnikovs. Checkpoints on roads out of Monrovia are remembered with particular horror. One consisted of a human intestine strung across the carriageway, and at another a monkey would decide on life or death. If touched by the monkey you were killed. Civilians fleeing as refugees were not safe. Incensed by Ghana's deployment of peacekeeping troops to Liberia, Taylor's gunmen executed scores of Ghanaian civilians who had lived in fishing communities on the coast for generations. Atrocity blurred into atrocity, cruelty into cruelty, reprisal into reprisal.

Worse still for the region, Liberia's conflict spilled over the frontier, sparking the civil war in Sierra Leone in 1991 when the Taylor-backed RUF attacked the east of the country, and causing further regional chaos as millions of refugees fled across the borders seeking sanctuary in Guinea and Ivory Coast. Liberia's war festered for more than six years, acted out on the ground by Taylor and other local warlords but heavily influenced by foreign powers, including, most importantly, Libya and Nigeria, before a lull allowed Taylor finally to take power in 1997 through a UN-backed election.

The international community was so desperate to put an end to Liberia's conflict that it was willing to tolerate the coronation of a murderous thug like Taylor even though the peace his reign brought about was always going to be illusory. Like Doe before him, Taylor ran a government of such venal corruption and incompetence that its violent demise was inevitable. The rebel force that eventually did for him was sponsored by Guinea, a country led by a regime with which he had fallen out, and called itself Liberians United for Reconciliation and Democracy (LURD). It was the advance by LURD rebels into Monrovia that had first brought me to Liberia as a reporter in June 2003. Although the Taylor regime boasted it would never surrender, within two months Taylor had fled for his life, avoiding the gory fate suffered by presidents Tolbert and Doe by taking sanctuary in Nigeria. Under intense diplomatic pressure, in 2006 Nigeria handed Taylor over to the United Nations for trial so, rarely among African warlords, he is being held to account for his actions as he faces trial under international law for alleged war crimes. Significantly, the charges all concern his role in Sierra Leone not Liberia, which has yet to decide how to deal with the sensitive issue of accountability for

wartime abuses. Before Taylor's arrest, all war crimes suspects in
Sierra Leone were tried in Freetown, but he is regarded as such a
threat to stability in the fragile country that his case has been moved
specially to the Hague.

Taylor left behind him a country both wrecked and traumatised.
The death toll from Liberia's post-1980 violence is not known for sure,
although public opinion in the country suggests more than 100,000
people lost their lives. But the fighting also left the pillars of Liberian
nationhood in tatters, with industry, healthcare, schooling and all other
infrastructure largely destroyed. When I reached Lofa County in 2009
the country might have enjoyed several years of relative peace but it
remained one of the world's most failed and scarred states.

The morning fog made for initially comfortable trekking conditions.
Johnson had complained of bad blisters since the first day, but David
had patched him with plasters and we opened at a good pace along a
well-beaten footpath. Grass on both sides left smears of moisture on
my trouser legs and when I used my *falloe*'s stick to flick low-hanging
branches out of the way, dewdrops would cascade to the ground. I
would catch a few from time to time and smear them refreshingly on
my face.

The trail led north-east for 8 miles to the town of Kolahun where it
was market day so we found ourselves not alone on the trail but
accompanied by numerous women with goods for sale balanced on
their heads: sacks of rice, rugby-ball-shaped lumps of cassava paste,
tubs of palm butter, gourds of palm oil. In the Greenes' day, the
women wore loincloths and nothing else, prompting plenty of observations by Graham Greene throughout *Journey Without Maps* about
breasts, nipples and thighs. Greene's sex life has become in recent
years a rather contentious issue, with some family members disappointed by the way his biographer, Sherry, focuses on it so heavily
in his three-volume biography, and the subject had inevitably figured
during my research. I had learned, for example, that Graham Greene
had four nipples, a physical quirk that led some to draw conclusions
about his libido, and that in an early draft of *Journey Without Maps* he
describes going in search of a brothel while in Freetown at the start of
the trip. He writes how Pa Oakley boasted about knowing a suitable

establishment but, by the time they got there, it was closed. This brothel reference did not make it into the published version of Graham Greene's book but nevertheless what struck me most about his writing was his frankness in addressing sex, something that feels way ahead of its time. Indeed, in the first edition of *Journey Without Maps*, while discussing his lack of sexual appetite during the walk, he proudly says he is unbiased racially when it came to women.

> I found it hard to believe in the need white men were said to find in the African bush for sleeping with native women. It certainly wasn't owing to colour prejudice; a black skin has always appealed to me and I no longer had any sense of smell. It was partly, I think, their lack of sexual self-consciousness.

His directness on matters sexual felt modern and I was disappointed to find they were excised from all later editions. As for his attitude towards sex on the 1935 trek, after experiencing the climate and rigour of the route, I found utterly convincing his observation that 'perhaps sexual vitality was lowered by the heat and the marches'.

Rivers and streams are still used as washroom and laundry in rural Liberia so I saw plenty of casual nudity but loincloths belonged to the past. The womenfolk we saw that morning walking into Kolahun wore more modern clothing, including T-shirts, cotton wraps and the occasional bra. Overtaking them became a bit of a game. With heavy loads locking their heads facing forwards, they had no idea there were foreigners walking their trail. As we passed there would be a teetering shudder of surprise as the periphery of their field of vision picked up the unexpected sight of white strangers. Some of the younger ones panicked, dropped their loads and ran screaming into the bush only to be reassured by Johnson speaking in Kissi, and by David and me in our own attempt at the local Krio. Just as Sierra Leone uses a modern relic of English with roots back to eighteenth-century British mariners, so Liberia retains its own broken version of American-English, known as 'Liberian English', brought by freed slaves from the Deep South, a Huck Finn vernacular rich with words like hog, catfish, creek, hollerin' and railroad.

It took two hours to reach Kolahun and the transformation in climate was phenomenal. As the dry season sun lifted the mist, down came the heat, knocking me almost senseless. By the time we emerged onto the un-shaded road leading into town I had started to feel groggy, such was the enervating power of the sun and the closeness of the humidity. The dry season might have meant there was no rain but there was plenty of moisture in the air and midday temperatures regularly surged over 35°C.

When the Greenes reached Kolahun they had an unexpected encounter with the country's leader, President Edwin Barclay, on a rare foray upcountry. The settler overlords of Liberia lived almost exclusively on the coast and were notorious for the distance they maintained from native people in the jungle-covered interior. The disconnection led to distrust and tension so when the slavery scandal broke in the late 1920s, it became positively dangerous for government representatives to trek inland as many tribes had turned hostile. The tension was described by Lord Lugard in a British parliamentary debate from 1934: 'Liberia claimed sovereignty over two million natives in the hinterland, among whom no Liberian dares to show his face unless supported by troops.'

It was President Barclay's squad of bodyguards that caught Graham Greene's eye when he reached Kolahun. They were parading up and down in a deliberate display of strength to the locals, so he approached and was told the president would see him.

President Barclay had come to power in the aftermath of the slavery scandal in 1930 when his predecessor had been forced to stand down. No matter that he had been serving as secretary of state at the time and was deeply implicated in profiting from slavery, President Barclay was hurried into office. Two years later his leadership was confirmed by an election, one where only the votes of property-owners, in other words Americo-Liberians, counted. It is fair to say elections in Liberia rarely had much to do with fairness even for the Americo-Liberian elite. In the 1923 poll, President King somehow gleaned 45,000 votes, even though the entire electorate numbered only 6,000.

Graham Greene felt self-conscious that his dusty trekking uniform of shirt and shorts was inappropriate for a meeting with the Head of State but President Barclay did not seem to mind as he welcomed the Greenes politely and chatted for some time, talking mostly about his grand plans for the development of the country and grumbling about the way Liberia had been treated by the foreign press. I smirked at

Graham Greene's diary entry noting how the president was particularly critical of the *Manchester Guardian*, precursor of the *Guardian*, a rival of my old employer, the *Telegraph*. The written accounts of the cousins vary slightly but both recorded President Barclay's description of the power he enjoyed as the country's leader.

'Once elected and in charge of the machine, I'm boss of the whole show,' he said. In 1930s Liberia, tucked away in a remote corner of West Africa and with few of the checks and balances associated with modern statehood, this was no overstatement.

The meeting with President Barclay was double-edged for the Greenes. In a way it was helpful to establish a rapport with the most powerful man in the country but it also meant they had drawn attention to a trip backed by British anti-slavery campaigners. For Graham Greene's mission of finding out if slavery continued in Liberia he would have to dissemble, although he writes 'it went against the grain' when he deceived the president over the route he and his cousin hoped to take.

There was no president for us to meet when we got to the war-damaged remnants of Kolahun. A small town, it lies on the main road that crosses Lofa County and in the short time we were there we saw a few trucks from the UN and aid groups thunder by, throwing up tumbling clouds of dust. Our priority was more mundane than a presidential encounter. We simply wanted to meet up with Mr Omaru, our new companion with two wheels to whom Johnson had entrusted our gear, and confirm the onward route to Kpangbalamai.

There was one roadside stall in town where we stopped and bought lukewarm Coke. Our breakfast back at Bolahun had consisted of the previous night's catfish and rice, unappetisingly re-heated, so the drink gave me a welcome blast of sugar. Mr Omaru was there, as arranged, a taciturn and earnest figure. Dressed in black and wearing ski gloves he watched carefully over his precious motorbike, another super reliable Yamaha AG, I was glad to see, and its heavy load of rucksacks strapped under a web of old inner tubes. He was not one for chat.

'I have found a way to reach Kpangbalamai by bike. I will see you there this evening,' he said, before setting off down the road at the head of his own modest dust devil.

We spent just a few minutes in the sanctuary of the stall's shade before Johnson hurried us back on to the trail. For the first time since I met him he looked a little nervous, so I took him to one side and asked him if everything was OK.

'Something happened to me near Kolahun during the war. It was the closest I came to being killed so I don't like this place,' he said.

Johnson was smart enough to know I wanted to hear more.

'It was 2000, I think, when Taylor was still in power in Monrovia but the LURD had appeared for the first time. They came from Guinea which is not far away and Kolahun was one of the first towns they passed through. When Taylor's people came here they wanted revenge, they accused the locals of helping LURD.

'Taylor's troops were commanded by Zigzag Marzah, the most terrifying man I have ever seen. He ordered his guys to collect a group of us to set an example, but me and a friend were caught by a child with a gun, a boy called Livingstone, who let us go. I don't know why he did it but I think it was perhaps through the hand of God.

'The others numbered thirty-four, women mostly. Zigzag ordered them locked into a container not far from where we are now, one of those things the aid groups bring food in on lorries. He then ordered it to be set on fire. They burned to death inside.'

Johnson delivered the story dispassionately with no sense of self-pity, no sense of using it as a way to ask anything of me. He was not looking for sympathy or charity. He was simply telling me of his own small experience of the broader pain of Liberia. But he made one crucial point that has long-term implications for the future of the country: since the war those known to be responsible for atrocities have not been held to account.

After the war ended in Liberia with Taylor's departure in 2003 the decision was deliberately taken to put off dealing with the killers and the warlords. A Truth and Reconciliation Commission was set up to establish the facts of what happened during the conflict in Liberia but not to hold people to account, so known perpetrators are currently free, their victims denied the chance of closure for the suffering they endured, their scars festering unhealed. The commission may one day resolve to pursue individuals but it was considered so important to end the fighting that any action which might fuel tension and violence was delayed.

This decision to withhold justice led to an extraordinary moment later on our journey when Johnson fell unnaturally silent as we walked past a group of villagers. His eyes dropped to the ground and his breath shortened but his stride picked up and he whispered something.

'That's him, that's J P.'

I was a little lost so, almost running to keep up, I asked him to explain.

'There in that group of men was J P, the man I told you about who burnt Yassadu, my village, to the ground. Let's go before he recognises me.'

The nervousness felt by Johnson in Kolahun disappeared as soon as we returned to a bush path, replaced by his default setting of energetic enthusiasm. The stall owner had given him directions for the next section of trail, saying something about 'passing over the big rock where the prints were left by the praying Muslim'. An hour or so later and our path climbed out of the forest and up a rocky flank. Johnson looked around for a minute or so and then pointed out two pale smudges on the rock surface and explained their significance.

'I had not heard the story before but back in Kolahun the shopkeepers told me the legend of this place. A Mandingo, a Muslim man, came to town one day a long, long time ago but was treated badly. Apparently he came here and prayed to his God, asking for punishment against the people who were bad to him. The legend says he prayed so hard his knees left marks on the rock.'

The legend of the curse continues today, blamed by the people of Kolahun whenever their crops fail, such is the power of Mandingos. Descendants of nomads who came to Liberia centuries ago from ancestral homes further north near the headwaters of the Niger River, Mandingos seeded Islam among the jungle communities in the region, creating what amounted to a significant ethnic minority. Tension between Liberia's Mandingos and other tribal groups has been a constant theme throughout the country's history, and the recent wars have exacerbated the isolation of Mandingo communities. Several times during our trek we would find them forced to live in their own jungle villages, apart from other tribes.

The heat out in the open of the rocky face was fierce and it was a relief to get back under the shade of trees. As the day went on I could see that Johnson was becoming less and less confident about directions.

He knew Kissi country intimately from his childhood and time as a tracing officer, but we had now moved into land shared between the Bande and Loma tribes and he was no longer on such familiar ground.

Back under the tree cover we met a man who gave Johnson a complicated list of fresh directions. They came in a long stream but I made out one section – 'turn left at the butter fruit tree'. I was curious about what this might mean until, a short while later, we turned left under a tree heavy with avocados.

My notebook got steadily more smudged as that day's journey wore on. When I later went over the day in my mind I broke it into three separate phases, each of increasing physical exhaustion. During the first I could comfortably wear both sunhat and glasses. As the hat got more and more soaked with sweat so my glasses steamed up and the second phase began when I was forced to take off my hat to keep the glasses clear enough for me to see. The final phase of tiredness came when I was sweating so much my glasses steamed up anyway. At this point I had to take them off and for the rest of the day my Liberian forest view was blurred at the edges.

There felt no shame in making such heavy going of it. Sir Alfred Sharpe, a British colonial administrator and old Africa hand, reached Kolahun on foot in the dry season of 1919, one of the first outsiders to do so. Bizarrely, he had taken a bicycle with him but found barely any stretches of track where it could be used, so it spent the entire trip on the shoulders of a porter. Later that year he described the rigours of his journey to an audience at the Royal Geographical Society in London.

'In the Liberian hinterland there are no roads; one follows native tracks, always in dense forest, and never on level ground. These paths take you up the steepest hills and down again; the surface is a mass of rocks and intertwined tree roots. I have never been in any part of Africa where the going was so bad.'

During my research I came across an even earlier written account of overland travel through this area. Published in 1857 by Reverend Samuel Williams, a descendant of former American slaves who spent four years in Liberia, it said 'that day we walked six miles, which is considered in Liberia a good walk'. Our trek that day from Bolahun to Kpangbalamai was a little under 19 miles.

For the last part of the journey, Johnson wisely conceded he needed his own guide. When we reached a forest hamlet called Pwenyeho he persuaded a young man, Amah, to lead us on the final leg of the day's trek. It was a sound decision as the trail was becoming increasingly erratic and difficult to follow. The young man agreed a price and set off carrying nothing but his cutlass, the buccaneering name in Liberian English for a machete, which he used to cut away tendrils, vines and branches. I was learning that the arrival of vehicle-worthy roads in the 1950s and 1960s, the period of slow economic growth in Liberia under American patronage, meant many of the old forest trails, the ones used by the Greenes in 1935, had fallen into disuse. Fortunately, Amah had known this section of the forest since childhood.

I entered that footsore zone of tiredness where all energy is focused simply on keeping going. The green screen of forest rolled by as I clambered over fallen tree-trunks, splashed through streambeds and, on slopes, picked my way down natural staircases formed by webs of exposed roots, all the time struggling to keep the sweat out of my eyes. Amah said nothing, concentrating hard on remembering the route, pausing now and then to orientate himself. To my eye there were no distinguishing landmarks under the never-ending tree cover but somehow Amah kept going in the right direction, an impressive display of bush navigation.

He had promised us 'two hours' to our destination. My watch-face had steamed up with a moisture cocktail of sweat and jungle humidity, but I could still see the hands sweep past the 120-minute mark with no sign of the village. I started to peer ahead through the forest, pathetically trying to convince myself I had seen a dip in the treetop canopy that might mean a village clearing. Without my specs, my eyes began to play tricks. I would swear I could see wood smoke in the distance, another sign of a village, but the smoke would vanish as we got closer and the trail would spin on and on.

Finally Amah paused, staring intensely downwards at the verge. He was looking for a thicket so memorable he would be able to find it again when he returned home that evening. When he found a suitable spot he discreetly slid his cutlass under cover, dusted off his shirt and walked on.

'It is rude for a stranger to arrive armed in a village,' whispered Johnson.

We turned a corner and there was Kpangbalamai.

*

The similarity between the village described by the Greenes and the one I saw now was unsettling. It was as if the Greenes had visited days ahead of us, not seventy-four years. The same mud huts, albeit with the occasional rusty corrugated-iron roof rather than thatch, were gathered around a large palaver house, an open-sided structure where visitors were met. Next to the palaver house was a tree and in its branches the same yellow-breasted rice birds gathering noisily to weave the same coconut-sized nests that hung from bare branches. And all around was the same dusty industriousness of African villagers caught up in the daily struggle for survival.

We had arrived unannounced but the village chief, Patrick M. Kollie, was welcoming, albeit in a perfunctory, dutiful way. He offered us shade in the palaver house, ordered rooms be made ready for us to sleep in and then began a long and quiet discussion with Johnson. For visitors like us there was no system of purchasing goods as there were no shops. Instead, a more indirect process of exchanging gifts, known as 'dashes', took place so that chicken and rice were given to us in the full and certain knowledge that we would dash something in return – money in our case, knives, watches and sewing-kits in the case of the Greenes.

Graham Greene describes the village as being roughly the same circular shape and size as the Round Pond, the ornamental lake in London's Kensington Gardens. The dimensions had not changed. After catching my breath I walked around the dusty edge of the village where it pressed up against a cliff of advancing jungle vegetation – a green barrier of banana trees at ground level overhung by branches from statuesque cotton trees. I saw the same busy level of activity both Greenes remarked on – villagers occupied with crushing palm kernels, smoking river shrimp, knotting rattan tree-climbing belts, spinning cotton, weaving fishing nets and so forth.

The setting sun was behind me as a man swinging a cutlass walked slowly into the village. He could not see me to begin with so he made no effort to conceal his tiredness, flecks of leaf pasted by runnels of sweat to the sinews standing proud of his neck, thin shins sloshing around inside tatty wellington boots. I thought of my father reciting his most cherished poem, Thomas Gray's 'Elegy Written in a Country Churchyard', with its romanticised view of rural life in eighteenth-century England where every evening 'the plowman homeward plods his weary way'.

I introduced myself to Sheraton Jallah, who turned out to be a visitor from Monrovia, and as we talked it soon became clear there was little romantic about life as a subsistence farmer in Liberia.

'I live in the city but life is hard and it is difficult to make enough money to survive, so every harvest season I come home to my birthplace to work the rice fields. It is not easy but rice is our only source of staple food so back we come, year after year, cutting back the jungle and trying to make enough to live on through the rainy season. We have no chainsaws, no tractors, no equipment. It is just us and a cutlass taking on the forest.'

I asked him about his boots. They looked horribly uncomfortable in the dry-season heat.

'I wear them because of the snakes. You never know when you will meet one. Each time you move a branch or a rock there is a chance one will be under it.'

I made a mental note to keep my *falloe*'s stick close by.

We walked through the village together and I asked him about the Greenes. He was forty-seven and had never heard of them, but he mentioned that one of his ancestors, Komowalla Jallah, had been village chief back in the 1930s. Graham Greene had written about the 'overpoweringly hospitable' chief of Kpangbalamai but Sheraton shook his head when I asked if, by some miracle, the man was still alive. He led me to a simple cement grave and headstone planted right in the middle of the village among the mud huts, a prized position only given to village chiefs. Into the cement someone had scoured a legend that was still legible: 'Here Lies Komowalla Jallah, died May 8 1954, lived about 100 yrs'.

Nearby was a building, once a school but now abandoned, and on one of its walls was a blast mark I recognised from my time as a war reporter. It had been made by a rocket-propelled grenade or a mortar strike. I asked Sheraton how Kpangbalamai had fared during Liberia's fighting.

'You know it came and went around here for so long I do not remember exactly what happened. We all fled to Guinea in the 1990s and when we came back we found our houses burned down. We built them anew, the same simple houses of wood, mud and thatch, and then the war began again in 2002 when a new set of rebels came through, the LURD who eventually got rid of Taylor. We had to flee

again and when we came back Taylor's soldiers arrived and accused us
of helping LURD. They killed my father, Myhango, and raped my
mother, Komasar. We never found their bodies and when we came
back for the final time again the houses were destroyed. We had to
rebuild everything.'

Like Johnson's story about the women being burnt in the container
near Kolahun, Sheraton's made me think about the lack of closure in
Liberia following the war. Sheraton knew his parents had been
murdered in appalling circumstances; how could he truly 'rebuild
everything' without a meaningful attempt being made to hold those
responsible to account? I could follow the logic of diplomats and
politicians desperate to end the war in Liberia when they focused on
the importance of bringing peace in the short term. But the decision
to withhold justice made me worried that in the longer term that peace
might vanish in retribution and retaliation.

Back at the palaver house Mr Omaru had arrived with his motorbike
and our rucksacks. He might have been the silent type but he was clearly
very efficient. Johnson, now limping quite badly because of his blisters,
said two rooms had been made ready in a hut for all four of us to sleep
in. After retrieving my towel I went to the communal washroom, an
open area of flagstones laid on the dirt behind a drystone wall, and did
my best to wash off the day's grime with a bucket of stream water that
had been heated over a fire. Dinner of rice, chicken and pumpkin
appeared shortly after sundown and all four of us sat chewing silently,
picking out the bone, gristle and claw. I did not mind the stringy meat
and watery squash. It was the lack of salt that I struggled with.

I felt too tired to talk, preferring instead to watch the cycle of day's
end in the village. The water that the women had used for cooking was
not wasted but used again to wash dishes and then to bathe numerous
children. A cupful would be poured over their heads, followed by a
scrub with fingertips dipped in palm oil, a quick rub with a cloth and
then the process was repeated on the next child. It was done with
assembly-line efficiency without enough time for the children to play
up, as if they already accepted life was a series of chores that everyone
has to take part in. Graham Greene writes that in all his time in
Liberia he never heard a child whine. Bath time at home for my young
children is never a quiet or efficient process and I watched with envy
to see if I could pick up tips.

Like all villages we were to pass through in Liberia Kpangbalamai had no power, so we sat in the gathering darkness and talked about our plan for the next day. After leaving here the Greenes had reached the village of Duogomai on one of the toughest days of walking on the whole trip. That day's journey was made worse as both had fallen ill in Kpangbalamai, victims of their cook's misguided attempt to bake bread using palm wine instead of yeast. I had known Johnson for only three days but I was already relying on his enthusiasm and initiative. While I had been washing he had hunted out the best local information about our route for the next day.

'Nobody from this village has walked as far as Duogomai in years,' he said. 'It is a long way and they say it is much easier to use taxis or motorbikes along the jeep road that goes on a longer loop through Lofa County. But I have found a boy who will guide us tomorrow for a few hours to the village of Kpademai, which is in the direction of Duogomai, and from there we will find other directions.'

Out of the darkness a shape loomed. It was Sheraton, the rice farmer I had met earlier. I flicked on my headtorch and offered him a place on the bamboo bench I was sitting on. He too had washed and was dressed in a smart collarless shirt embroidered with gold thread.

After Sheraton introduced himself to Johnson, David and Mr Omaru we sat in companionable silence for a few moments before he spoke.

'Why are you doing this, Mr Tim?' he asked. 'It does not make any sense when there are roads and vehicles. What is the real reason you are walking here? Are you looking for gold? Is it diamonds you are after? Are you investigating somebody after the war?'

I tried to reassure him, repeating what I had told him earlier about the Greenes. Under torchlight David got out his visual aids, the maps from Graham Greene's book showing the route that passed through Kpangbalamai. Sheraton looked at the book, listening closely to what we had to say, but as he wished us goodnight I could see he was not convinced. He had good reason to be sceptical: during decades of turmoil in Liberia outsiders had for the most part played the role of exploiters and profiteers.

In the darkness I got a strong feeling Mr Omaru shared Sheraton's doubts so I tried to win his confidence by talking to him properly for the first time. It was not easy. He was a man comfortable with silence.

'How was the ride today?' I asked. 'What was the road like?'

'There were no concerns for me. The road was long and the bike was heavy so I used a lot of fuel but from the main Lofa County road I was told where to turn off for Kpangbalamai. I got here in good time before sunset. It is important to arrive before it gets dark.'

I asked him why.

'It is not safe for you to go out on roads after dark. That is the time heartmen come out, killers who will take your heart. Only a fool goes out at night in Liberia.'

Rats. Every westerner who has slept in villages in rural Liberia makes mention of rats and the Greenes were no exception, referring often to the nightly appearance of the vermin. A nun at Bolahun memorably told the Greenes how she woke one night to find a rat sitting on her face licking the oil off strands of her hair. Barbara's own hair was to go un-brushed for the duration of the trek because on the first night in a hut the bristles of her hairbrush were chewed away by rats.

As soon as David and I settled into the single mud-walled room we had been given by the Kpangbalamai chief, the scurrying began. The floor was bare beaten earth and the roof an open structure of branches supporting banana-leaf thatch but, in spite of the lack of hiding places, my eyes were nowhere near sharp enough to spot the creatures. An old mosquito net, originally light blue in colour, had been strung over the homemade wooden bed I would be using with its mattress of straw covered by a blanket. On the net the beam of my headtorch picked up faded orange streaks of rat urine.

We tried in vain to spot the little blighters. We lay in the dark as the scratching and scurrying sounds grew louder, hoping to lull them into false confidence out in the open. But when we flicked on our torches, arms cocked to throw a boot, there would be nothing there. On top of the rats, the hut had trapped the day's heat like a slow cooker so, while the sun had long since set, the windowless room was stifling. I passed a clammy, vermin-disturbed night nose down, thinking of lassa fever and praying no rat urine would land on my face. I dreamed fitfully of my three-year-old son, Kit, a horrible dream where no matter what I said he kept asking me forlornly, 'Why are you not coming home, Daddy?' And no sooner had I finally fallen asleep than *Cock Idol* opened up outside, a cacophony of pre-dawn crowing by all the village cocks, all apparently trying to compete with one another for the loudest, longest delivery. Where I am from a single bird would crow once or twice to mark the start of the day and that would be it. In Liberian villages, the din went on for ever. I got up feeling utterly wretched.

That day's trek to Duogomai was for us, as it had been for the Greenes, one of the toughest of the entire journey. By jungle trail Duogomai lies 25 miles east of Kpangbalamai so we made sure we started early, leaving the village before sun-up. Following such a bad night's sleep, the day had a slightly dreamlike quality, as if I had just arrived after an intercontinental overnight flight. Sheraton had provided a teenager to guide Johnson, David and me through the first jungle section out of Kpangbalamai but all I can remember of the young man was the bling T-shirt he was wearing with Get Rich or Die Tryin' emblazoned across the front. America remains the dominant cultural reference point for Liberia, just as Britain is for Sierra Leone, and in both cases the original historic flow of people into these two West African experiments in post-slavery rehabilitation has long since been reversed. Today the most commonly held aspiration for young Liberians, even those living in jungle villages, is an American passport and the chance of a new life on the other side of the Atlantic.

It was during the trek to Duogomai that Johnson's blisters got so bad he had to stop, jumping up behind Mr Omaru on the motorbike and entrusting David and me to the care of a stranger for the only time during our whole trip. This was the moment when, tired, confused and wired by Mr Omaru's warnings about heartmen, I convinced myself I was in very real danger and started to leave a trail of broken branches in the forest in case I had to flee. David, I later discovered, was having exactly the same fears but we were too tired or, perhaps, too coy to discuss it at the time. Unknown to me, he was leaving a trail of coins at strategic junctions in the track to help us if we had to make a run for it.

Our fears were unfounded and we made it tired but safe to Duogomai, relieved to see Johnson, Mr Omaru and our bags again. As before, we found a village largely unchanged from the time of the Greenes' visit, with the same huts arranged in tight alleys on a bare hilltop with steep sides. It was dark by the time we arrived and the chief was the only villager with a torch. When he started to lead me to the wash area I noticed it was a novelty version so I asked him to stand still for a moment and point the torch at the flat wall of a hut. There in the middle of the faint circle of light the image of a man's face was projected. The face had long light brown hair and for a second I thought it might be Jesus but then I looked properly. It was an image of Lionel Messi, a football superstar from Argentina.

Graham Greene had risked rebellion among his porters by insisting on completing the 25-mile march all the way to Duogomai in one day. By evening the cousins had made it but the rest of the column was spread out behind them, split into groups of stragglers dispersed along the same jungle trails we used. It meant crucial parts of their gear, such as their campbeds, mosquito nets and water filter, had not arrived by nightfall so they tried to fall asleep upright in chairs, parched with thirst and sweltering under blankets wrapped round themselves to deter biting insects. Little wonder Graham Greene called Duogomai 'The Horrible Village' and tried to blank it out with alcohol. But even that turned out to be far from easy.

> . . . there was nothing else to do but drink. The difficulty was to get
> drunk; the spirit ran out in sweat almost as quickly as one drank it. The
> race between the night and drunkenness became furious as darkness
> fell. For I still feared the rats: I wanted something to make me sleep;
> but drink was quite useless for that purpose and most of the night I lay
> awake listening to the vermin cascading down the walls, racing over the
> boxes.

After my own rat-disturbed night in a cramped, filthy, sweltering hut in Duogomai I was introduced to the oldest villager, Mulbah Obelee. He did not know his date of birth but his eyebrows, whiskers and hair were frosted with age and he could only just walk, relying heavily on a stick. He started to tell me a story that soon banished all thoughts of discomfort from my mind.

'I remember the day a white man and white woman came to our village,' he said. I had a rush of excitement as I did the arithmetic in my head. The Greenes had been here seventy-four years before. If Mulbah was now in his mid-eighties, he could well have childhood memories of them.

'They stayed a day. I remember that. And he drank a lot of whisky. When they left, the bottle was taken by one of our people who put a spell in it, a message to the spirit world, and then took it out into the jungle and buried it.'

CHAPTER 8

Screams in the Jungle

Jungle Village, Liberia

Traditional wall decoration in rural Liberian villages with, top left, wartime graffiti

The trek through Lofa County covered 120 miles and took, including our rests, ten days. From the start, our target was the town of Zorzor way over on the eastern side of the county, where an aid worker contact had promised to put us up. It was close to where the Greenes had crossed from Liberia into Guinea and I thought it a good place to regroup and plan how to cross the frontier. But to get there we had to find a way through some of the toughest and most remote jungle terrain I have ever experienced. It took a bit of effort, but by consulting locals whenever we stopped, Johnson was able to find the places referred to by the Greenes, albeit with slight differences in the spelling. It meant we were able to follow exactly the rhythm of their journey, staying in the same villages and walking the same distances, even taking similar rest days after the longer and more difficult stretches. One by one, places I had imagined during my research became real – Bolahun, Kpangbalamai, Duogomai, Nekebozu, Zigida and Zorzor.

To begin with, David felt like a stranger but as we picked our way through Lofa County my attitude changed. He was no stranger. He was me as a younger man.

We were both graduates of Oxford University, where we had studied degrees that were not vocational, but rather had bought us time to decide what to do in life – theology for him a couple of years ago; politics, philosophy and economics for me twenty years earlier. We had both enjoyed a good education by winning scholarships to top private schools, although our parents had to make significant sacrifices to pay fees not covered by the awards. The choice of schooling exposed us both to a peer group that it would be difficult to keep up with later in life, sons of families so wealthy they would never face financial worries.

Curiosity and an eagerness to learn drew me towards journalism but David was still working out where his career should take him. To join me on the trip he had walked away from a lucrative banking job in London, a move few would have been brave enough to make. We were in the midst of a recession and credit crisis which left bankers jobless every day but he had willingly given it up. As we walked he talked about possibly joining the army or applying for the Foreign Office, conventional jobs that, I felt, would have received the approval of his father, Joe, my old contact from reporting days. But the thing that really drove David was travel, curiosity about what lies over the horizon, and it was this that had brought him on our trek. Later he would confide that back at his rented digs in London, on the wall of his room, he hung for inspiration a copy of a German oil painting entitled *Wanderer above the Sea Fog*. It shows a man staring out over a mysterious but tantalising wilderness of fog-bound crags. I teased him about it looking like an album cover from a 1980s New Romantic band but he remained firm and said he loved it. In many ways his journey with me was about finding what he wanted later in life, his own venture out into the wilderness.

His tolerance for hunger and discomfort were impressive but what I really valued was the way he knew when to keep his mouth shut. A footslog as exhausting as ours was bound to fray tempers. Indeed, the Greenes fell out so seriously towards the end of the trip that they would sit in consensual silence each evening. But somehow David and I managed to avoid this, largely because he had the invaluable knack of keeping quiet at the right moment. And he kept the promise he had made back in Freetown, allowing me to play the Alpha Male role as chief planner, organiser and leader, offering to help wherever he could but taking care not to appear competitive.

There were also times, especially on the longer, tougher stretches of the walk, where talk was called for just to pass the time. Then he would keep me going with his impressively comprehensive recall of quotes from the cult film *Withnail and I*. And I enjoyed probing his knowledge of religion, asking clumsy questions about the great schisms of Islam or the known provenance of the Gospels in the New Testament. I remember being so tired that I entered that half-awake world of international air travel, when you can consciously watch an in-flight movie only to completely blank it from memory seconds after it has finished. The content of what David said to me during these stretches became unimportant, its value being more in the fact he was saying something, distracting my mind from the effort of the hike.

But the thing that really endeared him to me was his clear pride in the whole adventure. The hunger, thirst, blisters, health threats and security risk would have made many fold, but David was not just determined to finish, he was proud of what we were doing. After one of our midday rests on the trackside, David gleefully relayed a conversation he had just overheard between Johnson and a local. Johnson did not know the local tribal language so they spoke in Liberian English that David could follow.

'The villager is suspicious about us so he asked Johnson what we are really up to. Johnson said we are walking across Liberia and the villager sounded sceptical so Johnson replied, "Believe me. These people have walked all the way from the border with Sierra Leone. Every step of the way, they have walked. They are crazy but they are honest. All they want to do is walk. Come along for a few hours and you will see for yourself." '

The story prompted an enthusiastic smile on David's unshaven, sweat-stained, haggard face, a smile that I shan't forget.

The walk to Kpangbalamai established the routine for those that followed: breakfast of reheated remnants of the previous night's dinner; load rucksacks onto Mr Omaru's bike; start walking as early as possible; hire local guides to help Johnson with the navigation; eke out five litres of clean water carried by each of us in a daypack; arrive thirsty, hungry and footsore in village before dusk for rendezvous with Mr Omaru; wash, eat, talk to the villagers and community leaders; try to sleep.

The assessment in 1919 by the frustrated cyclist, Sir Alfred Sharpe, of the physical demands of trekking through Liberia felt in no way exaggerated but we had modern medicines and good water puri-fication equipment to help us cope. And we had no need to rush so we could spend as long as we liked resting and planning in villages before slipping back into the jungle. With my Global Positioning System device it was possible to establish our exact location as long we were in an open area clear of trees where the GPS could 'see' the satellites it needed to make its calculation.

However, projecting that information onto my map, one produced by UN cartographers, was not particularly helpful, as the modern map was not much of an improvement on those complained about by

Graham Greene. Before setting out for Liberia he had found two maps, one published by the British government and the other by the United States War Department. Just like mine, his maps marked plenty of named places down on the coast but in the interior they grew steadily more blank.

Some of my earlier concerns vanished. Of the army worms, the pests that had supposedly inundated Lofa County just a few weeks earlier, we found no trace. I became steadily more acclimatised to the physical demands of the journey. My feet hardened, my weight dropped and my tolerance for putting on filthy clothes stiff with the previous day's grime improved. With the help of lifts on Mr Omaru's bike, Johnson's feet recovered and he was able to rejoin us on the trail, while David proved to be as strong and uncomplaining as his father had promised.

The nightly diet – invariably unsalted rice and chicken – meant food was always a major concern for us, as the physical effort of the trek was so considerable. Taking in enough to keep going was a constant struggle because our route was so remote we passed few villages big enough to have stalls where we could buy supplies like biscuits, canned drinks or tinned goods. Out in the jungle we would occasionally come across pineapples, beautiful things sprouting singly from a corona of sharp, blade-shaped fronds. The first time I saw one I took out my penknife and prepared to hack the fruit off its stem but Johnson shouted at me to stop. In the Liberian forest, I learned, consumables do not grow wild – from somewhere, someone had come to tend them and it was bad forest form to start scrumping. Whenever we reached a village Johnson would ask politely if there were any bananas, pineapples or other fruit to be traded but it was disappointing how rarely we actually found any.

On the morning before a particularly long hilly stretch, I remember with some horror the breakfast I forced down – stale crackers and a tin, allegedly, of luncheon meat acquired by Mr Omaru from some dusty roadside stall. The rectangular block of wet matter slid out of the tin with a shluck sound accompanied by a fragrance of off offal. It was all I could do to overcome my gag reflex but, without any other source of energy, I forced it down.

Throughout the walk we touched on some of the most remote parts of Lofa County, often finding ourselves on ancient tracks that had been used for centuries. The Greenes would have recognised the trails, save for one new feature – the litter. There was not much of it but every so often I would spot empty wrappers from the alcoholic popsicles I had seen back in Sierra Leone. I started to collect them and noted down their odd names: Old Soldier Herbal Bitters, 43% proof; Black Horse Gin, 42% proof; Pegapak Gin, 40 % proof.

On the fifth day of the trek, while walking between Duogomai and Nekebozu, we crossed a river known as the Lawa, using what the locals called a monkey bridge – an ancient and wonderfully intricate web design of knotted vines and rattan cords, elegantly suspended from high treetops on long cables made from twists of ivy. I could not see a single modern component in the entire structure; it was made entirely from material found in the jungle but quite who made it was a point of some debate.

In some parts of Liberia only senior members of the bush societies are allowed to take part in the construction of monkey bridges. The legend goes that while the society members twist the ropes and chords, it is a devil who magically flies backwards and forwards across the river to weave the structure. Unauthorised people who approach the crossing and try to catch sight of the devil are punished with death.

The bridge we crossed was identical to those described by the Greenes, although the name they used for them was hammock bridges. The one over the Lawa spanned a 40-foot gap and would have taken humans weeks to assemble. As I stepped along the split bamboo lengths laid along its floor the whole structure creaked and swung like a pendulum, making me clutch at its fibrous balustrades, but it delivered me safely enough to the other side.

'With monkey bridges like this you have to be careful how old they are,' Johnson explained. 'They only last one or two rainy seasons before they begin to rot and become unsafe.'

Five days later we would come across a monkey bridge spanning an even wider river, the Ulé. The design was finer and more elaborate than the one over the Lawa but we were told that this bridge had 'passed its time'. It looked sound enough to my eye but the locals insisted a little too forcefully it was dangerous to use and, instead, we were ferried underneath its graceful outline by dugout canoe. The angry way they reacted when I said I was willing to risk a crossing made me think that maybe there was some other mysterious force involved. Local reluctance to outsiders using monkey bridges was not new. When passing this same area Graham Greene noted in his diary that he and his cousin were also forbidden from using a bridge on the grounds it was 'not in repair'.

In the more remote jungle hamlets many of the huts were circular with low walls and steep, thatched roofs as tall and pointed as witches' hats. Invariably they were built on high ground, not so much as a defence mechanism against human attack but more as a way to survive seasonal rains. My visit to Liberia in 2003 had shown me just how formidable the wet season is in this part of West Africa where it is not uncommon for a deluge to last days without a moment's let-up. Building your village on a hilltop at least allows the rain to wash away and saves you from being swamped.

The huts are where villagers pass the night, doors locked, windows closed, but during daylight hours they spend little time indoors. As I spent time in the communities, I witnessed how time-consuming jungle survival is. There is always some chore that needs doing out in the ragged rice fields or back in the village. All cooking is done by women in separate 'kitchens', set some distance away from the huts in a vain attempt to keep rats from the sleeping quarters. The kitchens consist of a charcoal fire laid on the bare earth often under little more than a thatched shade supported by bare wooden poles. Without power for refrigeration or cold storage, cooking is a never-ending process. No sooner has one meal been eaten than preparations begin for the next, starting with the retrieval of water from a river, stream or, if the community is very fortunate, well. The extent of post-war development in Liberia can in large part be measured by the presence of a well in any particular village. With their concrete covers and depth, they provide an important leg-up for rural communities as they reduce considerably the risk of water pollution.

Near to the kitchen there would be a 'rice attic', a more substantial structure made up of a low, walled, thatched compartment, where the precious staple is stored, raised six or seven feet off the ground on lengths of timber stripped of all bark to defeat rats. Some villagers sprinkle pepper around the feet of the attic legs to deter weevils. Often the only other manmade structure in the village centre is a shrine to dead chiefs, flagstones arranged in a rough pattern, sometimes scoured with the names of the dead. The details of these remote communities are identical to those described by Graham Greene, Lady Dorothy Mills, Sir Alfred Sharpe and the other pioneers who first reached this region a hundred years or so ago.

There were some grim moments during those days in Lofa County. Shortly after hiking out of Kpangbalamai we found ourselves in an area of jungle infested by tsetse fly. They are as big as horse-flies with a bite to match but it is the sleeping-sickness and river-blindness they carry that makes them so dangerous. David was the first to be bitten, the insect's jaws cutting straight through his shirt as if it was not there, and within seconds all of us were jigging around, swatting them from our necks, arms and exposed areas of skin, momentarily forgetting our blisters and sprinting down the trail to get away from them. I was taking an antibiotic against malaria each morning and the following day I doubled my dose.

We had to learn from some silly beginners' mistakes. The hike to Duogomai had been so exhausting we decided to catch up on rest by sleeping in the next morning, confident that the map showed the following day's trail to Nekebozu as relatively short. But this meant we missed the comfortable cool around dawn and set out when the late-morning heat had already built up. It was almost suicidal. We had to walk only four hours that day but it was one of the most miserable days of the trip, as our walking hours coincided with the fiercest heat. Since the temperature difference between early morning and midday in rural Liberia is so huge, we resolved that the best way to deal with the climate was by starting early and then stopping at around 11 a.m., to find a shaded spot in which to lie down in for an hour or two. I have never been the lightest sleeper but during those midday breaks my internal computer would completely crash, allowing me to fall deeply asleep on the dirt floor, oblivious to the flies swarming greedily around the sweat rings on my clothes.

It was during one of these midday crashes that I was woken by what sounded like the crying of a tormented child. We had made it to a small village called Barziwen, about halfway between Duogomai and Nekebozu, and I stirred to find the screams were coming from an animal inside a homemade cage being poked with a stick by a little boy. After coming round, I walked over and looked inside to find a wretched-looking infant chimpanzee, clearly the survivor of a hunting trip on which its parents had been shot for the pot. I thought of Bala Amarasekaran and Bruno back in Sierra Leone, but when I later emailed Bala to ask him if there was anything he could do to help the animal I had seen, he explained that in Liberia there is no chimp sanctuary or government authority responsible for their protection.

'Unfortunately I am still attending to our local mess with the chimp situation and not authorised to accept chimps from other countries,' he wrote.

After a few miserable rat-disturbed nights inside crowded, stuffy huts, sharing single mattresses with David, I could not face another and decided to sleep outside. It meant more room inside for my three companions, as from then on I slept on the bare ground inside a small insect-proof tent I had bought specially for the trip. It consisted of a single, sealed chamber with walls of mosquito netting that would not keep out the rain. But I was happy to take my chances with the weather if only to get away from the vermin and the heat.

After an initial surge of interest from villagers who would gather round whenever I put the tent up, they would drift away as darkness fell and I would zip closed the door and make myself as comfortable as possible on the ground sheet. Its gauze walls allowed me to see out quite clearly, so from my voyeuristic capsule I would watch the day's end: mothers singing lullabies to nursing infants, little girls playing with dolls made of bamboo blocks planted with human hair, goatherds bringing their flocks back in from the jungle, teenagers joshing over mugs of palm wine, moonrise through the palm trees. The fresh night air was wonderful after the mugginess of the huts, although there were numerous occasions when a stray animal would disturb me in the small hours. One night I was woken by a domestic duck that was doing its best to roost on my head.

Whenever we reached a new village we found the locals curious about us and, for the most part, hospitable. I kept Johnson topped up with Liberian dollars and he took charge of all negotiations for food, water, shelter and guides, offering up appropriate 'dashes' whenever required. But what I found interesting was the varying power of the village chiefs, some of whom clearly commanded the respect of all in their charge while some were figures of mockery to be ignored, even abused, by their people. When the chief was weak it became a challenge to find the person in the village with the necessary authority to deal with our visit.

The chief of Nekebozu was named Forkpa Duolar and he was clearly in control. A solid man in his fifties he had tribal markings on his chest – scars cut in a traditional design during his initiation by the Poro bush society when he was a youngster. He carried a mobile telephone, even though it was not much use in Nekebozu where there was no signal, and he clearly had had experience of living beyond the confines of the village. The moment we arrived he called for buckets of hot water and I spent a very happy hour sitting next to Johnson as we both bathed our blistered feet, watched closely by a swarm of children who, quite understandably, found the sight of two topless men sitting with their feet in buckets comical. When we explained our mission, Chief Duolar said he was familiar with Graham Greene's trip and had even heard of *Journey Without Maps*.

'The book was very controversial here in Liberia,' he explained. 'The government banned it so people like me never had a chance to see it.'

Indeed, the Liberian government was irritated by the writings of both Greenes. Barbara Greene mentioned the president's suits being left to air on the balcony of the Executive Mansion in Monrovia, an irreverent detail that prompted a complaint from the Liberian authorities. But the reaction to her cousin's book was far more serious, as the government was deeply embarrassed by his description of corrupt officials from the coast exploiting the native population upcountry. It made Graham Greene *persona non grata* in Liberia to such an extent that when he asked MI6 to send him there during the Second World War, several years after the book was published, the authorities in Monrovia refused. Banned from Liberia, he ended up serving in Sierra Leone.

Even an authoritative chief has no guarantee of wealth or power reaching beyond the patch of beaten earth that makes up the village limits. As we waited for our rice that evening, Chief Duolar dis-appeared. I caught sight of him bent over a table writing by torchlight, but it was only after I had zipped myself up in my tent that I learned what he was working on. Through the netting I saw his shadowy form approach. He coughed formally, I unzipped the tent door and, without a word, he handed me this letter and disappeared. I read it by torchlight:

Nekebozu Town Chief
Nekebozu Town, Zorzor District, Lofa County
Febreuary 14 2009

Dear Sir
    Please help me with Motto Cycle. I do not have good foot.
    I was wounded with gun during the war. I usually attend meeting with my friend chief in long distances.
    This will enable me to over this distance.
    Contact Forkpa Duolar'

The unremitting poverty I encountered was acute, making the continued survival of the jungle communities all the more impressive. On the occasions our route took us close to the single main road through Lofa County we noticed signs from aid groups announcing completed projects, like the digging of a well or the construction of a palaver house. But in more remote places, further from the main artery, there was no evidence of any outside influence at all, whether from aid groups or central government. It was as if the rural people of Lofa County, passed over for more than a century by the Americo-Liberian government in Monrovia and savaged in more recent times by marauding rebels, had simply turned in on themselves, relying on the tough but proven forest survival methods of their forebears – subsistence farming, palm oil harvesting and hunting.

It meant the forest appeared, for the most part, a silent and barren place. The chance to eat protein is such a rare treat for rural Liberians that almost anything, from chimpanzees to frogs, is fair game – netted, shot or trapped, and served up as 'bushmeat soup' to garnish rice. We could walk for days without hearing birdlife or seeing any beast larger than a grasshopper springing across bare earth patches in the footpath, and the occasional scorpion – terrifying-looking things, matt black, about seven inches long with claws as mean as a crab's and a wicked stinger at the tip of their arched tail.

There was only one section of the trip when the forest truly came alive and that was because the trail passed through an area so remote and mountainous people had largely stopped venturing there. In 1935 the Greenes had found the trail to Zigida, one of the rare rural towns large enough to have a district commissioner sent up from Monrovia, clearly marked, but since the construction in the 1950s of Lofa County's main road which skirts the mountain range both the trail and the town have declined. Swallowed by the advancing jungle, the last time the track was used by any great number of people was in the 1990s during the war, when terrified villagers used it to flee on foot to sanctuary in nearby Guinea. Survivors described a hellish journey as half-starved adults carrying children fought their way through the thick bush, disorientated, parched and scared. Scores died, their bodies dumped in the undergrowth to be consumed by ants.

According to the Greenes, Zigida lay 12 miles almost due south of Nekebozu, a relatively short distance but one that took a full day of hiking because of the steep mountains that had to be crossed. It was to Chief Duolar that I appealed for help but while he appeared willing enough it took several hours to find anyone prepared to lead us over the hills. In the end two hunters from Nekebozu, Forkpa Zaza and Karmah Gayfor, agreed to help. They would earn a day's pay from us but the trek also gave them a good opportunity to go after quarry in a rarely visited patch of jungle. As well as the standard cutlass that almost every villager carries through the bush, they brought with them a single-barrelled shotgun and a torch. It is after dark, they said, that the forest comes alive with prey.

'It will take us all day to get to Zigida but we will come back in night and see what we can find,' Karmah explained.

We started out at first light, picking our way through sections of jungle where trees had been cut or burned down to make rice fields. A tall young boy appeared on the trail with a plastic bottle brimming with freshly drawn palm wine hanging from his wrist on a loop of grass. I remembered what Johnson had said about the need to be light and lithe for palm tree husbandry. Our two guides had clearly arranged this palm wine delivery because without a word the boy handed over the bottle and disappeared. Forkpa took a firm hold of the grass loop and continued on his way.

We reached a wall of undergrowth and the marked trail faded to nothing but with a slash of his cutlass Karmah forced an opening and we stepped through, entering a different Liberia, an older, more primeval version not so tamed by man. The jungle was thicker than any we had seen, the atmosphere stickier, the tree canopy higher, the drifts of leaf mulch deeper. For the first time on the trip I heard the trill of hornbills, distinctive African birds, front-heavy with their oversized beaks. When I looked up I caught glimpses of their dipping flight in the voids between the boughs of trees, rafters supporting a cathedral-like roof of green.

Like almost all other early explorers in Liberia, the Greenes soon tired of its jungle. The fuggy, closed-in embrace of the forest came to irritate them and throughout their books about the journey they complained about being bored, even stifled by the jungle. In a short story called 'A Chance for Mr Lever' that was set in West Africa, Graham Greene would write of 'the drab forest' as an unkempt garden with '. . . nature dying around you, the shrivelling of the weeds'. But on that mountain traverse to Zigida I felt completely different. I found the bush exciting and enthralling, a place of majesty and mystery.

Our guides' blades were busy that day, slashing and clearing, but every so often the two men would stop simultaneously, eyes straining upwards, ears picking up on a noise – the crack of distant branches being broken by monkeys or the screech of squabbling birds. They might not have been able to see much but through sound they were mapping the area for the night's hunt.

The trail took us up and down endless steep hills but the jungle choked any chance of a decent view. I was soon in my own sweaty, breathless world, focusing all my powers on keeping my footing and not tripping over roots or tumbling down steep banks. Whenever we stopped to rest, the two guides would take a few moments to make stools to sit on as they drank their palm wine. With their cutlasses they would cut three truncheon-length pieces of branch and then bundle them in one place around the middle with a length of ivy. Splaying the three ends on the ground would offer up a sort of cupped support between the upward ends, ten inches or so clear of the earth. The first time we stopped I did not bother with one of their stools, flopping down exhausted on a leafy bank. Within a few seconds I had ants all over my backside and was jigging up and down for the rest of our break trying to dislodge them.

In seven hours of trekking the only sign of man we saw was a table in a small clearing made from lengths of bamboo that had been split and then tied together with strands of ivy. It was blackened from a fire lit beneath it.

'A hunter made that for smoking bushmeat,' Johnson explained. 'Once an animal is shot you only have a few hours before it begins to rot. So you either eat it or smoke it so you can keep it for later.'

At the bottom of a little gorge we had to cross a marshy area of damp, black peaty soil. As I looked for firm footing to pick my way across I noticed a set of almost circular imprints, as if someone had pressed a dustbin lid repeatedly into the mud.

'Jungle elephant,' whispered Forkpa, looking around him anxiously. Karmah held up his hand to silence us and I watched as both men turned slowly through 360 degrees to try to pick up any sounds.

'Jungle elephant is the most dangerous animal in this type of bush,' Forkpa said after satisfying himself the tracks were old. 'You must never hunt them because they will ambush you. They are big but they move silently in these forests and you will never see them until you walk into their ambush.'

The primordial bush ended as abruptly as it started. One moment we were in its claustrophobic grasp and the next we had stepped out onto a footpath next to rice fields on the approaches to Zigida. Our two guides paused to swallow the last of their palm wine and then led us up the final slope towards a tightly bunched cluster of huts where a dumb mute groaned a greeting and I retired to a shaded bamboo bench to catch my breath.

In Zigida, Johnson got busy with his regular negotiations for food and shelter, explaining to the villagers our journey and our interest in the Greenes, while I tried to restore my feet once more in a bucket of hot water. After an hour or so a man approached and asked if I would like to meet someone who knew all about the Greenes. I was still thrilled by Mulbah Obelee's description of their whisky-drinking habits and I rather doubted that I could find anyone who could beat that anecdote. I was wrong.

Down on the northern edge of the village, the side facing the mountains we had just crossed, was a hut and outside it, on a bench, sat another Forkpa, this time Forkpa Argba, an elderly man with milky white eyes. Born in 1920, it was clear he could not now see. River-blindness, a nasty disease still common in Liberia, had struck in his sixties but it had given him a longer life than average, as he had been spared years of debilitating toil in the rice fields.

'I can remember the day those people came very clearly. I was a teenager of about fourteen or fifteen and they came from the north through the mountains. They had guides with them but we had problems understanding their language because the guides came, I think, from Sierra Leone.'

I could not believe my luck but the old man's account was incredibly detailed and, as far as I could tell, accurate. He even remembered the Greenes' companion. Barbara Greene refers several times to a pet monkey brought on the trip by Mark, the jester hired back at Bolahun, and she describes how it was tormented by some of the other team members. The first edition of *Journey Without Maps* even included a photograph of Mark with the animal clinging to his shoulders.

The old man went on: 'They arrived in hammocks. It's a difficult journey, you know, through those hills.'

I smiled. The Greenes had three hammocks with them, one heavy-duty version brought from Britain and the two lighter ones acquired from the missionaries at Bolahun. Barbara describes how from quite early in the trip she would walk some of the way and then rest while being carried in a hammock, before walking once more. In contrast, Graham Greene only admits using his towards the end of the trip when his fever got so bad that he was barely conscious.

The blind man went on: 'The thing I remember most about the man was how he wrote everything down. He had a notebook with him all the time and he wrote down everything that was said to him. I remember he was very interested in a man called Yassah Doweh because he could make lightning. He asked our elders many questions about that.'

'Is there anyone in the village today who can make lightning?' I asked.

'If you have the right training of course you can make lightning,' was his answer.

I asked him to explain more but he shook his head and mumbled something about tradition and secrecy.

As I walked up the slope to the centre of the village I looked back towards the mountain range we had crossed. Zigida has long had a reputation for having strong magical power, a place of rugged remoteness but great spiritual importance where senior devils of the bush societies can attain higher skills, such as the ability to conjure lightning or prepare poisons. The skyline of the hills was clearly lit by the setting sun and above all the peaks stood the sinister humpback shape of what is known in the local Loma dialect as 'Chimpanzee Mountain'. Graham Greene describes it as a 'thimble of almost perpendicular rock . . . the home of evil spirits', and mentions how it loomed over his two-night stay in Zigida, spooking him and the other members of his party. The sense of portent in Zigida reduced the bearers to a state of outright terror and they begged the Greenes to push on as early as possible. Barbara Greene later wrote that it was in Zigida that the illness that came close to killing her cousin began.

> Whether it was the power of ideas over the body or whether it was already the beginning of his illness I do not know. But from that last evening in Zigida his health began to suffer and for the rest of the trip and even for sometime after he got back to England, he was unwell.

Some time after I zipped myself into my tent that night in Zigida a woman walked slowly past me in the moonlight. There was nothing odd about the dark outline of her body, dressed in a vest and a skirt, but then she turned towards me and I saw her face. It was ghostly white with chalk. It might have been as innocent as a medicine or a balm for dry skin but I began to sense the same spookiness that had troubled the Greenes. I drew my knees up tight to my chest, screwed my eyes shut and urged on the arrival of daybreak.

And that was the feeling that came to dominate my mind as we crossed Lofa County, a strong sense of portent, of brushing up against the power of African spiritualism without truly understanding it. The devil who danced for us at Bolahun was a minstrel, an entertainer like other costumed devils who put on public displays across Liberia. Some even perform on stilts. But the dancing devil was also a symbol of much stronger forces, wizards and conjurers who would not show themselves to outsiders like me and who are believed to have powers that go far beyond entertainment, powers connected to the spirits that dwell in the forest.

All the way along our trek I spotted clues to their presence. On the approaches to villages I would often see a trackside shrine where food and drink had been left for ancestor spirits. The edge of one community was marked by an unbroken cable of knotted ivy that went around the entire village, like a boundary rope on a cricket pitch, but one with magical powers protecting the villagers from dark forces outside. In Duogomai, the village where Greene's empty whisky bottle had been snaffled by a conjurer, I noticed it was common for houses to be protected by bottles carrying charms. In the last house I slept in before resorting to my tent, a bottle had been sunk into the soil of the hearth, the lip of the neck just proud of ground level. When I asked what was in the bottle, our host smiled but stayed silent.

With Johnson as my interpreter I asked at several of our stops if the devil would meet us but was always politely refused. The villagers did not deny the existence of a devil but they would decline to discuss why it would not appear. As we got further and further from Johnson's own tribal territory it was fascinating to watch him trying to decode local traditions with which he was unfamiliar. Like many Liberians he was a Christian who had been initiated into the Poro bush society and, also like many Liberians, he refused to discuss with me, a non-initiate, what he had undergone. But when he saw unfamiliar things, such as a house in a village where the devil was said to live, he was as curious as me.

The only occasion in Lofa County when we met hostility was when we were accused of seeking to discover the secrets of devil societies. In Nekebozu some young men reacted angrily when we asked for guides through the jungle the following day.

'Why do you want to go there?' one of them shouted. 'There is a road you can use with a motorbike so why go through the bush? The forest has secrets and I think you are going to take them from us – you must not be allowed to go.'

It took the intervention of Chief Duolar to reassure the young men, although the next day I had the strong feeling that the guides he provided were also told to act as chaperones, keeping us tightly to the path.

Ever since anthropologists first learned of the existence of devil societies in Liberia a hundred years or so ago, they have struggled to discover exactly what rituals and beliefs are involved. Secrecy is key to the societies and intrusion by the uninitiated is shunned but a breakthrough of sorts came by accident in the early 1930s when a German missionary doctor in rural Liberia became the first white outsider to enter a Sande initiation school for girls out in the bush. An outbreak of smallpox in the region had reached the students and the elders of the Sande temporarily overcame their inhibitions, urging Dr Werner Junge to come and treat the sick initiates. His resulting description of the bush societies remains one of the most authoritative.

The whole initiation process, he said, presumed that until someone was initiated they did not truly exist. Initiation was so fundamentally important to followers of the bush societies that a person was not regarded as having been really born until initiated. One Liberian tribe even uses a word that means shadow or imitation to mean a young person and only after graduation from the bush school does an individual fill out into a person.

Key to the transformation that goes on in the bush schools is a process of symbolic death and rebirth. On entry to the society, the younger self is believed not just to have died but to have been eaten by a senior devil. For some tribes the ceremonial scars made on the bodies of initiates symbolise the tooth marks from when the young person is consumed by this omnipotent figure. After months, sometimes years, of training out in the remote bush, where students have to endure starvation, thirst and hardship, they are reborn as adults, often with new names, and finally allowed to return to their families. Many of the skills are practical, such as hunting or learning which trees in the forest have medicinal purposes, while many others are designed to ensure the continuity of the social order as the young are taught respect for the old. But the whole process is suffused with strong spiritualism and secrecy on many levels. Students are not just told to keep secret what they see, they are also told the powers of the devils are secret and only revealed to those with special training who climb up a hierarchy said to have ninety-nine ranks of seniority. The regime is notoriously tough and it is not uncommon for students to die while in the hands of the bush society, something that is accepted by their parents without complaint although they are never offered any explanation or body to bury.

'If one of them happens to have died his mother finds a jar of rice at her door on the night before his hoped-for return,' Dr Junge wrote in *African Jungle Doctor – Ten Years in Liberia*. 'This is the first and only news she will ever have of the fate of the son whom she sent into the Bush years before.'

Young men and young women go through similar procedures of education and initiation, and the whole process, Dr Junge stressed, is not to be spoken of to the uninitiated. Those who break the code of silence or who stumble accidentally across the schools out in the bush are put to death by poisoning.

Writing in the 1950s he felt confident the modernisation and development of Liberia would soon do away with these traditions: 'The time has no doubt come when this primeval institution must fall victim to the advance of civilisation'.

I thought of this conclusion one morning when we were about halfway across Lofa County. We were on a remote track a long way from any road suitable for cars when, from a distance, we started to hear faint moans. They did not sound like the cries of people expecting to be heard but of anguished wretches very much in the grip of terror. We were on flat terrain, with thick jungle on both sides of the trail, and I could not be sure if the voices, all male, were coming from in front of us or behind us. I started to look around but Johnson grabbed my arm and told me to leave well alone.

'They are asking for help, asking for food,' he whispered.

'But who are they?' I gasped, now struggling to keep up with Johnson's accelerated pace.

'It is a bush school run by the Poro. They are the students being trained before initiation and they are always treated badly with little food or water. It is really dangerous for us to stop because what happens there is secret. We have to keep going.'

Arriving in Zorzor after 110 miles of trekking from the Sierra Leonean border felt a bit like reconnecting with a more modern, less magical world. It was the first real town we had come across, with a busy mission hospital, roadside shops and even a restaurant, a good place for a pit-stop before we tried to enter Guinea on the next section of the trip. We had been using jungle trails through Lofa County but for the last stretch into Zorzor we were forced out onto the national highway, a wide dirt road that runs all the way to Monrovia, a couple of hundred miles to the south on the Atlantic coast. Without any tree cover we had no shade to help us cope with the heat so our pace dropped significantly, and the occasional passing traffic brought with it an irritating dousing in dust that clogged our breathing and stung our eyes. Worse still, the relatively even surface of the road meant my feet would strike the ground at exactly the same angle, step after step, putting repeated pressure on the same small area of my soles. I started to miss the uneven jungle trails when no two strides were the same and the entire underside of my foot was made to have a workout. The road section into town was only about 5 miles long but out of nowhere I sprouted a new set of blisters.

Zorzor lies on an old trade route into Guinea and because of its size it was fought over and destroyed repeatedly during the war. Very little reconstruction had taken place by the time we walked gingerly into town and the headquarters of the local police was nothing more than a thatched roadside hut. This was the first government building of any sort we had passed since entering the country and I felt now was the time to sort out our immigration status – without any entry stamps in our passports we could be regarded by nitpicking officials as 'illegals'.

At first sight the commander, Major Andy Russ Gborley, seemed like the officious type. Foreign nationals were monitored closely in Zorzor because of its proximity to an international border and when we arrived Maj. Gborley was bawling at an old man about an identity document irregularity. The unfortunate victim of his tirade kept repeating, 'I was born here, I was born here'.

David and I took our places on a bamboo bench and as we waited I saw a notice on the wall, signed by the major himself, saying, 'All officers to report to work in uniform and on time.' I then looked at the major again. He was not wearing any uniform.

When our turn came he listened closely to my account of our entry into the country on the other side of Lofa County, our interest in the Greenes and how there had been no border official to stamp us in at the entry point we used. He asked to look at our passports and then made a long call by mobile phone to a superior, the sort of phone conversation where the caller does a lot of silence and a great deal of head-shaking. I feared the worst but need not have because when he finished he smiled and said he would be happy to stamp us in himself. Furthermore, he gave us a handwritten note stamped with the mark of the Ministry of Justice urging all other Liberian government officials to give us 'all necessary assistance and protection needed while en route to and from your place of assignment'. This was my first encounter with Liberian officialdom in the post-Taylor age and I was impressed.

Throughout their trek, the Greenes had endless niggles with their porters who, after agreeing a price back in Bolahun, would complain about the difficulty of the terrain and threaten to go on strike unless given more money. Graham Greene describes the growing tension and endless discussions until, not far from Zorzor, the crisis point came and the porters said they were leaving. He handled it like a poker player, simply calling their bluff. That's it, he said, you can all go home now and I will simply find replacements from a local village. It was quite a risk, as hiring new porters would have been both hugely expensive and time-consuming, but the tactic worked and within moments the Bolahun men switched from being angry and self-righteous to meek and joshing. He had no more porter problems after that.

I faced similar issues in Zorzor when Johnson and Mr Omaru both approached me, despondently complaining about the way they were being treated. At first I could not work out what they were concerned about as they both gave rather rambling, incoherent accounts of their worries with mumbled threats about going home. It was the first time during our trip that they had appeared anything but willing and I thought initially that they were reluctant, for whatever reason, to go any further and cross into Guinea. When we started together back in Bolahun the agreement had been to travel together for a few days and then decide if we would go further, so perhaps they were exercising their escape clause.

And then slowly it became clear that they had every intention of accompanying David and me for the full journey and all they wanted was a cash advance. In Bolahun they had both agreed to be paid only on completion of the trip but, given that our journey was now going to take weeks instead of days, it was only fair for me to hand over an interim payment. I gave them several hundred dollars each and the mood of despond lifted immediately. They headed cheerfully into town but, as neither of them was a drinker, I knew they would not be blowing their money. I was touched when they came back wearing matching new black baseball caps and T-shirts.

'It is our team uniform,' Johnson said, smiling. 'We thought it would be good to have our own uniform when we head into Guinea.' They were clearly up for attempting an unorthodox border crossing.

Graham Greene was deeply disappointed by Zorzor. For the first time since Freetown his writing betrays contempt, even loathing, for outside influences on Africa.

> If Duogomai was the dirtiest place in the republic, Zorzor was the most desolate. It hadn't been left to itself; the whites had intruded, had not advanced, had simply stuck and withered there, leaving their pile of papers, relics of a religious impulse, sentimental, naïve, destined to failure.

His mood was not helped by his host, an eccentric Lutheran missionary, a hefty and troubled widow who seemed to have lost her senses living upcountry and who mumbled incoherently about the impossibility of dinner invitations. Graham Greene said she was so heavy she needed eighteen porters to carry her in a specially made hammock on the rare occasions she left town and Barbara Greene described her as a 'large white lump, like bread before it is put in the oven to be baked'.

The woman referred to by Graham Greene as Mrs Croup had long gone but the Lutherans still maintain a presence in Zorzor, battered by the war but refusing to accept the defeat Graham Greene suggested was inevitable. The original Lutheran church in the town centre is completely destroyed but the Curran Lutheran Hospital on a hilltop nearby has been partly rebuilt and is treating patients and training local health workers once again. It was founded ten years after the Greenes passed through, largely through the work of an American nurse and midwife, Esther Bacon. She would become a much-loved figure in the local community, cherished particularly for reducing the rate of Liberian mothers dying in childbirth.

As I walked through the grounds of the hospital I found her gravestone. It recorded how she gave her working life to Liberia, arriving in 1941 and dying in Zorzor of lassa fever at the age of fifty-six in 1972. Her headstone bore the same epitaph as the one I had seen back at Bolahun, 'The Lord is my Shepherd', and there was a memorial plate bearing a tribute I found particularly moving.

> This plaque is dedicated to her loving memory by her Liberian friends for whom she gave everything, even her life.

We stayed nearby in the local compound of Concern, an aid group with projects spread across Liberia. It has a well-built, single-storey house behind the obligatory high wall common to humanitarian groups. The security guards were so touchy they refused initially to let Mr Omaru and Johnson inside but my companions did not seem to mind, happy to head into town to look for accommodation. Concern's local head of office was away so David and I had the run of the place, washing our filthy clothes, dressing our feet and planning the next stretch of the journey.

While we were there we experienced our first major rainstorm, with thunder and lightning so strong it made the building shake. I was glad not to be outside in my netting tent that night. As well as being weather-proof, the house also had a gas ring, a generator and a well-stocked larder. I had tried to find food in town but the only meat available in the market was bushmeat, a rather malodorous and impossible-to-identify smoked animal body part, covered in flies and with its hands/paws/hooves balled by tendons tightened by the heat of a fire.

We had been told to make ourselves at home so, with rain pounding the roof of the house, I took a few tins of fish from a large pile stacked on the cement floor of the larder and David cooked up a huge pot of fishy pasta, a wonderful change after seven evening meals of bland rice and chicken. Both of us went to bed with swollen bellies and we slept long.

When I eventually got up the following morning I met the house-keeper employed by the aid group.

'I have a question for you,' she said after introducing herself. 'We have tins of cat food made from fish. This morning I found lots of empty tins. What did you do with it all?'

CHAPTER 9

Guinea Worm

Cotton Tree
Leafless in Harmattan Season

David Poraj-Wilczynski

The chief's voice carried clear and strong across the St Paul River but it failed to have the desired effect on the people I could make out on the far bank. The watercourse marks the international frontier between Liberia and Guinea and it was evident that the fishing community over on the Guinean side was too busy to respond to the shouted request for a ferryman. Women were wringing out clothes and bedding soaked in the previous night's storm, draping them over domed, igloo-shaped grass huts to dry. In midstream, a fisherman was not to be distracted from slowly casting and retrieving a circular net from his small canoe. The rising water level had improved the chance of a catch and no amount of shouting by Chief Peter Sumo of Kpaiyea, the last village in Liberia before the river, was going to disturb the morning's fishing.

'Don't worry,' Chief Sumo said, looking ever so slightly abashed. 'My nephew will go and find one of our own people from this side of the river to take us over.'

The chief, who was in his late fifties, gave orders to Moses, which had the teenager scurrying out of sight along a muddy river bank over which the hem of the jungle loomed. This was the only time during the whole trip that we were guided by a chief and it illustrated clearly that while their authority on home territory can be considerable, that power is limited very much by terrain. Step outside the village domain and it can dwindle to nothing.

The river, known locally as the Dianni but more widely as the St Paul, lies roughly 10 miles east from Zorzor and reaching it was an important moment on our journey. The coup that had brought a small and unknown cohort of junior officers to power in Guinea had taken place just a few weeks earlier and quite what this change of government's impact would be over on the other side of the river was unclear. Worryingly for us, there had been a bit of noise on the news wires from the newly installed regime warning the population to be on the lookout for 'white mercenaries' and 'international drug smugglers' bent on destabilising the new order, but I took the view that as we were not carrying anything dangerous like guns or narcotics it was still worth risking the river crossing. We had rested for two days in Zorzor and during that time Johnson had ridden with Mr Omaru to the main road crossing into Guinea and, through skilful sleight of hand involving modest cash donations and verbal flattery, had persuaded a border official to pre-stamp our passports as having entered Guinea. If we could find a way across the river our papers would be in order in the event that we encountered Guinean authorities.

There was, I concede, some personal vanity at work that morning. I had travelled extensively in Africa but never had I moved from one country to another across a jungle river frontier. It felt like a throwback to an earlier age and for me it had a nostalgic appeal. Back in the post-independence period, when the popular press still covered Africa, there was a famous rivalry between a gang of Fleet Street reporters who for years used river crossings as a way to outdo each other for what we call 'dramatic colour'. A favourite and often-used intro went something like, 'I crossed the crocodile-infested waters of an African river to bring you this report . . .' It was so common as to become a newspaper cliché, although the long-standing battle within the group was eventually won by a daring young reporter called Peter Younghusband from the *Daily Mail* when he reached Zanzibar during a rebellion in the late 1960s. No rival could top the intro he came up with on that occasion: 'I swam shark-infested waters to the riot-torn spice island of Zanzibar . . .'

Graham Greene records spotting what he believed to be alligators in the rivers on the frontier with Guinea so I had a good look that morning when our dugout eventually took us out onto the water, paddled by one of Chief Sumo's villagers. But with apologies to my journalistic forebears, I cannot honestly describe the St Paul as crocodile-infested, largely because any such creatures would have long since been shot for the pot. Instead, the river was dark, slow-moving and fouled with the jetsam of rainy-season torrents, half-sunk trunks of dead trees and boulders the size of houses. I felt rather smug that we had found a way across, a feat that was beyond an American rubber plantation executive who came to this exact same spot on horseback during a bush tour in the 1940s. Writing in his journal, H. H. Burgess describes how he rode from Zorzor to Kpaiyea:

I then sent the horse back and attempted to cross the St Paul. However, this well-marked crossing (on the map) did not exist, so we returned and trekked upstream.

In the dugout, Chief Sumo sat with his jaw jutting out, as if trying to restore some authority, while I shifted my camera bag to my lap and held on tight. The small boat was not nearly as stable as the pirogues I had slept on travelling down the Congo River and with our weight the tops of the boat's sides sank to within an inch or two of the river's surface. The slightest tilt would have us shipping water but if we tipped over I wanted to give my camera bag the best chance of surviving the soaking and had images of myself swimming one-armed, one arm held aloft like the Lady in the Lake, holding on to the bag. David was more worried about keeping his mouth shut. Guinea worm is one of Africa's nastier parasites and is caught by ingesting its larva from rivers such as the St Paul. Swallowing or even just splashing in rivers can cause infection, as it allows the waterborne larva to enter the body through abrasions, cuts or other breaks in the skin. When inside a human the grubs grow into worms that can reach prodigious lengths, sometimes as long as three feet, inflicting agony on the host who has the feeling of snakes worming through their lower limbs. For a long time the condition was known as fiery serpent disease.

To complete the life cycle the worms eventually cause a painful boil to grow on the victim's skin which erupts, spewing out thousands of fresh larvae. To remove it from the human body, you have to dig around in the boil cavity, find the tip of the worm and attach it to a twig which is then turned, drawing the creature out as if balling string. It's a delicate manoeuvre and if it breaks, leaving part of the worm still in one's body, the resulting infection can kill. Endemic to the region, it was named by seventeenth-century mariners who first reached the coast of West Africa, an area known for a long time as the Gulf of Guinea.

There were a few wobbly moments but our canoeist eventually delivered us dry and safe from Liberia, an African country heavily influenced by America, to Guinea, one just as heavily influenced by its old colonial overlord, France. I jumped out and slithered my way up the wet river bank, half-expecting to find some immigration officer or representative of *Le Pouvoir*. There was nothing. All I saw were some fishermen, clearly curious at the arrival of two white men, and some very simple thatched structures. They were nothing more than lean-tos, temporary shelters on the river bank knocked up from branches and palm fronds at the start of the dry season. Fishing is a seasonal business and the fishermen knew this area would be inundated during the rainy season so there was no point in building anything more substantial.

The fishermen were smoking the morning's catch over a fire laid on damp soil. In the still air a skein of smoke filtered my view as David and I got ourselves organised, Johnson paid off the canoeist, and Chief Sumo, looking as if pride had been restored, set off confidently to guide us down a narrow but well-marked track. I struck the ground with my *falloe*'s stick and took my first steps into Guinea.

The rain returned and I felt wonderfully at home. For the first time since we began our walk the terrain felt familiar, almost as if I were home in England. Take away the occasional palm tree and I could have been walking through the countryside of my rural childhood. The footpaths were muddy and thick with wet leaves, the view was closed in by grey sky and for the first time I saw what might be called hedges on either side of the track marking areas recognisable as fields. It took me back to the woods and lanes of Northamptonshire, where I spent long days exploring the wilderness, childishly careless of the mud and wet.

My enthusiasm for walking long distances continued into adulthood, something I felt I shared with Graham Greene. He had worked as a sub-editor on *The Times* in his mid-twenties but then bravely resigned so he could focus full time on writing. The paper never really forgave him, huffy in its view that nobody could thrive after turning their back on 'The Thunderer'. Within a few years he was indeed facing serious financial worries, living with his wife in a small rented cottage in the Cotswolds and writing novels that generated only a diminishing income. It got so bad that in 1932, when his brother, Hugh – whose journalism career would include service as a foreign correspondent for the *Telegraph* and later as Director General of the BBC – invited himself to stay for four nights in the Cotswolds, Graham Greene wrote back saying he was on the verge of bankruptcy and could only afford to host him for two.

Money worries aside, Graham Greene developed a Cotswolds

routine of writing each morning and then heading off after lunch on prodigious walks along the lanes of Gloucestershire and beyond. He once told his mother that he had clocked up 127 miles in a month and would soon be able to challenge the 'village postman's record of mileage'.

It was a little over two years later that he set about the journey through West Africa and I felt certain his Cotswolds walking had been good training. He used his hammock only very occasionally and the distances he achieved between village stops were truly impressive, something that acquaintances back in London struggled to believe. Walter Allen, the novelist, met Graham Greene some years after the Liberian trek and described how deceptively frail he appeared.

> . . . I remember thinking: how could this man have made such an expedition? He was very tall and thin; one felt a gust of wind would blow him over.

As I followed his route, blistered and exhausted, I learned to respect a very different part of Graham Greene's character to his creative, literary side. He was not only determined enough to take on a genuine physical and logistical challenge, but he was sufficiently tough and practically minded to see it through. Barbara Greene describes how he would stride out at the start of each day, setting a cracking pace at the head of the column which would soon become strung out behind him through the jungle. When the lead group came to junctions in the track someone would leave a branch across the way to indicate the route taken to those that followed, and though the system worked well enough it was near the St Paul River that things went badly wrong.

Graham Greene and a small group of porters had, as ever, forged ahead, but his cousin and the rest of the bearers missed a crucial junction in the trail, becoming hopelessly lost. It was only after crossing the river by raft and entering Guinea that Graham Greene thought to stop, waiting for several long, anxious hours on the muddy bank as he considered what to do. If he did not re-establish contact with her group then he feared 'we should have been permanently separated, for my cousin had no idea of the route I intended to follow'.

Forests can be terrifyingly disorientating. I remember that during my year in New Zealand I felt a morbid fascination as I read, in the country's early history, of British settlers who set up cabin homes in the thick rainforest that covered the North Island long before it was burned away to produce the open sheep pasture of today. There were instances when those pioneers would step out into the forest, even for a purpose as mundane as going for a pee, and become confused by the identical tree-trunks growing so close to each other that they appeared as a single, solid wall. Several early settlers perished after failing to make it back through the maze.

Barbara Greene describes her sense of stoicism when she and her bearers became aware of their predicament.

> Strangely enough I was not in the least worried. I had grown so stolid of late, so phlegmatic, and I simply decided that it would be a waste of precious energy to fuss till I was quite sure that my cousin had disappeared for ever.

With luck her group eventually reached the St Paul directly opposite the spot where the lead group was still waiting, a moment, she describes, of great relief.

> There, on the other side of the river, sat my cousin and his men, waving their arms excitedly. Even Amedoo allowed himself to show some feelings for once, for his relief knew no bounds . . . It was a ridiculous situation. To happen to run across one another in that great forest as if it had been a village street.

Chief Sumo had agreed to lead us to Bamakama, the first major village on the eastern side of the border, where we planned to rendezvous with Mr Omaru and our luggage. Our walk from Zorzor to the river and into Guinea only took a few hours, but it was much too tough for Mr Omaru to manage on the motorbike.

The plan had been for him to take our rucksacks to the main road crossing into Guinea from Liberia and, once he entered the country, find his way to Bamakama via a long but driveable road marked on my map. If we all set off from Zorzor just before first light, I guesstimated

Mr Omaru, who faced a time-consuming border crossing through both sets of customs and immigration, should reach the village about the same time as us, around the middle of the morning.

After our rest in Zorzor, I felt wonderfully strong on the rainy hike. African rain is usually something extreme, aqueous bullets pummelling the ground, taking out bridges and rearranging landscapes almost as if reasserting nature's authority by clearing away traces of man, but that morning in Guinea its nature had become much more benign. It was so delicate as to have become little more than a sensation of damp, and as I swept my hand through the air I could not see individual raindrops but my palm and fingers still ended up wet.

The bush in Guinea had a greater sense of order than I ever saw in the Liberian jungle. The path took us through tidy plantations of low trees with fleshy fruit the size of avocados growing straight out from trunks and boughs. Yellow, orange or purple in colour, I recognised them from a newspaper story I once wrote about chocolate. They were cocoa pods. And the first forest village the chief led us through had something I had not seen on the other side of the border – a rubbish dump. The poverty of Liberia ensures there is nothing left to waste, but in Guinea, still a poor country, rural communities actually have things to throw away, an unexpected but convincing hallmark of affluence.

As we continued walking east we would occasionally pass Guineans on the trail who greeted us in French. The river frontier might have been an arbitrary division created during the colonial period, with members of the same tribe distributed on both sides, but a hundred and fifty years or so of foreign influence has turned it into a meaningful barrier. A few miles to the west and almost nobody would understand French; here Liberian English is barely known.

Chief Sumo would speak a few words of greeting to each person in their shared Kpelle dialect, the language of the tribal group straddling the frontier, and they would invariably respond politely. But when we reached a young woman walking with a friend something quite extraordinary happened. The chief raised his hand in greeting, muttered a few words and carried on without missing a stride but the girl collapsed as if felled by a gunshot, her bag tumbling to the ground from its head-top perch, spilling its contents of rice. In the few seconds it took me to walk up level with her she fell silent but this was only because she was drawing in breath for a wail of such anguish it made me panic.

'Chief Sumo, Chief Sumo – what happened? What did you say to that woman?' I panted, having run to catch him up around a corner in the track.

'I told her that her mother has died,' he said flatly before turning back to the trail and starting to walk again.

We could not see the woman any more but her keening was growing more intense.

'What do you mean?' David asked, gently grabbing the chief's arm, obliging him to stop. David was livid.

'That woman comes from our village. She has been to Bamakama for a few days to buy rice and her mother fell sick and died. I just told her that.'

David persisted. 'Do you think you should say something else to her – something to explain, maybe, something to comfort her?'

The chief hesitated as he looked into David's face. It was the first time on the trip I saw my travelling companion truly assert himself. The stalemate lasted only a few seconds but from the glare in David's eyes, I knew there could only be one winner. The old man shrugged his shoulders, laid down the bag he was carrying and jogged back around the corner to the woman. For a few moments her wailing grew quieter and we heard muffled voices. Then back into view came the chief. He shouldered his bag and we set off again, the sound of the woman's grief following us far along the trail.

The night before we entered Guinea I had dreamed of storms washing away our trail but we reached Bamakama on foot without any major drama, as anticipated, around mid-morning. Mr Omaru and his motorbike, however, were not there.

The rain was stronger now so some villagers invited us to share a covered veranda in front of a small hovel while Johnson settled the guiding fee with Chief Sumo.

David and I shared lukewarm Coke bought at a roadside stall, my map of Guinea open on my lap. It was the best I could find but it was still rather pathetic, some photocopied pages from a Michelin guide. The Greenes' account of their journey becomes rather unclear in

Guinea, as they begin to leave out the names of some villages they passed through, but the last place they reached before crossing back into Liberia was Diecke, a name that survives to this day. According to my map, Diecke was three, maybe four days' walk south-east of us and I was keen to start, hoping to reach the village of Galaye by nightfall, one of the rare overnight stopping places recorded by the Greenes. But without Mr Omaru we could go nowhere.

The hours passed and I began to feel chill. Motionless on the veranda I had none of the heat generated by walking to dry my wet clothes so in spite of putting on a waterproof my core temperature dipped. David was doing his visual aids routine, showing the villagers the map from Graham Greene's book, as I began to worry. In my daypack I had water, a satellite phone, anti-malaria drugs, water purification tablets and some biscuits but no change of clothing and no bedding. We were more than 200 miles from our destination on the Atlantic and if Mr Omaru did not turn up with our gear there was no way we could complete the trip.

David finished his display and we began to discuss what could have happened. Mr Omaru might have had an accident somewhere along the trail, although throughout the time we spent together he had proved himself an ultra-cautious and skilful rider. Maybe the road was just longer than I had anticipated and it was taking more time than expected.

'You know the most likely thing is that he has had a problem with the officials at the border,' David suggested. 'He is by himself and yet he is carrying gear for four people – you, me, Johnson and himself. That's a hell of a load for one bike. If they spotted that and started asking him questions about it he would have problems. If he tries to explain he is travelling with two white guys who wanted to enter Guinea across a river in the jungle then we are all in trouble.'

In my heart I felt David was right. Our sense of good luck at having our passports stamped at the main border crossing now felt premature. Mr Omaru had most likely run into problems for trying to bring in our gear without us there to vouch for it. The question then became one of what we should do next. Sitting in Bamakama was not going to achieve much so I set a cut-off time of 1 p.m. If Mr Omaru had not appeared by then, we would go and find him ourselves, making our way back along the road we expected him to take, all the way to the main border crossing if necessary. As the hour approached, Johnson seemed to pick up my growing unease and he became increasingly animated. This was the first time our trip had run into a potentially major problem and he was desperate to sort it out.

'Let me go back by myself,' he suggested. 'You stay here with Mr David and I will go and find Mr Omaru.'

Mindful of the way the Greenes had become dangerously separated, I wanted to avoid splitting our small group further and so as the cut-off time approached we prepared to move as one. Bamakama might be on the Michelin map but it is a tiny community of rain-scoured dirt roads and petrol sold on the roadside in old beer bottles. It took a while to round up three young men with half-decent motorbikes but then we were off along the road leading north, back towards the main border crossing.

For a half hour or so it was *Wacky Races*, as the riders tried to outdo each other on a bending, dipping forest track slick with surface mud. I kept shouting for them all to slow down but they ignored me. A broken ankle at this point would stop our trek stone dead. My *falloe*'s stick saved me and my rider on a couple of occasions as the bike pitched to one side and I stabbed the stick down like a crutch to stop us toppling. After a few sharp jabs in his ribcage my rider finally got the message to slow down.

David was some way in the lead, about to go round a corner at the bottom of a hill, when I saw him raise his arms in triumph and his biker slide to a halt. From out of the trees phutted Mr Omaru on his trusty Yamaha AG, his recently purchased black baseball cap on his head. He was going slowly and carefully, his expression as imperturbable as ever.

'What are you doing out here on bikes?' he asked.

'We were worried you might have had some problems so we came to help,' I said.

'The road was slow and a bridge had been washed away so I had to take everything off the bike and ferry it across by canoe. It took a long time to pack everything properly again. But I said I would see you in Bamakama so you should have stayed there. I always do what I say I am going to do.' As he revved his engine and shot off, in his body language there was clear irritation at our doubting him. 'Good Old steady-Eddy Mr Omaru,' I thought as my biker turned round and began racing his two friends once more. I was so elated with relief that I gave up punching him in the ribs.

Once we had all safely reached Bamakama, I got out my map sheets and agreed with Mr Omaru on Galaye as our preferred overnight stop. The locals said a long route looping to the south and east would deliver Mr Omaru to the village while David, Johnson and I could use a more direct footpath. Confident that Mr Omaru would find his way we left him drinking coke and eating biscuits while the three of us set off through plantations of coffee, cocoa and, for the first time on the trek, rubber.

The palaver over Mr Omaru's border crossing seemed to have an energising effect on all three of us and we made good progress along a well-marked track, guided by a young man from Bamakama. The forest was as thick as in Liberia but, in contrast to its neighbour, the farming here was much more systematic and we started to see signboards announcing landowners' names and even the occasional piece of farming equipment like a tractor. Without the full-blown conflict that blighted Sierra Leone and Liberia, Guinea had been developed in relative peace, albeit at a glacially slow rate of economic growth, since becoming independent from France in 1958. A socialist dictator had ruled until 1984, followed by a more market-orientated successor, President Conté, whose death just before Christmas 2008 led to the coup and Captain Camara's unexpected rise to power.

Successful coups might take just a few hours but this only ever involves securing a few key strategic targets such as the national army headquarters, state media and the country's main international airport. To take full control of a nation, to put your own people in charge of all government departments and to see off your rivals, takes much longer. We were fortunate to reach Guinea in that honeymoon period when the impact of the coup outside Conakry, the capital city of Guinea way over on the country's Atlantic seaboard, was only marginal.

It was only five weeks after the coup when I had collected my Guinean visa at the shabby embassy in Freetown. It is one of Guinea's most important diplomatic missions and a main point of contact with a key regional neighbour but the loyalties of its staff soon became clear. They all owed their jobs to the old regime and were now facing a slow professional death, replaced whenever Capt. Camara's people eventually got round to dealing with the diplomatic corps. Above the consul's desk an official photograph of their country's leader did not show the new man but the recently deceased leader, President Conté. This honeymoon period in Guinea would last only nine months until September 2009 when a large crowd gathered in Conakry demanding clarity about the country's future, in particular the holding of elections. Troops commanded by the new regime ran amok, raping women at gunpoint and shooting dead at least 150 unarmed civilians, killings that brought out deep divisions within the ruling junta. A few months later Capt. Camara himself was shot in the head at point-blank range by another soldier and then whisked out of the country for emergency treatment in Morocco, leaving Guinea, a country that for so long had been a rare example of stability in West Africa, inching towards chaos.

It was during my journey across the Congo that I developed my favoured tactic for dealing with volatile, unstable African countries – travel quickly, quietly and as anonymously as possible. Guinea is an elongated country and the section we transited was admirably remote, two or three days' drive from Conakry and a world away from the immediate turbulence caused by the coup. Out here in the forested east we could pass through communities embroiled not in politics but in the daily struggle to make a living.

The villages we slept in were poor but they did not have quite the same edge-of-survival feeling that I had sensed in their Liberian counterparts. We saw more houses built with cement and plenty of non-rusty corrugated-iron sheeting as roofs. The roads were better maintained, roadside stalls better stocked and the people clearly more used to seeing white visitors. Our arrival in Guinean villages barely registered with most locals who often saw foreigners, mostly businessmen running the huge agricultural *sociétés*, or companies, responsible for the well-maintained plantations. After welcoming us the village chiefs would routinely ask for our *ordre de mission*, the official engagement letter carried by foreigners doing business in Guinea. We had to make do with the stamped letter provided by the helpful police officer back in Zorzor, Maj. Gborley.

Many of the LURD rebels who brought down Taylor in 2003 had come from Guinea and I had been warned that a large number had then returned home with their guns and their combat experience, a major security threat in Guinea's remote east. Johnson's linguistic skills were of little use here so I used my French to probe the issue, only to be assured that the LURD foot soldiers were long gone and had either returned to farming or moved on to Conakry.

As travellers moving through remote country we would have to have been very unlucky to bump into a group of armed men but for the villagers living in the region the odds were different. They had to accept the reality of being swamped by armed groups and foreign refugees at times of regional instability. During the wars in Sierra Leone and Liberia, Guinea's frontier had acted as a sort of buffer zone, inundated with civilian refugees from both countries, as well as gangs of unaccountable, armed militiamen. Several times I heard villagers express the fear that, after the honeymoon period, the latest coup could spark another cycle of cross-border turmoil or even full-blown conflict in Guinea. We had shown ourselves just how porous the borders of Guinea were and could see the huge disconnect between the provinces and the seat of power in Conakry. A cross-border raid into Liberia by Taylor's small force in 1989 was all it took to condemn that country to years of war. To me Guinea felt dangerously fragile.

But with the massacre of September 2009 still months into the future, we enjoyed the calm of the coup's immediate aftermath and in time I was able to stop fretting about security. Worry makes a good travelling companion, occupying the mind and sharpening the senses, so as I began to relax for the first time in the journey the walking began to feel like a chore. On the second day, between Galaye and Gbamou, we were told that there were no jungle footpaths in the direction of Diecke, only a dirt road suitable for vehicles, so we had no option other than to tramp down a relatively open track in the full glare of the sun, angering those same blisters from the road stretch into Zorzor. Without quite the same incentive as David and I had to keep going on foot, Johnson would sensibly rest by taking lifts with Mr Omaru from time to time, buzzing ahead on the motorbike and waiting for us to catch up. With only a single road to follow there was little chance of us losing our way.

On those long, open stretches of road my spirits begin to sag, an echo of the Greenes' experience. It was while in Guinea, with his

illness steadily getting worse, that Graham Greene began to despair of
the relentlessness of the trek.

> It was not that the villages were ever dull to me, and only here in
> French Guinea were their simplicity and hospitality a little tarnished
> by the touch of white rule, but the rising in the dark, the hurried
> breakfast, the seven hours of tramping along narrow paths through the
> hot-house forest with no view to either side and only occasional
> glimpses of sky above, this routine became almost unbearable.

As the Greenes' progress slowed in Guinea, a worsening sense not
just of tedium but of claustrophobia grips both their books. Barbara
Greene wrote of the 'utter boredom of walking for hours on end, when
the bush closed in so heavily on either side'.

To combat the tedium of the walk I kept my brain busy with
logistical details, plotting our route south through Guinea and the
crossing back into Liberia. But I also came to rely on Graham
Greene's writing. A paperback copy of *Journey Without Maps* was in
my daypack, not just as a source of inspiration for the trek but as
something to occupy my thoughts. It is not the most straightforward
travel book and on those long road stretches in Guinea I would take it
out from time to time and try to decode its more opaque passages and
what hints they gave about the author's character.

Graham Greene's fear of the mundane loomed over his entire life,
depressing him so fiercely as a young man he flirted with self-harm
and even suicide. In his teenage years he tried to poison and drown
himself, and during his time at Oxford he claimed to have played
Russian roulette with a First World War revolver hidden in a
bedroom cupboard at the Greene family home in Berkhamsted. To
run away from childhood troubles he would sneak off to the nearby
Berkhamsted Common, so back he went when he decided for the first
time to spin the pistol's cylinder and risk the ultimate escape. In his
autobiography, *A Sort of Life*, he described standing beneath giant
beech trees on the edge of the common, sodden wintry leaves
underfoot, as he put the muzzle to his right ear and pulled the trigger.
The resulting rush was something he could never forget.

The same fear of mediocrity towered over his writing, no more so than when he returned from the West African adventure. The idea of putting together a standard travel book drove him to despair and the only thing that saved him from giving up was the dread knowledge that he owed his publisher the £350 advance already spent funding the trip. In *Ways of Escape*, published more than forty years after the journey, he recalls his horror at the thought of writing a traditional travel book: 'I was haunted by the awful tedium of A to Z'. When he sat down to write the book (the working title evolved from *Journey in the Dark* to *Journey Without Maps* and then *The Mapless Journey*, before finally settling on *Journey Without Maps*) he flatly states in an early draft that 'this book does not pretend to be a travel book' although this remark was not included in the published edition. The same draft shows how Graham Greene initially withdrew himself completely from the adventure, ascribing it to an unnamed character X who was then crossed out and replaced by a character named Trench, the literary alter ego Graham Greene had used since writing poetry as a student. X reappears when Trench is crossed out and only on the fourth iteration does Graham Greene place himself in the journey, replacing the X/Trench/he references with I/me.

So to avoid a standard travel narrative he came up with a formula of melding two parallel journeys, one the slog through a remote corner of Africa, the other – one for which there truly were no maps – a more metaphysical journey back to private ideas or memories of quintessential importance. Several times within the book he borrows from the vernacular of psychoanalysis, drawn from the time when he underwent psychiatric treatment as a young man, writing of being taken back to 'repressed ideas' and 'primal memories'. For this internal journey Liberia was not important as a destination but as a means of unlocking the mind, a way not so much of going back physically *to* Africa but going back mentally *by* Africa, releasing memories, experiences and mental images, ones that sometimes sparked dark and sinister associations.

So his first travel book is deliberately punctuated by snapshots of seediness precisely because he viewed them as stepping stones back to lost primal innocence. An interest in seediness would be a feature of a writing career that would span sixty years, but in *Journey Without*

Maps, which he started drafting when he was still thirty, he gives perhaps the clearest account of what he saw as its virtue.

> . . . seediness has a very deep appeal: even the seediness of civilisation, of the sky-signs in Leicester Square, the 'tarts' in Bond Street, the smell of cooking greens off Tottenham Court Road, the little tight-waisted Jews in the Strand. It seems to satisfy, temporarily, the sense of nostalgia for something lost; it seems to represent a stage further back.

Throughout the book the reader is given extraordinary snapshots from Graham Greene's life, his own direct experience of seediness: an Old Etonian pervert in Kensington Gardens talking to strangers about caning schoolgirls; a vagrant who froze to death in a wintry Cotswolds cottage being dragged out by the police, his stiff corpse rattling down the stairs; an army Major telephoning a brothel on Savile Row and ordering girls, as if choosing a meal from a menu – young, fair, curved; an old Baltic aristocrat fallen on hard times, forced to carry tourists' luggage as a porter.

These images are used by Graham Greene in the book to reveal his distrust of the 'civilisation' represented by contemporary Britain and the developed world, and to justify the desire to go somewhere more base, pure and unspoiled.

> . . . but when one sees to what unhappiness, to what peril of extinction centuries of cerebration have brought us, one sometimes has a curiosity to discover if one can from what we have come, to recall at which point we went astray.

His trip to Liberia was what he called 'a smash-and-grab raid into the primitive' and he wrote that he found what he was looking for. While he sneered at those Africans like the Krios of Freetown who embraced western clothes and education, he found among the native tribes of the Liberian interior the existence of characteristics he saw as more admirable and honest – a sense of innocence, simplicity, even virginity that accentuated natural feelings, both good or bad.

> The sense of taste was finer, the sense of pleasure keener, the sense of terror deeper and purer.

He identified the same community-minded virtue that Laurens van der Post would later describe in the bushmen of the Kalahari. But while Van der Post was more interested in the anthropology of a people surviving as hunter-gatherers in an austere desert environment, Graham Greene appeared more focused on a moral search, perhaps linked to his conversion to Catholicism in his twenties. Several times he refers to looking for clues in Africa as to where modern man had gone wrong, as if he could discover something in primitive Liberia that might help right what he saw as the sins of the modern world. But while he found much to praise in the communal life of Liberia, he found no answer to this central question.

In many ways I too had come on this trek in the search for a better understanding of purity, but from my own experience of Sierra Leone and Liberia, the purity I was focused on was at the other end of the moral spectrum from Graham Greene's. The corruption, conflict and suffering here in recent years had destroyed whatever traces of innocence and simplicity Graham Greene identified. As our trek went on, so my search continued for an understanding of the pure evil witnessed here during the wars.

One feature of Graham Greene that I came to relish was his sense of humour. His religious conversion had taken place when he worked on a newspaper in Nottingham, a provincial town he teases in *Journey Without Maps*.

> you couldn't talk of darkest Africa with any conviction when you had known Nottingham well: the dog sick on the mat, the tinned salmon for tea and the hot potato chips for supper carried into the sub-editor's room ready-salted in strips of newspaper.

And the same light spirit showed itself unexpectedly during my research when I was looking into his time as a wartime spy in Africa working for MI6. For most of his life Graham Greene was a ceaseless communicator who wrote, according to one assessment, an average of seven letters a day for his entire adult life, as well as keeping diaries and notebooks on top of the published material – novels, plays, film scripts, non-fiction books and other works. But for reasons of security his letter-writing and diary-keeping tailed off after reaching Freetown just after New Year's Day 1942.

One of the rare references to Graham Greene in this period is an irreverent mention within the pages of *Never Judge a Man by his Umbrella*, the memoirs of another MI6 agent, Nicholas Elliott. During a journey by sea to Lagos in 1942, Elliott's ship put in to Freetown where he had a chance encounter.

> On the quayside I bumped into Graham Greene, who had the unrewarding task of trying to find out what was going on in Dakar. His *The Heart of the Matter* represents MI6's contribution to world literature, but his principal current preoccupation seemed to be the shortage of contraceptives in Sierra Leone; this we managed to alleviate through the generosity of some of our passengers. When, many years later, I reminded Graham of this episode he retorted that when I came ashore I was the tattiest Army officer he had ever seen. I had even, he said, omitted to put on my badges of rank.

Twenty-five years after serving as agent 59200 in Freetown, Graham Greene self-deprecatingly mocked his efforts as a spy, describing how he managed to muddle the combination of his safe, locking his crucial codebooks inside. They could only be retrieved with the help of a blow torch. One of the books did, however, contain a symbol for 'eunuch', something that fired his imagination, making him keen to come up with an official message that included the word. After much thought, he cabled his MI6 opposite number in Gambia to turn down an invitation to attend a regional meeting with the words 'as the chief eunuch said I cannot repeat cannot come'.

Official documents connecting him to MI6 remain rare but I came across a bundle, never before published, at the National Archives in London. Greene's humour illuminates an otherwise dreary collection of papers dating from the period after his deployment to Sierra Leone, when he had been moved back to Britain with responsibility for covering MI6 affairs in Portugal.

In a letter, classified 'Secret' and dated 29 December 1943, to a colleague at MI5, Graham Greene warns of suspicious activity by a British sailor serving as a fireman on a ship that docked at Lisbon. The sailor had been spotted in the city consorting with a known German agent, providing him with quinine. The letter is strictly formal, addressed without honorific, first name or initials – 'Dear Stopford'. But it has a wonderfully informal ending as Graham Greene suggests how MI5 might pick up the trail of the sailor when the boat returned to Britain.

> . . . our representative on December 20 reported that the fireman bought four canaries in Lisbon, and this may assist you to identify him.
>
> Your secretary has promised to reserve me one canary!

The letter sparked a mild flurry of canary-related activity within the British intelligence community, all of which is chronicled in the file. An agent reported officers on the ship had been seen buying birdseed, while another agent was able to report the section of the ship where the fireman had his quarters was too cramped to house a bird cage. In the end a letter, addressed 'Dear Greene', is sent from MI5 declaring the canary report a red herring.

The wonderful thing about intelligence matters, however, is the 'what if?' that clings to them, the way it is possible to come up with theories about secret services that, by the very nature of the intelligence world, can rarely be either proved or disproved. There have been plenty of commentators over the years who attributed to Graham Greene a sinister role as super spy and the canary story made me think they might find fresh support for their theory.

In 1943, at the time the canary letter was sent, the head of German military intelligence was trying covertly to contact the British government to express his loss of faith in the way the war was being run by Hitler. Several attempts to establish a line of communication with MI6 were made through its agents in Lisbon and Madrid but they were suppressed by Graham Greene's boss, Kim Philby. In the 1960s Philby was revealed as a Soviet spy who would have been under orders from Moscow back in 1943 to block attempts by moderate Nazis to reach an accommodation with Britain and the western allies. Any peace on Germany's western front would have allowed it to focus all its efforts on the eastern front against Russia, something Moscow was anxious to avoid.

The name of the German military intelligence chief, a man who would eventually be executed as a traitor by Hitler's loyalists, was Admiral Wilhelm Canaris. I wondered if Greene's letter about

canaries was part of a ploy to get round Philby by informing MI5 that
Admiral Canaris was in play.

David and I became so anxious to avoid walking along the open road
in Guinea that we were willing to take jungle tracks, even if that meant
lengthy diversions and the cost of hiring additional guides. At the end
of our second day in Guinea, and after a hike of 20 miles, we reached
a village called Gbamou where we were so determined to return to the
bush the following day that we made the mistake of ignoring
Johnson's advice.

After bathing and putting up my tent in the dirt outside the chief's
hut, I had strolled into the centre of the village which was dominated
by a huge tree hung with thousands of nests woven by rice birds.
There was a restful end-of-day calm about the place until suddenly,
from behind the tree, came a commotion. A dozen giggling children
were chasing after a sprightly kid that had escaped from its owner,
who in turn rushed past me and launched himself at the escapee,
rugby tackling it in a muddle of dust and bleats.

With the goat firmly settled around his neck and holding on tight
to its front and back legs, Musa Koroma-Gbembu greeted me in
Liberian English, a language not commonly spoken in Guinea. He
had a mild stammer but I was still able to understand as he explained
how he had been forced by the war to move from his birthplace across
the border into Guinea.

'For a long time there was a big refugee camp just outside Gbamou,'
he said. 'I am from the Kpelle tribe and there were many other Kpelle
in the camp, as well as other Liberians from other tribes. But I liked it
here in Guinea because the hunting is good and I took my second and
third wife here. I can go back whenever I want as the border is easy to
cross but I can earn money here from the animals I hunt so this is now
my home and I know all the forest trails around here.'

There was a sparkle in his eye, one that Johnson took against
immediately when he came to the chief's hut in the twilight to discuss
leading us through the forest to Diecke the following morning. We
were all seated on bamboo chairs outside the hut in earnest discussion
as a rat walked into view, raised its nose to sniff and then disappeared
nonchalantly round the corner.

'I don't think he can be trusted,' Johnson whispered after Musa had agreed to collect us for a 6 a.m. start.

Mr Omaru rarely passed judgement on people but out of the darkness came his verdict: 'That man speaks too much.'

Musa was an hour late the following morning. I had been packed and ready to go at 6 a.m., keen to start the third day of trekking through Guinea, and was growing increasingly angry. But not knowing where his hut was there was nothing we could do other than wait. When he finally showed up he did not register our irritation as he clapped his hands and led David and me away from the road and into the forest, leaving Mr Omaru and Johnson to head to Diecke by bike.

There then began a frustrating five hours as Musa charged in circles down forest trails, got lost, cut back on himself and generally wasted a lot of our time and effort. I was not scared, as I had been back in Liberia when Johnson had been forced to leave us, I was plain annoyed. Mouthing silent prayers against guinea worm, we were forced to wade rivers and cut through areas of undergrowth where there was clearly no trail. It became apparent Musa was a rogue and not a very likeable one.

At one village he stopped to find some friends. 'Five minutes,' he said, returning after half an hour with two other men. It took just a moment to work out what their role was. They were Musa's old drinking pals and they had agreed to lead him to a palm wine tree known to be ready for tapping.

Hidden in the undergrowth near the tree was a 'ladder', a length of stout bamboo with footholds cut every twenty inches or so along its length. One of the men leaned it against the tree and then climbed up to where the palm fronds spread from its top. He tied a length of vine between two fronds and braced his back against it for support as he wheedled his machete blade into the soft heart of the tree to reach the white sap. Filling a large plastic bottle he stuffed a leaf in its top, lowered it to the ground on a string and then repeated the process. I remembered how our taxi driver back in Sierra Leone had said a good tree could produce a gallon of palm wine in one go.

Down at ground level Musa sat on the trunk of a fallen tree and drank deep. He offered David and me a mouthful but I had tasted enough palm wine and was feeling too annoyed with our slow progress to want to humour Musa any further. Eventually we left the two men

filling more bottles and followed a clearly giddy Musa for the last pull
into Diecke.

Of course, the walk took longer than expected and meant we were
still walking when the midday heat reached a critical level. By the time
we reached Diecke and parted company with Musa, David and I were
desperate for shade. The town was bigger than any we had seen in
Guinea and after finding a large roadside stall we both stretched out
on wooden benches and fell asleep. I woke to find Johnson leaning
over me, mumbling something about cow meat and the police. I sat up
and came round surrounded by posters of American rappers and soft-
porn stars decorating the stall, while customers drank from oversized
bottles of beer and shouted into mobile phones struggling on a weak
local network.

'Here is some cow meat for you to eat,' said Johnson. 'Be quick
because the local police chief wants to speak to you.'

Unlike in Liberia, keeping cows is relatively common in Guinea
and outside the bar a girl cooked skewers of beef over charcoal in an
upturned oil drum. The smell alone revived me and I was soon
wolfing them down by the handful. The cubes of meat were gristly
and hot enough to burn the roof of my mouth, but after so many bland
meals they tasted great. Feeling stronger, we walked through town to
the gendarmerie where we had our first encounter with Guinean
officialdom. Diecke is a sufficiently large town to warrant a police and
security headquarters, and it was there that our passports were
checked and found to be in order. The officials were polite and formal,
although the police chief, Inspector Moussa Suma, guffawed loudly
when he heard we were on foot.

'But we have good roads in Guinea. Why do you not use a car?' he
asked, smiling.

David started to proffer the map from Graham Greene's book but
the inspector was not interested, simply waving his hand dismissively.
Between sniggers I am pretty sure he said *bon voyage*.

The Guinean police on the border were not quite as friendly when
we got there around sunset after four hours of tramping south along
another road, this time through stifling rubber plantations. In the
tumbled muddle of the West African forest these areas stood out with
their symmetry and straight lines. The rubber trees were evenly
separated in long rows and, planted at the same time, they had all

reached roughly the same size, with trunks about the thickness of my thigh. A few feet off the ground the mottled bark of each tree had been scoured in upward swirls by tappers to release the valuable latex, a white milky secretion that can be collected each day. I had read about the rubber industry and knew that the earlier the tappers came each morning the better their harvest, as latex flows fastest when cool and coagulates in the heat. A bit like our walking, I thought to myself, as I explored a particularly sweltering stand of trees.

In spite of developments in the production of manmade rubber, the natural form still commands higher prices on international markets. The world's best surgeons still prefer using latex gloves for their most delicate work and the world's buyers of condoms choose latex versions over synthetic alternatives. It means natural rubber remains so valuable that when tappers leave the plantations each day they tie beakers to the tree-trunks to catch any last drops that might ooze out later.

I bent down to look at where a tree-trunk had been delicately cut. It takes skill and months of training to be able to remove just enough bark to release the latex but not so much that the tree dies. The margin for error is tiny. At the bottom of the swirl was a small, yellowing gobbet. It came off the tree easily enough and I rolled it between my fingers, feeling the spring in its texture, and I then stretched it as far as it would go. It was like a Dennis the Menace bogey, reaching as far as my arm could stretch before snapping back sharply to its original shape.

Guinean border formalities were spread out over a mile or so of track approaching the border and it soon became apparent why. Four separate agencies – police, immigration, customs and army – all ran their own checkpoints, which they deliberately wanted to be out of sight from each other. This allowed all four to demand 'fees' for crossing. The bribes were not expensive for foreigners like us but they would have eaten into the pockets of Johnson and Mr Omaru had I not been covering their costs. I was struck by the lack of shame in the faces of officials fleecing everyone entering or leaving the country. It is such a fact of life in Africa, both for the bribers and the bribed, that nobody bothers to react. Just as before in Sierra Leone, I had the feeling that a corrupt individual or checkpoint would not do too much harm in Guinea but, taken collectively and over time, these seemingly insignificant instances ground to a halt the workings of the state.

The Guinean border south of Diecke is formed by the St John River but, instead of crossing by canoe, an elderly box-girder bridge led us out of Francophone Africa and back into Liberia. After walking 65 miles through Guinea in three days, I felt a sense of recognition, homecoming even, as we crossed the bridge and entered Nimba County. As we trudged the mile or so into the town of Ganta, the post-apocalyptic array of war-damaged buildings looked reassuringly familiar, as did the potholed roads, hawkers selling sachets of alcohol and the roadside health notice in English urging people to 'bury all poopoo'.

Graham Greene in Liberia – 'rather thin and anemic but "game"'

CHAPTER 10

The Cry of the Bull-Roarer

Dancing Devil, Bolahun

Johnson Boie

What I remember most clearly about Emma Konnah is that her feet were widely splayed and calloused. I had the opportunity to study them closely because when we arrived for an evening appointment at her house in Ganta, she did not stir from her position lounging in an armchair, legs stretched in front of her on a stool, bare soles outwards. From this angle, her feet were ugly but her manner was uglier still.

'Who are you to come to my house without any notice?' she said sharply, without looking up.

Her sitting-room, already hot, suddenly felt a lot more sticky and uncomfortable. A transistor radio blared, its weak signal hissing, but she did not care to turn it down. Above the din I tried to say something about telephoning in advance but she ignored me.

'Why should I not be suspicious of you coming here to Liberia without telling the authorities? Where are your documents authorised by my government? Who are you working for? What are you up to?'

Again I tried to interrupt politely, saying something about my visa and proffering a letter of introduction I had had signed that day at the office of the superintendent of Nimba County. Mrs Konnah was a district commissioner, outranked several times by the superintendent, and the letter surely must persuade her, I thought. Still not looking towards me she glanced at a lackey who had appeared out of nowhere behind me and flicked her head in my direction. He immediately snatched from my hand the piece of paper bearing the letterhead of 'Ministry of Internal Affairs, Republic of Liberia' and read it out above the blaring radio that was now really beginning to irritate me.

When he got to the paragraph urging all government representatives to give us 'official courtesy, maximum protection and assistance' I felt certain Mrs Konnah would fold. Not a bit of it. A big woman, she lumbered to her feet and grabbed the letter, read it for herself and then snorted in derision.

'This is nothing. If a foreigner comes to my area they must write to me in advance and only with my agreement can they enter. You must go now and I will investigate why you are really here.'

Mumbling more threats, she sank back into the armchair with a sneer that indicated our meeting had reached its end. On the wall I saw a picture of a dancing devil, masked, in costume and standing on stilts. It could have been mocking me as I stepped back into the pitch black of Ganta, an annoying end to a day that had begun with much hope and excitement.

Ganta is the second largest city in Liberia but one that still has no power or mains water, and where meaningful post-war reconstruction remains largely an illusion. Mr Omaru, Johnson, David and I had been given lodging at the headquarters of Equip Liberia, a small but active aid group that does a lot of work in Nimba County, providing support to schools and public health clinics, and after a day's rest we had returned to the Greenes' trail, leaving at dawn to walk 8 miles east to the small village of Zuluyi.

It was meant to be one of the most picturesque days of the journey as it was near Zuluyi that the Greenes discovered a memorably beautiful waterfall. Over the days of trekking in Guinea I had begun to share with the Greenes a certain frustration with the jungle, in part because it felt so restrictive, so lifeless. The breeze barely penetrated the cover of the tree canopy so the undergrowth below rarely stirred and one's outlook was forever dominated by an uninspiring colour of green, washed pale by the dry-season heat. The rain we had encountered as we entered Guinea had lasted only a few hours, replaced by temperatures so formidable they crushed the life out of the forest. Graham Greene would reminisce warmly about his trek as the occasion when he lost his heart to West Africa, but the one thing he did complain about was the jungle's lack of contrast.

By the time they left Ganta the Greenes were both feeling bored. They had been told of a waterfall near Zuluyi but neither of them expected it to be anything but a disappointment, a rather dismal attitude expressed forcefully by Barbara Greene:

> . . . as we climbed I was preparing myself for another anticlimax . . .
> what would it lead to? Probably some little pool and a small splash of

water that only the most romantically minded traveller could get really thrilled with.

They were both astounded by what they found, a roaring 60-foot cascade of water that crashed into a rocky dell, whipping up a permanent presence of cooling spray. It was a scene of movement, noise and, finally, contrast, utterly different to anything they had seen on their trek so far. Even the colour had come alive, with the moisture in the air creating a glade of luxuriant green. Their enthusiasm was infectious and I was excited about seeing the waterfall for myself. We made good time on the trail to Zuluyi, first passing an old leper colony on the edge of Ganta and then enjoying the protection of the morning mist. We were walking towards the rising sun and the first we saw of it that day was as a watery disc decorating the leafless limbs of a cotton tree on the horizon. But when we got to the village our journey began to stall. By this stage we had been walking for two weeks but for the first time we were in real danger of losing the trail of the Greenes.

To begin with there seemed nothing untoward about our arrival in Zuluyi. The sun was now high so David, Johnson and I looked for some shade to sit under while we asked for local advice on how to get to the waterfall. Graham Greene noted it was located near a village called Zugbei and when we mentioned the name there was, as ever, much scratching of heads and discussion among the locals. Then an elderly hunter stepped forward saying he knew the waterfall well and could lead us there. His name was Wesley Wuo and, at seventy years of age, he had an admirable gravitas about him.

'It is a place where fish cannot go down and fish cannot go up,' he declaimed formally. 'And it is a place that is cold, colder than anywhere I know in the jungle.'

His description chimed perfectly with that of the Greenes, adding to my sense of anticipation, as Johnson led him to one side to negotiate a price for his guiding services. After a few minutes all arrangements seemed to have been made but as I stood up to get going, a young man hurried over to us and said the local chief wanted to know what we were up to. This all felt perfectly natural and in keeping with our experience of Liberia so far, so Johnson set off to talk to the local chief while David got out the book to show Mr Wuo and a small group of

villagers the map of the Greenes' trip and their reference to the
waterfall.

Johnson was gone a suspiciously long time, and when he returned I
could tell from his downbeat expression we had problems.

'The chief said he does not have the authority to let us go to the
waterfall without the permission of the paramount chief,' he said.
'And the paramount chief is not here at the moment.'

I took Johnson to one side.

'Is it a matter of money? Should we offer to pay the chief something
to let us go?'

'I don't think so. There is something strange about the way they are
talking. I will go back and ask once more,' he replied.

This time Johnson was gone for an hour, enough time for Mr Wuo
to tell me a little about his life. He said he was one of ninety-seven
children sired by the same father and he explained how he had learned
to hunt after spending a full year out in the bush being initiated into
the Poro society. He remembered meeting Dr George Harley, an
American medic turned anthropologist who arrived in Ganta in 1926
as a Methodist missionary and lived there for thirty-four years,
studying as closely as any outsider the workings of the bush societies.
These secret groups function across much of central and northern
Liberia and nowhere are they more powerful than among the Mano
tribe living around Ganta. Dr Harley had put the Greenes up for three
nights and when he heard about the waterfall he accompanied them on
their walk, curious about its possible role as a ceremonial site used by
the bush societies.

Mr Wuo talked on but there was still no sign of Johnson. A young
man offered me a pineapple so, after whittling away at its husk with
my penknife, I devoured the gorgeous syrupy chunks, my fingers
running with juice. Still no sign of Johnson. I walked around the
village, a typical collection of huts, bamboo benches and rice stores,
although it had a proper road running through it which brought the
occasional truck roaring past. Still no sign of Johnson. A rather
unpleasant smell caught my attention and I went to investigate. A
woman was preparing a meal of fermenting cassava, a foodstuff that
smelled to me like rotting fish but is eaten in Liberia enthusiastically
as a 'soup' – a term that covers any sauce, often containing chicken,
fish or bushmeat, that is served as a garnish to rice. In the absence of

refrigeration it made good sense to come up with a way of eating cassava that had been allowed basically to rot, but I was never able to quite get over my squeamishness at its aroma. Nearby, another woman was involved in an early stage of cassava preparation, squeezing water from the pulp of freshly soaked roots. She was using a hinged press made from branches of wood lashed together with plant fibre, a design which made me think of the mangle used by my grandmother to wring out laundry. Still no sign of Johnson.

Finally, he came back and I could tell by his expression that we had made no progress.

'We eventually got in contact by phone with the paramount chief but he would not give us permission without the agreement of the district commissioner, a woman called Emma Konnah, but she will not be available until this evening,' he said. Irritatingly, Mrs Konnah lived in Ganta so we would have to backtrack and return to where we started the day.

We spent the rest of that frustrating day on motorbikes. As long as we made sure we picked up the Greenes' route from Zuluyi after we had sorted out the access problem it did not feel like cheating to head by bike to the capital of Nimba County, Sanniquellie, 20 miles further east, to ask the county superintendent, the most senior government figure in the area, for help. I felt confident that as long as we were patient, Mrs Konnah could be persuaded to grant her permission but, as insurance, a letter from the superintendent would not hurt.

It seemed odd to be climbing the stairs to the office of the superintendent, the Honourable Robert Kamei, in Sanniquellie, a town that was terribly damaged by the conflict in Liberia and which has barely been touched by reconstruction efforts since the war ended in 2003. Those stairs were the first I had used in almost 200 miles of walking and it felt like I was using a new set of muscles in my legs as I climbed. Mr Kamei kindly made time to meet us and offered to help, sending us to his secretary where a letter of introduction would be prepared. His secretary was not in the next-door office but about a mile away in a room adjacent to the local UN military base. The government headquarters where Mr Kamei was located had no electricity so all secretarial matters were dealt with on a computer that drew power from a UN generator.

The secretary was almost entirely computer illiterate and it took him an hour to produce the short letter. The computer had to be rebooted several times as he managed to do things that made the software freeze but, eventually, he handed it over and we headed back to Ganta. I was confident that the letter would see us back on the Greenes' trail the following day, searching through the forest for the waterfall, but I had not factored in the possibility that Mrs Konnah might completely ignore the orders of her superior. Clearly something was up, some other authority was in control over and above the hierarchy of Liberian local government.

It was only after we got back to our lodgings at the Equip Liberia headquarters in Ganta that I learned what this might be from our host, a remarkable Canadian aid worker called Dave Waines. For twenty-three years, a span that included the most violent spasms of the civil war, Dave had made his home in Liberia. But not for him the relative comfort of Monrovia; he had preferred to live up in Nimba County, the crucible of the original uprising led by Taylor and an area overrun countless times by violent militia.

Dave listened closely to my account of our failed attempts to reach the waterfall and, when I finished, he smiled, nodded his head gently and spoke.

'That is the power of the Poro,' he said. 'The waterfall is being used by them and they clearly don't want strangers dropping by. All the government letters in the world are not going to get round the power of the Poro.'

Spending time in Ganta with Dave felt like a re-run of the days the Greenes passed there with Dr Harley. Their trek had made them curious about the spirit world of Liberia and it was Dr Harley who sought to decode it for them. Seven decades later Dave Waines did the same for us.

He was a large man in both body and character. Even though he was not physically there on the evening we walked up from the Guinean border to his charity's base, Dave's spirit filled the place. After coming to Liberia in 1986 when he was twenty-seven, he had been the founding force behind Equip Liberia and all its subsequent achievements – pupils put through school, healthcare provided in remote areas, support given to the development of the rule-of-law – were mostly down to him. He had designed and built the modest head-quarters on a hilltop to the east of the centre of Ganta, a single-storey structure a bit like a school with an open hall off which ran a few basic bedrooms and a washroom. When word came on the third night of our stay that he was driving up from Monrovia the next morning, I watched as the staff cleaned the place from top to bottom, but I was sure their hard work stemmed more from love than fear.

A robust Christian, his faith had an earthiness about it that made it admirably accessible. He asked about my children and I told him how much I was missing three-year-old Kit and Tess, only eighteen months old, and how they kept coming to me in my dreams.

'When all is said and done, there is nothing that comes close in life to the children that we bring up,' he said. 'They are the ones that open our horizons, who make us believe we can make a difference.'

Getting him to talk about the bush societies was not particularly easy and he preferred instead to start by discussing the work of his predecessor, Dr Harley. The drive from Monrovia had taken him much of the day but there was still enough daylight for a tour so we jumped into his jeep with Dave at the wheel. The road was bumpy but short and we were soon in the grounds of the nearby Ganta United Methodist Mission, a remarkably impressive complex dating mostly from the 1940s that spread over a wide area. It was made up of stone-built clinics, classrooms, sport halls and administration blocks arranged around a central avenue shaded by two carefully aligned rows of tall palm trees. Some of the buildings were a bit tatty, with windows broken and fittings missing, but compared to the rest of Ganta it looked as if the war had passed this place by. It could have been the campus of a university in Britain, an image helped by the presence of a weathered stone building with Norman windows and a bell niche on its roof. Limited funding and more pressing demands to build a dispensary, clinic and school meant it would take Dr Harley and his family thirty years to complete the Miller McAllister Memorial church. It was eventually finished in 1956, just four years before he and his wife retired and moved home to America. On his death in 1966, Dr Harley's ashes would be sent to Ganta and buried next to the cornerstone of the church.

'He really was the most amazing man, George Way Harley,' Dave said. 'He was responsible for building pretty much everything you see. He taught the locals how to quarry stone, how to fire bricks, how to make roof tiles, how to shape roof beams from timber – everything that was needed to build a school and a hospital that has lasted more than half a century.

'When he got here there was not a single road in the interior of Liberia, let alone a car, so you know what he did? He arranged for a mile-long road to be cut through the bush here in Ganta and set about bringing in a car. First he had a Model A Ford shipped over from America to Monrovia, and then he had it broken down into components and carried here through the jungle piece by piece. That's a trip of more than 150 miles. It took weeks and weeks, especially the heavy engine block, which had to be carried by an entire crew of four men, but eventually it all arrived and he reassembled the car and fired up the engine. That must have been some moment when an engine sounded in the forest for the first time and he drove down his road.'

Dave said the doctor soon earned a reputation for driving flat out, engine straining and tyres pounding over the uneven road surface, locals wide-eyed in astonishment.

Originally Dr Harley had come here with his wife, Winifred, to work as a physician, but something happened in 1932 to undermine his faith in medicine. By then the couple had had three boys, all born in Ganta, and the family had grown used to dealing with the health problems associated with living in the tropics. In the early hours of Saturday 5 March, the oldest boy, Robert, aged five, had developed a slight fever and Mrs Harley had gone to him several times, dosing him with quinine. Tragically, she left the bottle of tablets on a table in the boy's bedroom and at daybreak, as she rested from her disturbed night, her middle son, Charles, aged four, found the bottle and swallowed its entire contents. Effective in small quantities to fight malaria, quinine can be highly toxic in large doses.

'It took the boy ten hours to die,' Dave said. 'The fact that in all that time his medical knowledge could not save his child meant from then on Dr Harley had a huge loss of confidence and within a few years he had stopped practising medicine altogether. Instead, he devoted his time to anthropology, education and technical training.'

When the Greenes reached Ganta in February 1935 they noted the Harley family was still in mourning, an air of melancholy made more acute because their visit coincided with the birthday of the dead child. Barbara Greene describes Dr Harley's 'deep mournful eyes' and Mrs Harley as an ethereal figure 'all soul and no flesh . . . I began to wonder if she were really there, or if I was the only one that was seeing an apparition'.

During my research I uncovered a letter written in March 1935 by Mrs Harley that showed she was very much there during the Greenes' visit. Indeed, from her perspective it was the apparent frailty of Graham Greene, by that time already ill, that was worth commenting on.

> The next week . . . we had two English people here, a Mr Graham Greene – writer – rather thin and anemic but 'game', and his cousin, Miss Barbara Greene . . . They descended with only an hour's notice but Miss Hooks had left the day before so we could give them her quarters and not worry much . . . They were surprisingly agreeable and unopinionated, and we enjoyed their stay very much.

Her son's grave is still there on the campus near where the Harleys' original wooden home stood, although it is difficult to find in the long grass. The house was burned down by raiders during the war. Dave pointed it out but the light was failing and he was anxious to take us on to the leper colony where he first worked on arriving in Ganta as a volunteer. The sight of his jeep prompted greetings and waves on all sides as we drove in.

'You know, this was one of the few places the rebels left alone during the war,' he said with a smile. 'There are not many times being a leper feels like a good thing but the war in Liberia was one of them.'

It was now so dark he flicked on the jeep's lights, making a woman shy away from the glare. She blinked extravagantly but her face broke into a smile when Dave greeted her through the open window. Behind her a boy of about six years of age, slick with soapy water, stood upright in a tin bucket and when he recognised Dave's voice he jumped out and ran towards the jeep.

'How are you, little Dave Waines?' said Dave, extravagantly lifting the boy in the air and spinning him round. 'Not so little any more.'

He could see I was confused.

'His father is a leper and we have been friends for years. They did me the great honour of naming their son after me, Dave Waines.'

'Come here, Dave Waines,' the grinning mother cried and both meekly obeyed.

Our evening tour had one more destination, the village of Gbuyee, over on the other western side of Ganta, where Dave wanted us to see the house he lived in when he moved out of the leper colony. The road was narrow and pitted but after ten minutes or so the headlights picked up a few huts and then, on another open section of track, the shadowy figure of a man. He had a piece of string tied round his head under which a torch had been tucked so its beam would point onto the ground in front of him. In his hand he had a long, thin staff on the end of which had been attached three pieces of wire to make a primitive trident. 'Frog hunting,' said Dave, before winding down the window and chatting for a few seconds to the hunter, an old acquaintance called Aaron. He was in late middle-age, thin and with sinewy muscles like lengths of cord. Over his torso he wore a T-shirt so threadbare its cloth had the texture of a teabag.

We got to Dave's old turret-like house, now abandoned and rather time-worn, next to a school which was in bad need of repair. It was pitch black but the headlights picked out the torn mosquito netting over the windows and a door hanging off its hinges. Dave reminisced about a powerful dream he had had on a Christian retreat back home in Canada in the mid 1980s. It began with visions of suffering and death in Africa, acts of cruelty by people he did not recognise. But slowly the dream's atmosphere changed as the people began to work together, building wells and fighting disease. By the time he woke he did not want the dream to ever end.

He was drawn to East Africa to begin with but when he eventually reached Liberia he recognised snapshots from the dream: people, both good and bad; events, both terrifying and uplifting. As much as anything else it was the dream that persuaded him to make his home in the Liberian hinterland, a fateful choice that gave him a ringside seat for the war. Ganta is the largest town in Nimba County, the part of Liberia first invaded by Taylor and his small rebel force when they slipped across the border from Ivory Coast on Christmas Eve 1989. Dave witnessed much of the subsequent fighting and he also had a close-up view of the power of the Poro.

'You know, until you live out here in a bush village all the talk of the Poro society and the devils really does not mean much. It's only when you get to know a rural community in Liberia, and I mean really get to know a village, that you see the strength of the Poro and how deep it reaches into the communities. It's like a contract, a secret contract that everyone is involved with in some way or other.'

When Dr Harley spoke to the Greenes about the Poro, he took no chances. Such was the power of the taboo around the bush societies that he waited until all the local staff were outside the house and there was no risk of being overheard. Since arriving in Ganta he had come to know as much about the Poro as any non-initiate, although he freely admitted this did not mean he understood everything. The code of secrecy was observed so intensely and policed so fiercely that Dr Harley's understanding was assembled only piecemeal from snippets of information gleaned over the years from a variety of individuals, often medical patients, with whom he had been able to build slowly a bond of trust.

Asking questions about the Poro in Liberia was a dangerous business both for Dr Harley and for his informants. It was said the three men who gave him most help were found out by the society elders and punished by being poisoned to death. Barbara Greene describes how terribly on-edge Dr Harley appeared when he spoke about the Poro, forever throwing the door open suddenly to check if someone was eavesdropping.

> They were after him, he said. His boys thought that he knew too much. One day they would kill him. He expected it all the time . . . just a little poison in the food . . . a sudden stab in the dark. Soon they would get him.

Her description made me wonder about the death threat placed on me by Taylor when I had written in the *Telegraph*, all those years ago, about the growing use of cannibalistic ritualism by the warlord and his inner circle. Perhaps my report had done nothing more than challenge the same taboos taken on by Dr Harley.

Dr Harley waited until after dark to let the Greenes in on the more sinister side of his discoveries, taking them to the locked room where he kept his prized collection of wooden masks, the ones worn by devils and senior figures within the bush societies. Masks are key to West African bush societies, both the source of spiritual power and the store where it resides to be passed down through the generations, and Dr Harley had gone to great lengths and not inconsiderable personal risk, to acquire them. His collection would eventually number more than four hundred, all individually carved, some with purely human characteristics, some more animalistic. Dr Harley had built up the collection over the years, gleaning as much information as possible about the symbolic meaning and religious role of each one. It was an unsettling encounter for Barbara Greene.

> Cruel faces grinned at us, and others, ugly and grotesque, seemed almost alive. We were surrounded by them, and they were hideous, though carved with great skill . . . One I saw was not intended for the eyes of women. It was a wicked thing, roughly carved, but strong and evil in expression. I could find no beauty in any of them . . .

Dr Harley's mask collection and the details surrounding their function formed the centrepiece of the papers that he wrote and published in the 1940s and 1950s on behalf of Harvard University's Peabody Museum of American Archaeology and Ethnology. The papers remain among the most important published sources on the Poro and Sande, as well as wider spiritualism in Liberia.

In them, Dr Harley admits from the outset that in spite of his years living in Ganta he had built up only a partial understanding of the topic. He also makes the point that while secret societies led by masked figures operate in much of Liberia, the name Poro is used only by some of them, with the others having their own nomenclature. Based in Ganta he was living among the Mano tribe, one of the most prolific followers of the Poro, so he focused much of his writing on Mano traditions. It was an interesting choice. Among all of Liberia's tribes, the Mano have perhaps the worst reputation for ritual cannibalism, a reputation that spread far and wide. Laminah, Barbara Greene's attendant, came from Sierra Leone but he was fully aware of the notorious Mano tribe. 'These people bad, they chop men,' he said to Graham Greene. In Krio to chop is to eat.

Dr Harley showed no squeamishness in his account of how ritual human sacrifice and cannibalism lay at the centre of the Poro.

According to him, before a group of young initiates could be taken out into the bush for training in the society's ways, a human sacrifice had to be made by the society elders. Normally the victim was a slave boy but for some rituals senior Poro members were obliged to make a more personal sacrifice, offering up their own sons to be put to death. He wrote that it was crucial the victim did not cry out so he was numbed with a drug that silenced his screams as his heart or liver was removed. The organs would then be cooked and eaten by senior Poro figures, including masked devils. Special body parts like the skin of the forehead and the palms of the hands were removed and cooked in potions used to anoint sacred items like fetishes and celts, whetstones passed down between generations. In some ceremonies no blood was allowed to drip on the floor so it was carefully collected and later drunk by the senior society members or used to 'feed' one of the fetishes. The penis of the sacrificial victim might be used by a senior priest to hunt down youngsters who had tried to hide and avoid being taken out into the bush school. The penis acted like a diviner, supposedly twitching to indicate where the fugitive was hiding.

The doctor gave away some of the tricks used by the Poro, such as a stunt used to symbolise the death and rebirth of the initiate. He described how in some communities young men were shown to be stabbed with a spear and then tossed over a curtain screen where they would be heard to land with a thud, supposedly dead, then to be reborn through the magic of the Poro. Dr Harley wrote that this was often a piece of carefully constructed theatre, with the victims protected by a wad of plantain stalk worn under their clothes. This would protect them from the spear while at the same time a small bladder of chicken blood was burst to make the stabbing look authentic.

The style of his writing is very academic but the subject matter is chilling. The ceremonies he described are predicated on fear, on keeping the Poro initiates and members to heel through terror. A tray of fingers and toes was kept on show, supposedly taken from people executed for breaking the taboo surrounding the society. And to scare away strangers, a bull-roarer was used in the ceremonies, a voice-distorter that delivered a bloodcurdling stream of unintelligible sounds in a rolling falsetto. It was made of a tube with holes cut into the sides over which were spread discs of membrane cut from the egg sacs of a particular type of spider. When a person spoke into the tube, the membranes would resonate, creating a strange, unnerving sound that made the ceremonies even more terrifying.

He explained that while it was common for visitors to see dancing devils, such as the one I came across in Bolahun, these were lowly figures at the bottom of a complex hierarchy. The name 'zo' was given to more senior figures with special powers and atop the pile was a 'zo of zoes' to whom all others deferred. A zo would preside over the main elements of the initiation process in the bush society, although Dr Harley admits he had been unable to find out anything meaningful about how a member of the Poro reached the level of zo. He chose, however, an interesting term to describe the skills the senior figures attained. He calls these dark arts 'frightfulness'.

There was, perhaps, one redeeming feature in Dr Harley's account. In 1941 he wrote that the more cruel ceremonies, especially those involving human sacrifice, no longer occurred in the region. Dave Waines disagreed.

'Unfortunately Harley was very wrong. For most it is a taboo subject but newspapers, human rights groups and other sources have documented many, many cases of human sacrifice each and every year since I arrived in 1986 and right up to today.'

In my rucksack I had a copy of a Freetown newspaper, the *Independent Observer*, which was published the day I flew into Sierra Leone at the start of this trip. I had kept the paper not just because it reported the recent murder of a village girl, named as Mointeeyae, but because the killing was not deemed shocking enough to make it to the front page. The girl had been decapitated and had her womb ritualistically removed.

We were still sitting in his jeep near the village of Gbuyee when Dave embarked on his own assessment of the Poro and, importantly, its power today.

'I have been in Liberia at a time when outside influences have in some ways had a greater impact than ever before, with foreign investors in the 1980s and, more recently, UN peacekeepers and mobile phone technology. But no matter how strong these modern things are, they come up against the Poro,' he said.

'We were living out here one time in Gbuyee when five friends we knew in the village said they wanted to become Christian, to be baptised. We worried this could cause them some problems but we gave them all our support and help, until the evening before the baptism when we heard this terrible noise coming from the village.

'I was with some other friends visiting from overseas and we were walking home at the time as it was after dark. The noise came from the bull-roarer and it seemed to follow us, growing louder and louder. I knew it was something to do with Poro and our Christian friends in the village but to begin with I did not know what to do. I was scared.'

For effect, he cupped his hands around his mouth and made a series of salivary screeches that he said imitated perfectly the scream of the bull-roarer. As a terror tool it worked perfectly on me.

'We stopped on the track and we joined hands and we prayed. It was a great moment. Suddenly, my fear was gone and I knew what we should do. We would go back into the village and help our friends.'

Turning around, they then strode into Gbuyee and found a crowd of people mobbing the hut where their friends lived.

'We came round the corner and something – somebody even – moved really quickly. It was so fast I felt sure it was not human and I did not get a good look. All I saw was a presence, a shape, and the speed it moved at convinced me it was not human. It was a devil, a senior Poro figure, inside a raffia costume and behind a mask of wood and he did not want to be seen by us. Then the crowd, wearing cloaks and black coverings over their heads, turned from us and walked slowly away.'

He paused and looked out into the dark almost as if he had lost the thread. Then he spoke again.

'You have to understand, Tim, Dr Harley's writing contains one deliberate inaccuracy. The Poro has not gone away and the methods it uses today can be as cruel as those he described, involving sacrifice and ritual murder. The reason Dr Harley wrote like that was survival. He could not have gone on living here in Ganta, among the Poro believers, unless he pretended their cruel practices were finished.

'That night in the village we helped our friends by staying with them until dawn but eventually they had to leave their homes. You cannot take on the Poro and continue to live in these villages. That is the reality of Liberia.'

I asked about the current power of the Poro and if the local authorities do anything to challenge it.

'Last year we had a case in a village east of Ganta where a young man called Hastings Tokpa had also decided to become a Christian. The problem was his father is a zo, and for the Poro Hastings' choice was the worst insult.

'It took ages to find out what happened but eventually witnesses came forward to say a Poro mob had grabbed Hastings and told him he had to be initiated, he had to join Poro. He refused and refused and they argued and argued. So they cut off his head.

'The body was thrown in the river, never found, but the head was buried and when it was finally discovered a case could be built. The local police don't like to take on the Poro killings but in this case the local church took up the case, and we helped all we could. Eventually enough witnesses came forward that a case could be built and, after weeks and weeks on the run, the ringleader was tracked down and arrested. Do you know his name? He was called "Don't Fool The Man".

'The case came to court and we were thrilled because it convicted all five suspects. This was historic, the first major Poro killing conviction since the war. But then what? All five were freed a few weeks back on appeal. The witnesses have gone into hiding.'

Thinking about the apparently unbeatable power of the Poro seemed to get Dave down and his voice faded as we drove back into the unlit town centre of Ganta. He said he was certain ritual murder continued today and his assessment was that hundreds if not thousands of executions take place every year. The reason you don't often hear about them, he said, is that 'the police are either unwilling or incapable of investigating them'. In all of Nimba County the police force, which itself is full of Poro members, has only one jeep and much of the county is reachable only by footpaths.

We pulled up outside Abuja, one of the two functioning restaurants in the town centre, and took our places at plastic picnic tables arranged on the veranda, faintly lit by low-power light bulbs. One by one we went through items on the menu and one by one the waitress said they were not available. Instead, we each made do with a large bottle of Club beer. It was one of the first chilled drinks I had had since Freetown so I wiped the lip of the bottleneck eagerly and joined Dave in taking a deep gulp. It seemed to revive him a little.

'You know, we must not give up, Tim. No matter how strong the Poro might be in Liberia there is a way we can take on these people but you know how we are going to do it? We are going to chase the devil back to hell through prayer.'

Johnson and Mr Omaru were delighted when the time finally came to leave Ganta. They had been rather subdued ever since we arrived, a mood that was only worsened by the unpleasant encounter over the waterfall with Emma Konnah. Johnson later confided in me.

'Those Manos have a bad reputation, you know,' he whispered one day. 'I have never been here before but when I got through to my wife on the phone to say we were here she got really scared.'

Dave Waines and his colleagues at Equip Liberia had been good hosts, allowing us to rest and prepare for the final trek to the coast. One day I had limped into the house in obvious discomfort as my trousers had become shredded where my legs rubbed together and the chafing had left me tender. One of the nurses did not even blink, tossing me a memorably named tube of ointment from Canada where mothers use it for their babies' nappy rash. It was called Boudreaux's Butt Paste and was wonderfully effective.

We ate well in Ganta thanks mostly to a Guinean immigrant who had recently built a basic oven in town that churned out small baguettes, a rather pleasant hangover from the French colonial project. Another Equip Liberia staff member allowed David and me to raid his precious supply of olive oil and fresh salt, so we would sit in the shade of the veranda of the group's headquarters, mopping up oil and salt from a china plate with the chunks of bread as if we were in a smart West London brasserie. David's appetite was prodigious, although he stopped eating in shock one night when I started playing with one of the bigger blisters on my right foot, nicking it slightly and sending a needle of high-pressure blister juice jetting across the cement floor.

After five nights at the house the time came to get back out on to the trail. There was no way around the waterfall issue so we would simply have to miss it out and hope to pick up the Greenes' route further on. It was disappointing but Dave convinced me there was no point going to the local authorities again as they were powerless over the Poro. He had lived in Ganta for a long time and had never been allowed anywhere near the waterfall.

Looking at the map showed we were embarking on the final part of the trek. For almost 200 miles we had been walking mostly east but from Ganta we would start to swing back on ourselves, picking up a trail running south-west straight to the Atlantic and the end of the walk. By the time the Greenes left Dr Harley's hospitality, they were both fed up with sleeping in vermin-infested villages and trekking day after day through the closed-in, sweaty jungle. The thought of finally leaving the forest and reaching the coast, with its promise of a boat to Monrovia and then home to Britain, became an obsession for Graham Greene. In the words of his cousin, he talked incessantly about the coastal village they were aiming for 'as if it was going to turn out to be a heaven on earth' and his desire to arrive at the sea was like 'a pilgrim craving to get to a holy city'.

David also started to fantasise about the end of the walk, talking enthusiastically about what he began to call 'the victory march' onto the beach. But before we got there we would have to cross the area of jungle where illness almost claimed Graham Greene's life.

CHAPTER 11

Daventry Calling

Pandinus Imperator
(Emperor Scorpion)

Mr Omaru

After all the talk about the spirit world in Ganta, it felt somehow appropriate to leave under cover of night. By the light of our headtorches we slipped out of town before dawn, picking our way through the grid of unlit, uneven roads to begin the last part of the trek. All was quiet, except for the regular sound of my *falloe*'s stick striking the ground, and dark, apart from a self-sufficient UN military base glowing on the town's southern approaches. The arrival in 2003 of the peacekeeping mission, one of the largest ever deployed by the UN, helped end the conflict in Liberia, as the foreign troops made the country whole again by reopening roads and setting up bases in territory long since given up to rebels. But by the time of our hike, the impetus of the mission had been spent and the three UN bases we passed during the trip all had a forlorn air about them, places where peacekeepers were holed up, passing the time until they could go home for good. Diplomats back at UN headquarters in New York bickered over the cost of the mission and the manning levels but pretty much the one thing they agreed on was that a UN peacekeeping mission was still needed in Liberia. Without it, conflict would almost certainly return.

Mr Omaru had mentioned his fear of heartmen several times during the trip, and from Ganta onwards he became increasingly jumpy. Over the years such murders have been reported by numerous witnesses, including Dr Junge, the German medic who gained rare access to bush societies in the early 1930s. He helped to investigate the murder of a little girl whose liver had been removed and body mutilated by killers using blades designed to resemble a leopard's claw. The killing was later shown to be the work of members of the Leopard Society, a small but sinister offshoot of the bush society culture. The Greenes themselves came across a case of ritualistic murder just before they entered Liberia, when a district commissioner in Sierra Leone reported the killing of a child by members of a group calling itself the Gorilla Society. The victim's body had also been disfigured with what Graham Greene describes as 'a gorilla knife with curved prongs to make the rough clawing wounds'.

Mr Omaru's anxiety was so acute that it was a struggle to persuade him to venture out on his motorbike in the half-light before dawn. And this became impossible a few days after leaving Ganta when news reached us of a motorcyclist killed in a nearby town called Gbarnga. Reports said two attackers had struck under cover of darkness but what they did not say was what had happened to the body. Dave Waines told me over the phone that he had sent his medical officer to check the corpse and he found the victim's brain had been removed by the killers. Hearing that, Mr Omaru said he would only move during daylight hours.

Mr Omaru's state of mind was not helped when, early on the second morning out of Ganta, he fell heavily from his motorbike as he tried to pick his way past a tree felled across the track in one of the increasingly frequent overnight storms. He was one of the most meticulous riders I have ever seen and this was the only mishap in our entire journey, but it was quite a spill. It scoured the fuel tank, skewed the handlebars and squashed the clutch lever out of shape. More importantly, it left Mr Omaru with a right shoulder so bruised and painful he could no longer pick up his bike, let alone ride it.

We managed to get him to the nearby village of Duo, a rather unfortunate choice of place to regroup. Back in Ganta, a nurse had warned me of an outbreak of lassa fever in Duo which had just killed two people and infected several others. With Mr Omaru in obvious pain I decided not to fuss too much about lassa contamination, and helped him towards a fire that had just been lit by some Duo women on the threshold of a hut. David gave him some painkilling spray but he also wanted to use local methods.

'I need chalk,' Mr Omaru kept saying as he took off his jacket and shirt. 'I need chalk.'

The village medicine man was roused and within half an hour or so, Mr Omaru's right shoulder and upper torso had been painted with a pale clay-like substance that had the appearance of chalk. I have no idea what ingredients went into the balm but it was enough to comfort Mr Omaru and, after settling down in the glow of the fire, he stopped groaning.

He was one of the most sober men I have ever come across,

scrupulously efficient and free of anything hinting at frivolity and, oftentimes, emotion. But I knew from a recent conversation how pained he would be by the damage to his motorbike, one of his most prized possessions.

It had taken me until this last stage of the trek to get past his very private, taciturn exterior but slowly he opened up about the tough rural Liberian life he had endured, made tougher by war. Although only forty-three, two years older than me, he had the mature even stately air of a village elder. Educated into his late teens at the Bolahun mission school, he had barely begun working at the iron ore mine at Bong, one of Liberia's few meaningful industrial programmes, when Taylor's force invaded in 1989, sparking civil unrest that would soon lead to the mine, along with other commercial projects in rural Liberia, being abandoned as workers fled for their lives. After making it northwards to his home at Bolahun, Mr Omaru, like much of the civilian population of Lofa County, soon had to flee once more, spending many of the next thirteen years as a refugee across the border in Sierra Leone. He clearly had presence, as he rose to the elected position of chairman of the Liberian community within his camp, and was later taken on by the Red Cross to help reconnect Liberian families divided by the war. When he eventually ventured home to Bolahun in the late 1990s fighting erupted again and his first wife did something he could never forgive.

It was not a subject he would readily talk about, but over three weeks of travelling and living together he saw from the questions I asked of the villagers we met that I was trying to understand life in rural Liberia and, importantly, why the war had festered for so long and so brutally in this region. When he told me the story of his wife, I felt it might have been his own attempt to help me understand.

'Her name was Kpanna and we had three children together but when the rebels came that last time to Bolahun she told them I had a motorbike.' As ever, Mr Omaru spoke quietly but the bitterness was strong in his voice.

'You could get killed for owning a plate back then. They stole everything and, to make sure there would never be any follow-up, they were willing to kill the owner as well. It was anarchy. So to tell them about my motorbike was to endanger my life – they could have killed me for the bike as easily as anything. I could never forgive her.

'She ran away soon after with one of the rebel leaders and we got a divorce, so I am married again, with another child. I hope life will be better for us now because I earned enough from the Red Cross to plan a little for the future. I bought land and planted four hundred palm trees. It takes about five or six years before they begin to fruit so we must be patient.'

I asked him why Kpanna did what she did and he thought for several moments before replying.

'We had known each other for years and loved each other as man and wife. But she grew jealous of something, maybe my job with the Red Cross, my money, my travelling. She never said what it was but in Africa jealousy can be a terrible thing. Even between loved ones, people can become so jealous they don't just bring each other down, they destroy everything.'

Warmed by the fire, Mr Omaru's morale picked up and he assured us he would be well enough to travel pillion on a motorbike later that day. He let Johnson take responsibility for the scratched but still roadworthy bike. We would set off as a threesome going at our slow walking pace and Mr Omaru would catch us up later in the day down the trail, whenever he got his strength up enough to ride behind a biker he would hire in Duo. According to the map and local advice, there was only one main track so we should not get lost. The plan was a bit clumsy, but it was the best I could do in the circumstances to maintain the momentum of the journey.

It was a short time after leaving Mr Omaru that I had one of the most unexpected experiences of the trip. In all our time in Liberia we had been trekking not just through primitive jungle but through communities scarcely more developed than those seen by the Greenes in 1935, an environment where people lived in houses walled with mud from streambeds and thatched with branches cut from jungle palms, and where to cross a river you used a monkey bridge or canoe. But a little over 30 miles south of Ganta, in bush as thick as any I had seen, I discovered something utterly alien from what I had experienced so far in Liberia – modern, hi-tech, heavy industry.

The sound reached us first. We had just walked through a small forest village where a litter of piglets had squealed loudly. Pigs, or hogs as they are called in Liberian English, are a rarity but, in the few villages where I saw them, they played the role of refuse-recycler, eating pretty much anything they could find, no matter its provenance. From personal experience, I know that they happily spend much of the day snuffling around the village latrines. With the squeal still in my mind, I heard another high-pitched noise so far off as to be formless. I thought at first it too might be something to do with livestock, but it hardened into a beep – a regular, repeating beep that simply had to be manmade. Then I heard a distant metallic rumble and the sound of a man shouting.

Johnson was having a rest, parked up on the motorbike in the shade somewhere behind us, so David and I exchanged a baffled look before edging forward, ever so slightly, nervously. With the beep growing louder, the trail turned a corner, the undergrowth parted and there before us was a large, well-resourced gang of railway workers.

The men were all wearing pristine high-visibility vests and white, industrial workplace hard-hats. The shouting came from a surveyor with a very modern-looking piece of equipment that used a laser to measure distances, and the beep was from a large, yellow, wheeled forklift reversing with its heavy load of ballast to reinforce an embankment next to railway tracks that ran arrow-straight out of sight in both directions through the jungle. Nearby was a fully intact box-girder rail bridge spanning a river and, as if to prove it was in working order, a jeep, gleaming white and with its headlights blazing, was driving across it on a specially designed set of small metal wheels that locked onto the underside of the chassis. The apparatus made a loud, grating noise but it allowed the road vehicle to run safely along the rails.

The workers were friendly, although rather surprised to find two white men walking past their remote jungle worksite. One expatriate worker, who was being driven past in a new Toyota pick-up, asked his driver to stop so he could ask what we were up to. When he opened the door I was close enough to sense the unnatural waft of something I had not felt for weeks – air-conditioning. Kindly he offered us bottles of water from the jeep's onboard fridge, a welcome break from our own tepid supplies. The water was so cold it made my sinuses ache.

I had heard about a contract to rehabilitate the railway line connecting Liberia's Atlantic coastline to the rich Yekepa iron ore deposits way up on the country's mountainous north-east border, but had no idea about the scale of the operation. Completed in the 1960s by a Liberian-American-Swedish consortium known as LAMCO, the 160-mile-long track was, for a long time, Liberia's single most important piece of transport infrastructure. Much of the iron ore was found in a single peak so, like termites setting about a fallen tree, the miners spent the 1970s and 1980s dynamiting and bulldozing their way through the entire mountain, changing for ever the area's skyline. The resulting ore – millions of tons of it – was shunted by train across the width of the country to the coastal town of Buchanan. Close to the beach, LAMCO built huge machines to wash the ore and pack it into pellets. The company also built a large harbour where cargo vessels could be loaded with the precious ore for shipment to steel smelters around the world.

But this functioning business ran into the buffers during Liberia's war. The mineworkers fled, foreign investors pulled out and looters set about the once elaborate infrastructure installed by the company. After securing Buchanan in the early 1990s, Nigerian peacekeepers added to their reputation for criminal opportunism when they systematically dismantled the processing plant and shipped it home as scrap. Nearby villas, built for LAMCO employees behind security fences and arranged in circular loops like middle-class homes in suburbia, were picked clean.

In our modern on-line world, it is possible to see virtually what life must have been like in the mine's heyday as home movies from LAMCO employees are on YouTube. One shows Scandinavian-looking children idling away sunny, pre-war days, splashing around a huge swimming pool set among the rolling forested hills of Yekepa, and in another it is possible to ride with one of the locomotives as the film was shot from the driver's cab of an iron ore train creeping through the jungle.

During the war some of the rails were removed for scrap but largescale theft was not easy without expensive lifting, cutting and moving equipment, so most of the track was simply left alone. Prodigious annual rains mean roads have to be carefully looked after in Liberia, so when the maintenance workers fled the conflict the road network fell apart. In desperation, rebel groups started to use the railway piecemeal, customising the axles of trucks so they could run along the rails. It was enterprising but dangerous, with numerous bloody crashes.

After the war ended in 2003, the world's largest steel manufacturer, ArcelorMittal, began to look covetously at the iron ore deposits in Liberia. In the eyes of the company's planners, Yekepa was still so rich it might be worth refurbishing the railway and port so that largescale shipments could start again. The costs were daunting, as the entire LAMCO infrastructure needed work. Every inch of track, embankment, bridge and building would have to be refurbished all the way from Buchanan up to Yekepa on the other side of the country. Local Liberian industry was so damaged and unreliable after the war that, even though the country has some of the world's best timber resources, it could not even be relied on to produce the thousands of new wooden sleepers needed for the track. So they would be expensively imported from overseas, along with almost every other item needed for the project, from heavy plant machinery to the fried potatoes cooked at the works cafeteria for the legion of expat engineers and technicians brought in to oversee the refurbishment.

But, as is common in Africa, the profits from the project promised such riches that it still made sense to take on these prodigious investment costs. Contracts were signed by ArcelorMittal with the post-war Liberian government and, although some clauses were later disputed and had to be renegotiated, work began in 2006. The scene we stumbled across in the jungle was a small part of the refurbishment, the single most valuable commercial project in post-conflict Liberia.

When you invest on this scale in Africa, however, you do not just play the role of business partner. In the absence of other meaningful economic activity or effective government, you become something much more important. Buchanan was the place on the coast where the Greenes finished their trek (although they knew it by its 1930s name of Grand Bassa) so, as we picked up their route again south of Ganta, we found ourselves following the rough direction of the railway track. This meant we often heard first-hand accounts from local communities about the impact of ArcelorMittal's work. The villagers spoke not just of their high expectations for jobs and wealth from the railway, but also of their strong belief that the rehabilitation would be the panacea for all problems born of Liberia's war, turmoil and decay.

Those hopes were to be badly disappointed. The global economic downturn saw a fall in demand for steel, so in 2009 the accountants at

ArcelorMittal redid their sums. A few weeks after we came across this jungle scene of hi-tech industriousness, all work on rehabilitating the track ceased. Thousands of local workers lost their only source of income and the estimated date for the first export of Yekepa ore slipped indefinitely. The beeps from reversing forklifts were no longer heard out in the jungle and the company was forced to refocus its expenditure from refurbishment to security, with guards paid to protect equipment that had been so expensively shipped in.

On leaving the bustle of the rail gang it took only a few paces to return to the default setting of the Liberian hinterland: silence, sweat and the closed-in, washed-out green embrace of the jungle. Our routine was, as before, to trek from dawn until late morning, take a couple of hours' rest to avoid the midday heat, and then head back on the trail until a suitable village could be found at twilight where we might find food, a hut for David, Johnson and Mr Omaru, and space where I could put up my mozzie-proof tent.

At the end of the first day's walk, roughly 30 miles south of Ganta, we left Nimba County and entered Bong County when we crossed a bridge over the St John. We had seen it first upstream where a section of the river forms the border between Guinea and Liberia, but from there it cuts into Liberia proper, meandering its way across the lowlands until it reaches the Atlantic. We would cross it a total of three times and always have to fight the temptation to take a dip. The river level was low because of the dry season, exposing huge flanks of pinkish rock where the water gathered in still, deep pools, almost irresistible in the cloying discomfort of our march. The only way I kept from throwing myself in was to picture guinea worm parasites climbing like toxic ivy up the insides of my legs.

In Bong County we found villages almost identical to those up in Lofa – mud-brick huts with thatched roofs and, every so often, a tin roof, arranged around a jungle clearing, with 'kitchens' set away from the dwellings. Trackside stalls were a rarity, electrical power non-existent and water came from local streams and the occasional well. But I began to notice decoration on the hut walls for the first time, repetitive hand-prints or swirls of paint in tones of ochre, brown, black and red. It was the only artistic expression I saw in rural Liberia, with the exception of initiation tattoos on the chests of men, and I grew to like it so much that as we came to each village I would search out the most interesting-looking designs to photograph.

After three days of trekking from Ganta we crossed from Bong County into Grand Bassa County and spent the night in a roadside village called Barseegiah, which had a feature unique to our walk – a female chief. Etta Barseegiah was forty-nine, and I found her deeply impressive. Chiefdoms have a hereditary component in Liberia, although members of the ruling family have to win a vote to take over, proof that democracy is strongly rooted here, albeit democracy that always comes second to the power of the Poro. Chief Barseegiah could not have been more different to Emma Konneh, the district commissioner who had been so hostile and unhelpful back in Ganta, and, with her businesslike efficiency, I had no doubt Etta won her chiefdom vote on merit. She lived in a small dwelling which, like countless others we had seen, was overrun by vermin but kept as clean as possible in the circumstances. David and I were done in when we got to Barseegiah having just walked 29 miles, one of the longest days of the trip, but Etta dropped everything to help us, arranging food and hot water for bucket showers.

After washing and getting my breath back, we began to talk. All Liberians from the hinterland have a tribal language as a mother tongue but most, especially a community leader such as Etta, also speak Liberian English. It's a simple form of English, Americanised and with the peculiarity of adding '– oh' on the end of the last word of any statement as a sort of lyrical sign-off. While Johnson could help translate some of the tribal languages, over time I picked up a working understanding of Liberian English.

Through Etta I got a sense of how glacially slow the regeneration has been in rural Liberia since the war. By coincidence we had arrived on an important day in the village's history – just hours earlier a jeep had brought important visitors.

'We used to have a school here run by Pentecostal missionaries,' she recounted. 'It was set up way back in the 1960s and everyone from the nearby villages studied there. I myself learned English there. But with the war it became too dangerous and the missionaries all left in 1990.

'I never thought they would come back but today, just a few hours ago, some of them returned to see what is left of their school. One of them was called Aunt Shelley and I remember her from before. There she was back among us today, once more in Barseegiah. It was a great day.'

I asked what she thought would happen now.

'Sadly there is not much left of the school. Our village was overrun many times during the war and we all had to flee. My husband gave me nine children, but he was killed in 1996 down in Monrovia. When we got back here our homes had been burned and we had to build again.

'Aunt Shelley said the missionaries might be coming back. That would be very special, to have the school working again.'

I asked about the elected, post-war government of Liberia which, like the village of Barseegiah, is also run by a woman. While African governments have occasionally in the past been led by women, President Ellen Johnson Sirleaf is the first to come to power in a national election. Her victory at the polls in 2005 was in large part because she was the chosen representative of the remarkable women who had campaigned so nobly in Monrovia during the war, the ones I saw back in 2003 standing on a muddy, rainy field chanting slogans that called for an end to fighting. I wanted to know from Etta what impact the elected government was having on projects such as schooling in her community.

'This country has always been run from Monrovia by people from Monrovia who don't care about what happens outside Monrovia. The only way a school like ours will be rebuilt is if foreign missionaries like Aunt Shelley come back.'

In her view, Liberia's old divide between country people and Americo-Liberians remains the same as ever, a divide between haves and have-nots.

I went to sleep in Barseegiah in my mozzie-proof capsule watching fireflies through the mesh, pinpricks of light in motion that petered out like dying sparklers the moment my eye caught up with them. They gave me quite a light show alongside the flicker of distant electrical storms that promised an early end to the dry season. I went to sleep thinking we were going to have to pick up the pace if we were going to avoid the rains.

Our trek brought us steadily closer to sea-level and, as the terrain flattened and the climate got even warmer, we entered Liberian rubber country for the first time. From our days in Guinea I knew what well-kept plantations look like: serried ranks of trees, each with a black beaker tied at the same height sitting snugly against the trunk below identically placed cuts in the bark, catching every available drop of valuable latex. When I saw the Liberian plantations, it was as if I was looking at the same scene through a hall-of-mirrors. No two trees were the same. There were branchless saplings the width of my wrist next to giants as thick as my torso, with boles as misshapen as recently-fed pythons. Untended lanes between the trees were choked head-high with vegetation and where in Guinea there had been order, in Liberia there was none. Trunks starburst in all directions, some knocked sideways by seasonal storms, others corkscrewing upwards seeking sunlight from breaks in the high canopy. It took quite some leap of faith to believe rubber production had ever taken place here, but every so often I would spot a black beaker clinging to a rusted twist of wire.

The chaos was due to years of wartime neglect as rubber planters and tappers had been forced to flee, crippling an industry that had once promised to be the making of Liberia. Just as diamonds had raised the prospect of economic salvation for Sierra Leone, so rubber had created hopes of sustainable growth. From its founding in 1847 until the 1920s, Liberia's economic performance was dire, its trickle of earnings from import/export tariffs swallowed up servicing bank loans, so meaningful development was impossible. In 1923, Henry Fenwick Reeve, a long-serving British colonial officer who had spent much of his career in Gambia, published a book on Liberia called *The Black Republic* which castigated its failures at nation-building.

Since 1894, when the writer first visited West Africa, he has witnessed the great regeneration of the whole of that part of the continent – with the exception of Liberia. She alone has stagnated, and is even now with less hope of making a successful African State than ever . . .

Liberia's gloomy prospects were to change completely the very year Reeve's book was published when two senior representatives of the Firestone Tire & Rubber Company from Akron, Ohio arrived by ship. The government was then too poor to build a proper harbour in Monrovia, so the prospectors had to come ashore in a tiny, unstable surfboat, surging past the dangerous sandbar at the river mouth below Cape Mesurado, the promontory that dominates Liberia's capital. The city they discovered was a strange mixture of old and new. A few large buildings had been erected on a grid of wide, modern-looking streets but the absence of regular vehicular traffic meant grass grew long and untended in the thoroughfares, a playground for children and a pasture for livestock. Down on the water's edge was a more traditional crowded shantytown of dilapidated huts and uneven alleyways.

The peculiarities of urban Monrovia were not the concern of the two visitors, however. They were much more interested in what lay outside the city limits, a terrain and a climate that they judged perfect for large-scale rubber production.

Firestone, then in the process of establishing itself as America's leading tyre manufacturer, had found itself dangerously exposed after the First World War to a price-fixing scheme organised by the dominant force in global rubber production, British planters in Malaya and the Far East. To avoid paying what it saw as inflated British prices for the raw material, Firestone sought its own source of supply. Liberia promised exactly what the company was looking for, somewhere the company could create its own large-scale production.

It took three years to agree the final deal, largely because the Firestone plan for Liberia was much more ambitious than anything the weak West African state had ever dealt with before, but in 1926 the Liberian government leased a million acres of forest to the company for ninety-nine years. It is a deal that still represents, on paper, the largest single rubber-growing project in the world. In theory, tens of thousands of Liberians would be offered steady employment planting and maintaining rubber trees, and if the plan worked the government of Liberia would, for the first time, enjoy the guarantee of meaningful revenues.

But, as ArcelorMittal was to find out with its rail project so many years later, Firestone discovered that its role in Liberia went beyond that of financial partner. The tyre company became both the great hope of the country and the scapegoat for local wrangling. Within a few years of the agreement being signed, the firm got caught up indirectly in the slavery scandal investigated by the League of Nations, accused of using unpaid labour on its plantations. Local chiefs, it was alleged, were co-opting tribal rivals and forcing them to work at what had already become known simply as 'Firestone'. Any pay was then pocketed by these unscrupulous chiefs.

Firestone was later cleared of all slavery charges, but this did not stop critics of American foreign policy accusing the firm of promoting US economic imperialism. Allegations of exploitation and mal-practice have gnawed away at Firestone throughout its decades of involvement in Liberia. Production largely ceased during the fighting of the 1990s and even in recent post-war years, when the company has sought to restart production, harmful new allegations have surfaced, this time concerning the use of child labour.

The million-acre dream was never fulfilled, as only a small fraction of the land was ever developed and the country's ambitious hopes for sustainable economic growth on the back of the rubber industry were never met. Just like diamonds in Sierra Leone, rubber in Liberia promised more than it delivered.

More than any other time in the trip, the five-day hike after Ganta felt like a route march because our final destination, the port of Buchanan, was now in reach. We began to see yellow signboards, relics of LAMCO days, marking the distance to the port but they had an unsettling effect because, for the first time in the journey, it somehow became important to know exactly the mileage we were covering. The first one told us we had 118 miles to go and the fact that we had seen one sign raised the expectation of others. I started to look out for them and when I spotted one, poking clear of the foliage, I would eagerly anticipate what distance it would show. But just as the watched clock in double physics lessons at school turns more slowly, so the longed-for signboards never quite showed the mileage I had hoped.

With the countdown to the finish begun, I thought of what I might take from my journey. For those trying to make sense of modern Africa, Liberia has always been a problem. As an African nation that was not colonised by white outsiders, the example of Liberia undercuts those who blame white colonialism for all the continent's problems. Outsiders settled in Liberia where they enjoyed disproportionate status but the country was never in the possession of a foreign power. By touching on both Sierra Leone, a former white colony, and Liberia, never a white colony, I felt the trip allowed me get away from the stranglehold of colour-obsessed analysis and consider their common problems.

When I first went to both countries as a reporter it had been a time not just of war but of barbarity. The cruelty of the RUF in Sierra Leone and the ritualistic atrocities committed by wig-wearing militia in Liberia were so vile I had struggled for understanding. It meant the background for my journey could not have been more different from Graham Greene's. He came in the 1930s at a time when fascism was on the rise in Europe and the world's economy was struggling to recover from the Great Depression. He was eager to find what made this part of Africa different from the rest of the world but his antipathy to his own 1930s world, I felt, coloured his conclusions. He found here purity, simplicity and virtue.

Greene's analysis simply cannot explain what has happened in recent decades, the corruption in both countries that has led to resentment, jealousy and eventually war. He had failed, I felt, to fully account for the role of the Poro, something he regarded as no longer being active or relevant. But my journey through Sierra Leone and Liberia convinced me he was wrong on both counts.

When I had first read about the Poro, before my journey, I admit to being in some way relieved. Devil-worshipping secret societies appeared reassuringly alien, allowing me, as a white European, to distance myself from the cruelties they were blamed for in both countries. Faced with wartime atrocities, it was comforting to blame the Poro, an impenetrable, inexplicable side of Africa that was in some fundamental way different from the value system I was familiar with as an outsider.

But as I trudged along on the last days of the trail, I realised that my opinions had been changed. What had appeared alien and illogical had slowly come to make sense. I did not approve but I felt I better understood. Village life in this environment is so remorselessly tough that people can only survive if they work together: preparing common fields where food is grown, keeping water sources clean, sharing knowledge about herbal medicines capable of fighting disease. From my trek I learned that to survive alone out here is effectively impossible – the individual has to surrender to the community, every person playing their part in an order overseen by a hierarchy of knowledge-keepers capable of making sense of the harsh natural environment. That they were called zo or devil was unimportant. What was much more important was that they represented the best hope for people subsisting in the jungle as they protected proven tenets of knowledge, refined over the centuries, on how to survive. Some of the Poro's ceremonies and internal discipline were vile and cruel but I begrudgingly accepted the rationale that lay behind it. If you believe, as many in the Poro do, that a person does not exist fully as a human unless initiated, then the killing of a non-initiate for ritual reasons is, in many ways, no worse than the killing of an animal for the pot.

With its devil nomenclature and fetishism, Poro is darkly dramatic, but it is essentially no different from similar initiation belief systems observed by aboriginal communities around the world. Writing in the 1940s, Dr Harley identified parallels with initiation ceremonies in Australia and the Pacific Islands. And ritual murder associated with such animistic beliefs is today not limited to Liberia and Sierra Leone. In African countries as far apart as Uganda and South Africa, specialist police units exist to investigate murders committed for ritual purposes. When the headless, limbless torso of a young Nigerian boy was found floating in the Thames in 2001, British police eventually concluded his murder – still unsolved – was connected to African ritualism. To outsiders like me the killings are inexcusable but to the believer they can be justified in a number of ways, often on the grounds that the victim is not actually a human but a spirit in human form.

I feel sure that some of the brutal atrocities of the Liberian and Sierra Leonean wars were committed by individuals motivated by an interpretation of the Poro's values. Modest attempts had been made early in the twentieth century by both governments to suppress the Poro but the wars allowed it back as law and order, in the sense of a state-wide police force or criminal justice system, collapsed. It is undeniable that ritual cannibalism took place during the fighting, often the consumption of human organs as a way for the winner to gain strength. But my journey taught me that to focus purely on these horrific acts is, in fact, to overlook a more pernicious and corrosive impact of the secret societies, one that I feel holds back the development of those African nations where they play a role.

The trek showed me an intense spirit to survive in Sierra Leone and Liberia, whether in the vermin-infested shanties of Freetown or the lassa-ridden villages of Nimba County. Millions of people in this region lost everything during the wars and were condemned to flee to forest camps, returning home to find houses destroyed and property stolen. And yet they managed to rebuild lives and dwell not on what was lost in the past but on what might come in the future. Theirs is an arduous life, a subsistence existence relying on water drawn from rivers, rice eked out from jungle clearings and health problems treated with little more than traditional medicine. But it is at least life, something provided by their fighting spirit.

While the spirit to survive is strong, the spirit to thrive is not and this, I came to believe, is because of the deadweight of traditional taboo, such as the Poro. It is a community-focused phenomenon, born from the necessity of surviving in the tough West African bush, and by its nature it stresses the value of the group over the individual, of developing at the pace of the lowest common denominator, not the advanced outlier. And it is this feature of Poro, and any other secret society found elsewhere in Africa, that condemns its followers to flat-lining stagnation. Stephen Ellis, an academic who has studied the role of tribal religion and spiritualism in Liberia, describes the Poro as 'highly egalitarian', not allowing for individualism, private initiative or personal success. In *The Mask of Anarchy*, published in 1999, Ellis says great effort is made by the Poro to present devils as non-humans. He wrote they deliberately wear costumes and masks to deprive themselves of their individuality as a human so as to avoid any sense of that person claiming to be *primus inter pares*. His observations reminded me of Graham Greene's description of the devil's assistant near Bolahun carefully brushing down the raffia skirts of the dancing devil 'lest a foot or arm should show'.

One of the Poro's key features is its ferocious demand for all members to adhere to rules and hierarchy. Its defenders say these rules are its strength, the means to glue society together, but, for me, these rules, these tribal taboos, are key to understanding the weakness of countries like Sierra Leone and Liberia.

The totems and taboos worked when tribal groups were modest in size, before the era of the nation state in Africa, when an individual's place in society could be defined by their place in the immediate community, whether it be the village, clan or tribe, and success by the achievement of survival and procreation. But the founding of nation states in Africa from the nineteenth century onwards called for a new sense of community, a commitment to a different public good connected with the broader nation, not the narrow tribe. It is, I believe, the failure of this new national public good to dominate over atomistic tribal interests that has led to so many of modern Africa's problems. In the case of Liberia, with twenty recognisably different tribal groups and many more sub-groups, it is the failure to force the devil to cede his power that has undermined the country's development and made it prone to civil strife and, ultimately, war.

It might sound perverse but while Africans survive in Africa, to thrive they go elsewhere. In the diaspora, they do incredibly well, whether as doctors shoring up the National Health Service or as sporting superstars in the United States, and their success can be measured in purely financial terms by the scale of financial remittances. Wangari Maathai, the Kenyan environmentalist who won the Nobel Peace Prize for pursuing environmentally sustainable projects in the face of fierce political oppression from a corrupt regime in Kenya, gave figures for remittances in her 2009 book *The Challenge for Africa*. Her figures showed Africans living abroad each year send more money back to their families than foreign companies invest in the entire continent.

As I trekked through the bush I thought of how individual success in Africa makes that person a target. Until that reality is changed I fear the continent is condemned to fall behind the rest of the world. The devil – the senior, tyrannical figure atop a suffocating belief system of secret, unaccountable, rules that crush the individual – must be chased away.

The final section of the Greenes' trek was, in many ways, the most significant part of their journey and would have an enormous long-term impact on both of them. The depressive author, who had once flirted with suicide, would learn a fresh zeal for life, and his cousin would find reserves of stamina and common sense she never knew she had.

Long before coming to Africa, Graham Greene admitted how danger and discomfort got him through his darker moods. Writing in 1925 to his future wife, Vivien Dayrell-Browning, he urged her to forgive his depression and understand that taking risks was how he best dealt with it. 'The only thing worth doing at the moment seems to be to go and get killed somehow in an exciting manner,' he wrote.

Agreeing to explore Liberia for the anti-slavery campaigners brought him closer than any of his adventures to meeting a premature end. After absentmindedly leaving the expedition's medicine chest back in Freetown, he had little more than Epsom salts with which to fight the illness first spotted by Barbara Greene back in Zigida. She begins to describe in great detail how he came out in boils, his hands started to shake and a nervous tic above his right eye got stronger but, as the illness worsened, it was fever that really concerned her. They had bought a large new tin of Epsom salts from Dr Harley in Ganta and Graham Greene would heap spoonful after spoonful into his tea in the hope of easing his fever but it didn't work. Delirious and barely conscious he had to be carried in his hammock.

Barbara Greene's description of the final days of the trek reads like a medical journal as she charts her cousin's nausea, rollercoaster temperature and worsening lethargy. On one occasion she wrote that he began to totter like a drunk and when he finally agreed to be put to bed she looked at his grey, sunken features and readied herself for the worst.

> Graham would die. I never doubted it for a minute. He looked like a dead man already . . . I took Graham's temperature again, and it had gone up. I felt quite calm at the thought of Graham's death. To my own horror I felt unemotional about it. My mind kept telling me that I was really very upset, but actually I was so tired that . . . I was incapable of feeling anything. I worked out quietly how I would have my cousin buried, how I would go down to the coast, to whom I would send telegrams.

Much to her astonishment he made it through the night. The hollow cheeks and dark rings around his eyes were as bad as the night before but, she noted, his fighting spirit soon returned. When she suggested he rest, he flatly refused, insisting on pushing on for the coast, desperate to end the tedium that he had come to loathe. Graham Greene would later play down the danger he was in, subtitling the relevant passage in his book 'A Touch of Fever', but he readily admitted the experience had brought about in him a fundamental change of heart about the relative merits of life and death.

> I had made a discovery during the night which interested me. I had discovered in myself a passionate interest in living. I had always assumed before, as a matter of course, that death was desirable. It seemed that night like an important discovery . . . one may be able to strengthen oneself with the intellectual idea that once one had been completely convinced of the beauty and desirability of the mere act of living.

Almost as if in counterbalance to her cousin, Barbara Greene got stronger on the last section of the trail, taking on more of the responsibilities, such as arranging food and shelter for the expedition whenever they reached a village. In her diary she noted how 'this weather agrees with me' and for a short while she led the column, with her Freetown-hired servant, Laminah, loyally walking so close at her side that once he was able to save her from stepping on a snake.

As their journey neared its end, Graham Greene grew prickly, complaining for the first time since Sierra Leone of the creeping, coercive impact of white influence the closer they got to the coast. Gone was the purity of the untainted African villages he had eulogised about back in Guinea. Trudging down from the higher, hillier area around Ganta, temperatures soared and the expedition's food supplies petered out so the pair fantasised about the food they missed most. Both of them had to throw away their walking boots as the soles had worn through, leaving them with nothing to walk in but sport shoes. Barbara Greene complained about the new footwear as she could feel every stone she stepped on.

A mutual tetchiness developed and they began to fall out over trivialities. Barbara Greene developed an irrational anger with the way her cousin's socks kept falling down, while he grew incensed by the peculiar shape of the shorts she had had made back in Freetown.

It took David, Johnson, Mr Omaru and me five days to cover roughly 150 miles from Ganta to the sea, our average daily distance now much higher than when we started back in Lofa County. But the daily averages were going up not just because we were getting fitter and more acclimatised. We all began to feel we had had enough and, like the Greenes in this same terrain in 1935, wanted the end of the trek to come.

There was, fortunately, little chance of David and me falling out with each other. Not only was he too tactful for that; we were simply too tired at the end of each day to squabble. For sustained exhaustion the trek through Liberia and Guinea was the most demanding thing I have ever done and when we stopped in the evenings it was all I could do to wash, take down my notes and make ready my tent. Anyway, David was not my only travelling companion. The worry that stems from being responsible for a dangerous expedition kept me company. I still had to work out where we were going to stay in Buchanan and how we were going to get from there to Monrovia by sea, as the Greenes had done. There was little time or energy left for petty infighting.

My own diary records headaches and occasional dizziness but, as the miles and nights rolled by, nothing like Graham Greene's fever. I remember sleeping particularly heavily, perhaps because of our approach to sea-level, and having dreams that crossed the line into the realm of nightmares. The one that troubled me most was a suburban scene, a street where people were milling about carrying burnished steel dustpans. Looking closer, it dawned on me, with the slow, inexorable realisation of a nightmare, that the edges of the pans had been sharpened like cutlass blades. As the understanding crystallised that they were weapons I started to run, chased by dustpan-waving madmen until I hid in the boot of a Mercedes crammed full of amputated limbs.

Graham Greene's dreams according to his diary, often turned to his wife, Vivien, and their infant daughter, Lucy Caroline, and he writes repeatedly about how much he was missing them. In 1935 their marriage was strong and in the diary Graham Greene describes 'longing inexpressibly for V'. The entry on the day after he almost died includes a letter to her in which he says 'I've never never loved you more dearly and more longingly and deeply than on this silly trip'. When the first edition of *Journey Without Maps* came out in 1936 it was dedicated 'To My Wife' with a William Plomer quotation saying 'I carry you like a passport everywhere'. Their marriage would fail in the 1940s meaning the dedication would be removed from later editions.

For the first time in the trip David had started to have serious problems. His left shin, low down and just above the boot, was really troubling him. He would start the day well enough, pumped full of painkillers, but as the day progressed he would fall some distance behind me. I would wait for him from time to time but when he finally caught up his limp would be noticeable. He is a determined young man and he refused to give up the chance of the victory march into Buchanan.

On the fourth day, we reached a village called Siahn and after washing and making ready for bed I had an unsettling exchange with Mr Omaru. That day had been the first when he was well enough to ride his bike again after his fall and towards the end of the day he had done something rather odd. We had just passed three men on the trail carrying cutlasses and walking in the same direction as us and, for some reason, Mr Omaru had all of a sudden appeared on his motorbike from nowhere and taken up position right behind us, separating us from the three men, the engine just ticking over as he kept our, by then, slow pace.

After darkness had fallen Mr Omaru asked me quietly if I remembered anything odd about the three men. I said no.

'They were going to embarrass you, Mr Tim.'

At first I did not know what he meant by 'embarrass'.

'I heard them talking and they had decided to attack you and steal your things. I followed you closely to protect you.'

Impossible to verify, the story sounded plausible enough, if only because Mr Omaru was not one for hyperbole. I went to bed feeling as if I had another reason to want the trek over.

Graham Greene might have been sick on those last days but his journalistic luck – the luck that has you in the right place at the right time – did not desert him. His diary shows how lucky he and his cousin were from the outset as a yellow fever outbreak struck Freetown shortly after they left on the train. Had it been discovered just a day earlier the Greenes would not have been allowed to travel because of quarantine rules. Luck had played a part in their meeting the president in Lofa County, and it returned once more on this final leg of their trip as they ran into another important Liberian figure, Colonel Elwood Davis. To meet Col. Davis was the equivalent of bumping into Ratko Mladic, the Bosnian Serb military commander and wanted war criminal, in the Balkans. Col. Davis was one of the most controversial figures in the entire country, centrally involved in atrocities allegedly committed by Barclay's government in its attempt to subjugate the native country people of Liberia. In British government papers he was accused of killing women and children during a campaign against the Kru tribe, so time spent with Col. Davis would be of considerable help to Graham Greene's mission to build up the human rights picture of Liberia for the anti-slavery society. From his description of the meeting, Graham Greene appeared to rather fall for Col. Davis, an American who had served as a junior soldier in the US army before crossing the Atlantic and being made commander-in-chief of Liberia's armed forces. The pair of them drank their way through a substantial part of the Greenes' dwindling stock of whisky.

I met no Liberian military commander but on our last morning of walking I did stumble across a sad relic of the war, a dreadlocked madman staggering down the track firing an 'air machine gun' into the forest. He was unshod and wearing rags, with the same eye tics I saw in the Harlequin we had encountered back on the walk into Bolahun. The noise of his pretend gun – 'digga–dig, digga–dig, digga–dig' – picked up as we got closer and not once did he stop aiming into the trees. That was where his imaginary enemies were hiding and his body language and glances over his shoulder suggested he was protecting us as allies. Johnson was not convinced, however, and he urged us to walk on by as quickly as possible.

Graham Greene's luck struck again a day's walk from the coast when, in the middle of the bush, he came across the only working truck in the area. It meant an end to what had become, for the Greenes and their entourage, an ordeal. He writes:

> I wanted to laugh and shout and cry; it was the end, the end to the worst boredom I had ever experienced, the worst fear and the worst exhaustion.

All the trekkers – the Greenes, the three servants taken on in Freetown, the teenage jester hired in Bolahun and the twenty-four remaining bearers – squeezed on board and set off shrieking with glee in a cloud of stinking exhaust fumes. After so many footsore miles, Barbara Greene describes the sensation of being driven as 'one of the most utterly satisfying experiences I have ever had'.

With their trek nearing the end, Graham Greene could have picked from numerous yardsticks to measure his return to civilisation but, for me, his choice felt like synchronicity. He writes how he would know his venture into the unknown was over when he would be able to listen on a radio to 'the Empire programme from Daventry'. Daventry, a modest town in Northamptonshire, rarely makes it into works by great literary figures. I know this because it is five miles from the village where I was brought up, and over many childhood years of reading I looked out keenly for mentions of my local town. The best I ever found was an entry in *The Guinness Book of Records* from the mid 1970s, categorising, if I recall correctly, the town's car-part distribution centre, as 'the largest, single-storey building in Europe'.

During my research for the trip through West Africa I can remember how special it felt to spot Greene's reference to Dav, as we locals know it. The BBC Empire Service, the precursor to today's BBC World Service, was first broadcast in 1932 from radio masts erected on hills near to the town, and for many early listeners the first words they heard when tuning in would have been the announcement 'Daventry Calling'. Graham Greene's mention gave me a strange sense of connection with his expedition, a reassuring omen for my risky adventure.

The last stretch to Buchanan ended with a prayer, a suitable bookend for a trek that had started back in Bolahun with Brother Frank's 'Prayer Before a Journey'. The coastal plain of Grand Bassa County was flat and the LAMCO signboards had petered out so I had no idea quite how close we were to the coast when, a little before midday on Sunday 1 March 2009, we reached a junction in a dirt road. There had been no trees around for the past few hours so we had no alternative other than to walk in increasingly hot, open country, and when we got to the turning all I was interested in was getting under the shade of a thatched roadside stall. There I found a woman who was selling packets of biscuits covered in a thick coating of road dust.

'Please ask the lady how far we have to go to Buchanan,' I mumbled to Johnson as I stretched out gratefully on a rough plank balanced on two rocks.

But Nyonkondo Gbor understood me and she said something that had me jumping back up with excitement.

'What do you mean "how far to Buchanan"? – This is Buchanan; you are here already.'

I looked around. To the north-east was the open country we had walked through and to the south-west all I could see was the flat horizon along a low tree-line.

'Behind those trees is the town and then there is the sea. It is just a short walk from here.'

When Johnson explained to her that we had come all the way from the border with Sierra Leone on foot, she uttered a long 'eeesh' in astonishment before composing herself and formally offering to say a prayer. So David, Johnson, Mr Omaru and I all stood up and bowed our heads under the thatch as she began to speak. She spoke in Bassa so none of us, including Johnson and Mr Omaru whose linguistic skills were focused around their homes back in Lofa County, could understand what she was saying. But her reverential tone and solemn body language felt appropriate enough and she finished with words that even I understood – 'tanks to God'.

David and I were thrilled but Mr Omaru's mood suddenly changed things. As practical and inscrutable as ever, he formally demanded payment so he could set off for his journey home.

'But don't you want to finish the last few miles with us? Don't you want to celebrate?' I asked, not really appreciating how serious he was.

'No, thank you. I do not know this place and once you have given me my money I will be a target for robbers. I want to leave now and ride to Monrovia where I know people.'

As ever, Mr Omaru was being both cautious and wise. When the Greenes paid off their bearers here, the men frittered most of their month's earnings on a night of revelry much lubricated by local palm wine and sugar cane spirit, while corrupt Liberian government officials lay in wait to squeeze them for backhanders. Johnson looked forlorn. He was much more interested in reaching the bitter end of the trek and celebrating but he knew that if Mr Omaru left he would have to go with him as a passenger. Mr Omaru's bike was his best bet for starting the long journey home to Lofa County.

It meant a brutally truncated end to our shared adventure. The others looked to one side as I fished my dollar bundle out from where I had secreted it in my daypack and started to pay both Mr Omaru and Johnson. For what had basically been three weeks' work they each received dollars worth well over £700, a sum representing about forty times what they would expect to earn normally in a month.

'You are a good man, Mr Tim,' Mr Omaru said formally. 'You do what you say you are going to do. You said you would walk across Liberia and you did that. And you said you would pay me this money and you did that. Now, I must go.'

Johnson was genuinely upset. I arranged some group photographs outside the roadside stall. In them Mr Omaru and Johnson have taken off their team baseball caps and while Mr Omaru looks content enough poor Johnson's cheerful default setting is deflated. He had suffered through the trip, not just from the terrible blisters back in the first days, but from the worry of feeling responsible for two foreigners as we ventured into parts of Liberia and Guinea he himself had never been to. After sorting out our 'luggages' one last time, he put on a forced smile, hugged David and me warmly and mounted up behind Mr Omaru. Over the roar of the Yamaha's engine I heard him shout, 'I will see you again, *falloe*'.

There was one final thing we had to do to complete our mission. Breaking our rule of avoiding the midday sun, we emerged from the shade of the thatched stall and started walking one last time, David doing his best to conceal his limp. Those last few miles felt a little strange without Johnson and Mr Omaru, but by then I was focused on just one thing: reaching the beach. The track took us through the old LAMCO compound, built at the terminal of the iron ore railway, where we saw rusting hulks of abandoned machinery, the only equipment left by looters back in the 1990s. It passed the tents of UN peacekeepers deployed to Buchanan, the only meaningful port in Liberia outside Monrovia. And it skirted old villas recently refurbished for ArcelorMittal employees.

The terrain could not have been flatter and, against a wide, low horizon of reed thickets and long grass, it was a struggle to believe we were making any progress. Finally, we emerged through yet another patch of low scrub and there in front of us was a manmade wall of huge boulders, the breakwater of the old LAMCO harbour, looming above head height. The rocks were hot to the touch as we clambered up, lizards skittering away at our approach, my *falloe*'s stick helping me one last time to keep my balance.

Then with one final heave, we reached the top and there in front of us was the true end of our trek, the Atlantic Ocean, which we had last seen under the baobabs at Cape Sierra in Freetown. For what felt like the first time in weeks I felt a breeze, a lung-venting, sweat-lifting, shirt-flapping breeze. It was heaven.

Dropping down onto the soft sand, I unlaced my boots, stripped and ran into the waves. My forearms were creosote brown from the sun, the rest of my body pastier and thinner than I recognised. Giddy with glee, I did not feel the burn of the saltwater under the torn flaps of skin on my feet, plunging myself time after time into the water. The walk was finished – *da wok don don*.

CHAPTER 12

The Devil's Last Dance

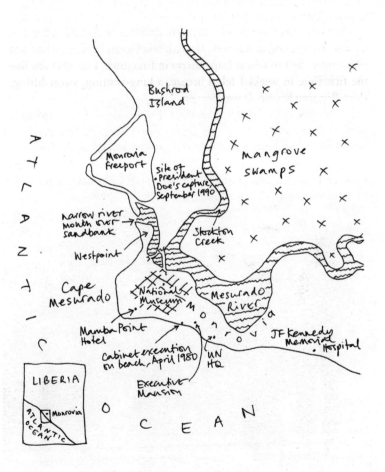

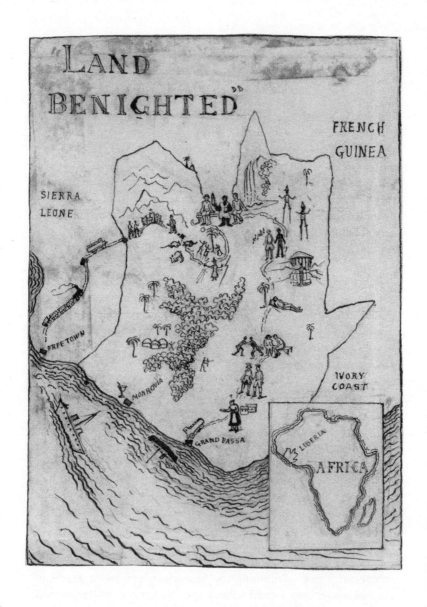

Map depicting the Greenes' 1935 route, believed to have been drawn by
Barbara Greene

After the thrill of completing the overland hike our adventure had one final act, a 60-mile sea journey from Buchanan to Monrovia. During the planning stage I had imagined it would be the easiest part of the whole trip but, on journeys into the unknown, expectation and reality rarely marry. While it took the Greenes only a few hours before they found a boat, by 2009 sea travel along the coast of Liberia had dwindled almost to nothing because a jungle road had been built to the capital city offering an easier, albeit bumpier, means of travel. Without a ferry service, our only hope was to persuade a fisherman to take us.

Buchanan had once been a thriving port but war had left little of the town intact. The main road leading to the beach was pockmarked with potholes and its once grand houses were reduced to occasional patches of rubble roughly defined by the moss-covered stubs of collapsed walls no higher than my waist. In what passed as the town centre it was possible to spot a few recently refurbished buildings, such as a general trading store owned by a Lebanese businessman. Immigrants from the Levant have thrived not just in Sierra Leone but across much of West Africa, nowhere more so than in Liberia. I retained fond memories of the Lebanese owner of the Mamba Point Hotel in Monrovia occasionally providing mezze back in 2003, during lulls in the rebel attack on the city. Inside the shop, members of the owner's family busied themselves stacking slabs of imported beer and checking stock levels for the tinned fish, batteries and basic dry goods piled on the shelves. A quiver of cheap, Chinese-made umbrellas stood next to the till, ready for the imminent rainy season. Looting remained such a threat that the shop was set up a little bit like a fortress, with crudely cut lengths of metal welded over the windows and security guards manning the front door, policing a gaggle of beggars who milled around outside and hassled the few foreign aid workers and ArcelorMittal employees wealthy enough to shop there.

I noticed that some churches had also reopened. Their newly painted walls and noticeboards, fluttering with evangelising messages, suggested they enjoyed good local support. A portentous poster from the Church of Pentecost caught my eye with its promise of a national crusade under the theme 'Oh! Pharaoh, Let My People Go'. Nearby, a billboard announced the post-war relaunch of the Liberian postal service with a jaunty motto of 'Rain or Shine, Mail Must Go'. Back in 2003 I had visited the central post office in Monrovia and remembered it as a symbol of how dysfunctional the nation had become under Taylor's regime. The plate-glass windows of the 1970s building had been shot out and airlines had stopped taking bags of airmail letters because they were owed so much in arrears. I try to write to my godchildren whenever I travel overseas no matter how turbulent the country, but the post worker in Monrovia told me not to bother. The thought that the postal system had come back on stream was comforting.

On our first morning in Buchanan I heard what could have been gunshots as we headed to the town-centre beach, so when I stepped from under a screen of coconut palms onto the sand I did so rather gingerly. Hand-painted flags streamed in the onshore breeze from the bows of dozens of beached fishing canoes. Made from rough, sun-bleached lengths of timber, at a distance the armada could be mistaken for flotsam from some biblical flood, an image reinforced by the religious messages borne by the flags. They were quotations from Christian scripture, imploring God to look benevolently on each small vessel and its crew. Every so often the wind would gust, making the bigger flags crack as loudly as bullwhips. After the close confinement of the jungle, the colour, movement, sound and open-ocean backdrop were giddying, so for several moments I stood motionless in the shade of a time-tilted palm and recalibrated my sense of horizon.

'Please sit down,' said a boat-owner I was introduced to in the warren of shanties erected just up from the surfline. They were little more than shacks with planking walls planted straight on the sand, topped with plastic sheeting. They had the same temporary air that I last saw in the fishermen's grass huts on the banks of the river frontier between Liberia and Guinea.

Sea-fishing is a notoriously itinerant business in West Africa. Not only do the fishermen face fluctuations from Mother Nature, such as seasonal movements of their quarry, changes in feeding patterns and the like, they also face manmade crises such as war and instability.

Almost all the fishermen I met in Buchanan were originally from Ghana, two countries along the coast from Liberia, but overfishing in their homewaters had forced them to move a generation or so earlier. The older ones had been in Liberia for decades and they remembered how, when fighting reached here in the 1990s, they simply put out to sea, turned their banana boats east and moved, temporarily, to the beaches of neighbouring Ivory Coast. The wandering life meant the fishing industry is never much more than artisanal – small canoes, modest nets, limited catches, temporary dwellings, shifting sands – and it was never powerful enough to compete with the huge, unregulated foreign trawlers that since the 1980s have been plundering the waters off West Africa, driving down fish stocks and changing annual migration patterns.

The boat-owner listened patiently to my pitch, which basically amounted to one simple question: how much would it cost to take David and me from here to Monrovia? In a canoe with an outboard motor this represented a one-way journey of about seven hours. He was bare-chested and while we talked every muscular fibre in his torso was being worked as he mended a net hooked over his toes. Leaning back to strain the mesh as taut as possible, he gripped it firmly with one hand while working a large, threaded needle with the other. He paused for a long time before giving his answer. My interest represented a rare opportunity to earn extra money but he did not want to overplay his hand and ask for too much. After several moments mumbling about the crew and extra fuel for the outboard engine he came up with his price – $1,200.

He had blown it. This was way too much and there was no point even starting a negotiation at that price. If he came down halfway, that would still be more than I could afford. I thanked him for his time and shuffled out through the sand under the plastic roof of his shack. Buchanan's beach was a place for industry, not leisure, and even though the palm-fringed shoreline would have been gobbled up by tourism developers in the Caribbean, in Africa it was put to much more prosaic use. I watched as men and women took turns to walk down to where the sand was churned by ankle-deep surf. They then squatted down and defecated.

Finding an affordable boat ride to Monrovia was a frustrating process. After fruitless hours spent trudging through the sandy, malodorous alleys of the fishing community, an aid worker friend suggested, as a last resort, speaking to one of his contacts, the Liberian owner of a medium-sized fishing canoe crewed by Ghanaians. The owner was said to be working in the old LAMCO harbour, the one built for iron ore shipments back in the 1960s, so I set off to find him in my friend's air-conditioned jeep. It was only a mile or so along a rutted road but by the time we arrived my body was already relishing the cool. When I opened the door and felt, once more, the suffocating heat outside I could scarcely believe that less than twenty-four hours earlier I had been willing to trudge on foot through the same conditions.

The coastline of Liberia is notorious for its lack of natural harbours and its hazardous coastal currents. There are plenty of river mouths but, unlike the estuary of the Sierra Leone River where Freetown was established, the river currents are rarely strong enough to wash away sandbars deposited by Atlantic rollers, so approaching them by sea is very hazardous. Only tiny boats such as canoes have a shallow enough draft to avoid being trapped on the sandbars. Furthermore, the rips and undertows in local inshore waters claim lives regularly. Since the war ended, numerous foreigners, NGO workers mostly, have drowned in Liberia's benign-looking but lethal sea.

LAMCO's construction of a large harbour in Buchanan offered a rare sanctuary along a treacherous coastline. It is a simple enough design with two rocky breakwaters reaching out into the Atlantic and a few wharves, but in the absence of any other major ports in the area it became known as the place for ships to go to in times of trouble. Today a huge Soviet-era trawler from the 1980s, so large you can see it clearly on Google Earth, rots quietly in the tropical sun where it was run aground next to the old commercial wharf after limping into the harbour. Nobody could tell me quite how long it had been there but it must have been many years. A seed that had germinated on one of its upper decks had had enough time to grow into a mature tree and the rust near the old Hammer-and-Sickle emblem was so advanced it had perforated plate steel into a brandy snap-like wafer. A diving expert told me that over the years dozens of trawlers, coasters and other ships had made it into the lee of the breakwaters only to sink, so ArcelorMittal, the new de facto owner of the harbour, would not be able to start shipping iron ore using large cargo vessels until safe passage through the underwater wrecks had been established.

A small Nigerian boat, shallow enough in draft to use the commercial wharf, was loading up with large yellow blocks of latex when I got there. It took some time to talk my way past the ArcelorMittal security men at the gate but eventually I managed to extricate the Liberian businessman I was looking for, Mr Gree, from the stevedores, guards and hangers-on gathered noisily next to the ship. Armed security was needed because the wharf, a simple enough block of stone and concrete, represented a major national asset in Liberia. With so few other ports along the coast, whoever controlled the wharf controlled a potentially lucrative source of income. It was from this wharf that illegal timber was smuggled out of the country in large quantities during the war. Hardwood trees from the high rainforest were cut down upcountry, cleared of their branches, and then dragged by truck and tractor all the way to this harbour before the bare trunks were loaded on ships and taken overseas to be made into flooring, furniture and fittings. Alongside the smuggling of Sierra Leonean diamonds, unregulated shipment of timber from upcountry Liberia was one of the major sources of income for Taylor's regime.

Mr Gree beckoned me over to the shade provided by a broken-down gantry crane and politely listened to my request to use his fishing boat. We chatted for a while and I explained the connection with the Greenes and how, if we were able to leave the next morning, we would be sailing by coincidence on exactly the same calendar day, 3 March, when they had sailed in 1935. This symmetry seemed to rather appeal to him so, after a few minutes' consideration, Mr Gree said for the right price he would be willing to send his fishing boat all the way to Monrovia. His crew would be under orders to drop us off first and then work their way back along the coast, fishing waters rarely reached by the Buchanan boats. With luck the catch would generate significant additional earnings. We danced a bit around the price for our passage, with him suggesting $500 initially, me responding with $300 and then us both agreeing on $350. But when we shook hands, I felt sure that I had finally found a way of reaching Monrovia by boat. He needed $200 upfront to buy fuel, so I handed over the money with the promise of paying the balance on reaching our destination.

Mr Gree suggested we make contact with his Ghanaian crew, so back along the beach I drove, to a section of beachfront known as Fontayn Town. Down among its temporary huts I met two brothers, Kofi and Kojo, who by the time we got there had already been informed by mobile phone about the deal. Ghanaian men are traditionally given first names according to the day of the week when they are born so Kofi – just like Kofi Annan, the former UN Secretary-General – was born on Friday, while Kojo was a Monday child. They walked us down to the water's edge and pointed at an uncovered banana boat, called *The Skipper*, moored just beyond the surf.

'That's the boat we will take tomorrow,' Kofi said. 'Make sure you are here by five-thirty a.m. and we will have a chance of getting to Monrovia in the early afternoon.'

I left them making arrangements for the fuel and headed back into town where David insisted, presciently, on stopping off at the Lebanese store to buy two umbrellas as sun shades. Excited at the prospect of nearing the end of our journey, we were even happier to be invited into the ArcelorMittal compound to eat at the company cafeteria, a well-stocked establishment run by a meticulous French-Moroccan chef. Feeling sheepish in our filthy walking clothes, David and I tried to appear as nonchalant as possible when we reached the building, with its polished tables and clean floors. But there was no hiding our thrill when we saw a buffet offering braised steak, crumbed fish, chicken curry, endless salads – and all in limitless quantities. Small groups of expat employees sat eating in near silence, clearly used to this array of choice but David and I nattered away excitedly about our selection as the chef freshened the trays of food and told us that every last ingredient had to be imported.

The sight that really threw me, that really drove home the chasm between the rural Liberia I had seen and the Liberia as experienced by this foreign company, came at the end of the meal. On a huge platter quivered the richest crème caramel I have ever seen, oily with syrup and crowned perfectly with a luscious tan layer of caramelised sugar.

I have a weakness for crème caramel and could not help myself spooning out a large bowlful. Ambrosia itself could never have tasted finer for the Gods of Mount Olympus. But my body had been changed somewhat by weeks of village food and my stomach could not cope with the deluge of rich food. Somewhere on the bloated stagger back to our digs in Buchanan, I threw up the lot.

Pre-dawn the next morning and Fontayn Town looked like a photo-shoot for a Robert Mapplethorpe masterpiece. It was almost pitch black but in the feeble beam of my headtorch appeared the heaving, muscular forms of numerous naked men. Good to their word, Kofi and Kojo had roused the crew of *The Skipper* early and the fishermen were making certain they kept their single set of clothes dry as they waded backwards and forwards to the boat, carrying all the gear needed for the trip. First went the outboard engine, balanced precariously on the head of the tallest of the crew, then drums of fuel, sacks of charcoal, a large sack of rice, tub of palm butter, barrels of drinking water and, finally, clothes folded neatly with other personal items in large plastic margarine containers with sealable lids. It should take us only a day to get to Monrovia but, if the fishing was good, the crew could take as long as a week to work their way back to Buchanan.

One of the crew offered to carry me but I preferred to wade out unshod, soaking my trouser legs before clambering up and over the coarse timbers of the boat. David passed me our rucksacks, which I stowed, before the pair of us settled on a thwart trying to keep out of the way. The boat was about 25 feet long and felt rather crowded when the last of the eleven-strong crew jumped on board, flicked the saltwater off their lower limbs and dressed.

Kojo had stayed ashore so it was Kofi who took command from the sternpost. The design of the boat could not have been simpler – an open, planked canoe with a draft of less than two feet and gunwales standing only three feet above the water level. The anchor was a rusted driveshaft from an ancient truck engine, the shape sufficiently angular to snag the seabed. A wooden flange stuck out from the right-hand side of the boat near the stern and on it the single outboard engine had been mounted, fed by a fuel line worming up from the bottom of the boat where the petrol drums were stored.

Everyone fell silent in the darkness except for Kofi who gave commands to unmoor. With the engine barely ticking over, he then nudged us free of a web of mooring lines attached to other Buchanan boats. The sun had yet to show itself but the shaggy skyline of palm treetops on the beach could just be made out against a glow from the distant ArcelorMittal compound. The town itself, unlit and unreconstructed since the war, slipped away unseen as Kofi, happy that we were clear of all other obstacles, gunned the engine and set us on our way.

In the early-morning chill I soon understood why the crew had taken such care to keep their clothes dry. Trying to shelter from the wind below the gunwales I felt truly cold for the first time since flying into Freetown thirty-five days earlier. From a rarely visited corner of my pack I retrieved a grubby fleece, put it on and discussed with David what the Greenes went through when they covered the same stretch of sea seventy-four years earlier to the day. They too had taken passage on an open boat, similar to ours although a little bigger, carrying a large group of opposition politicians to Monrovia for a political rally. Recently bought second-hand, its new owner wanted to make as much money as possible on his first trip so, even though the boat was already dangerously low in the water, he invited the Greenes and their three Sierra Leonean servants to pile on board. Graham Greene writes that most of the passengers got 'roaring drunk', nearly tipping the boat over in their staggering inebriation, and Barbara Greene's account is just as riotous:

> I fell asleep, and when I woke up a few hours later nearly every one was drunk . . . The captain looked as if he too had indulged in a few drinks, and I was glad, for the sake of my peace of mind, that I could not see the engineer. The boat chugged on its staggering way hour after hour. The sun beat down, and on every side I was pressed in by intoxicated politicians.

Our crew were a more sober lot. With only one man needed at the tiller, Kofi and his nine other colleagues were all asleep within moments of unmooring and it was only long after the sun was up that they stirred. First, the youngest crew member, a cabin-boy, albeit one with no cabin, leaned over the side and used seawater to scrub clean a large pot. He then placed some charcoal in a cast-iron stove on an empty thwart, lit it and prepared a massive heap of rice. Only when it was fully cooked did Kofi order the tillerman to seek out another fishing boat.

Since first light I had noticed that we were never truly alone on the sea. We were always within a mile or two of the beach and throughout the journey it was possible to spot in the offing other fishing boats, varying from tiny, hollowed-out tree-trunk canoes crewed by a single man to larger versions more like ours.

With the rice pot steaming, we came alongside a three-man canoe with the message 'Mother Blessing' painted on the side. Its crew was busy dragging in a net and unpicking small fish trapped in its mesh. From the tip of their boat poked a length of wood, a mast, round which was bundled a sail made of sacks sewn together. The bags in which food aid is delivered by the UN and NGOs had been found to make excellent sailcloth if unpicked and reassembled as a single canvas, so several times during the journey I saw canoes under way beneath patchwork sails bearing the names of food donors. Without a single word being spoken, the men in the smaller boat started to throw some of their catch over to ours. After a few minutes Kofi was satisfied and he ordered *The Skipper* to head on its way. I was curious to see that no money had changed hands so Kofi offered an explanation.

'Almost all of us fishermen here on the coast are Christians, many coming originally from Ghana. We believe in sharing, so if fishermen come up to you with nothing, you offer them whatever you can. I have never met those men before but they know that if they meet us on the way back from Monrovia they could have the pick of our catch.'

The cabin-boy then fried the fish with onions in red palm oil. The stove was mad hot and it took just a few minutes before he pronounced the meal ready. The engine was turned off and we drifted in the gentle heave of the oily Atlantic as the crew ate en masse. Gathered around the single rice pot with its garnish of the freshest fish, they helped themselves to handful after handful, balling the rice and fish into sticky gobbets, chewing contentedly and every so often ejecting bones from their mouths onto the top of clenched fists. After my crème caramel experience I did not feel up to eating, preferring to nurse on bottled water bought at the shop in Buchanan.

The coastline acted as a handrail for our journey. As long as it was in sight, to our starboard, we could not get lost. Between Buchanan and Monrovia there are no meaningful coastal towns so the view was unchanging, a broad blue canvas of cloudless sky and calm sea divided in two by a wavering but unbroken line of butter yellow sand and

green palm trees. The sense of moving without any effort felt
wonderful after the footslog through the jungle and no matter how
slowly the boat phutted along, I kept telling myself we were making
better progress than anything we could have managed on foot. As the
sun grew fiercer David's umbrellas proved their value and during the
dead hours of the journey I sat under mine, twirling it every so often
like a promenading Edwardian dame.

The green thread of this coastline was used by Conrad in *Heart of
Darkness* to set the scene for clumsy colonial aloofness. As Marlow
steams towards his upriver rendezvous with the mysterious Mr
Kurtz, he describes a French warship at anchor near here, riding the
Atlantic swell and settling some pointless tribal dispute by firing her
guns aimlessly towards the tree line: '. . . there she was, incom-
prehensible, firing into a continent.'

Life was to imitate art when, in 1918, a German U-boat surfaced off
Monrovia and began to fire into the city without causing any major
damage. The country's links with America brought on this feeble
display of German military power and drew Liberia into the Great
War in spite of its remoteness. When the allied powers gathered for
the Paris Peace Conference in 1919, Liberia took its place alongside
France, Britain and the United States, the only black-ruled African
nation to attend.

Our voyage took a little longer than expected but some time in the
early afternoon I noticed first proof that Monrovia was in range – my
mobile phone found a signal. Then I saw the occasional beachfront
property among the palms, then a radio mast with a bright red
warning light on top and then began an unbroken line of huts and
shacks slowly growing in size and sophistication along the foreshore.
The city reached further than I remembered but eventually I spotted
an unmistakable squat, rectangular shape rising above the single-
storey buildings: the John F. Kennedy Memorial Hospital, a place all
journalists visited in 2003 to measure the human cost of the rebel
advance that finally did for Taylor.

But the thing that I wanted to see most, that had me closing my
parasol and taking a seat at the prow of the boat studying the shoreline
intensely, was not the hospital. It was a stretch of beach a short
distance further on, and as it got nearer I began to feel more and more
agitated. It was the site where a friend of mine, a newspaperman, had

an experience that changed him for ever. There he watched thirteen men put to death.

When I first joined the *Telegraph* in 1990 it was a paper rich with mavericks. One of the quirkier members of staff was a lifer called Brian Silk, a single man who had worked his entire career at the paper. His reporting days included a golden period when he was entrusted by the editor with the prestigious role of 'fireman', jetting round the globe whenever a dramatic news story broke. An occasionally gruff individual, he was the one who volunteered to work Christmas and Bank Holidays, a person with the appearance of having no family other than the *Telegraph*. By the time I arrived he was approaching retirement and had long since taken up the position of Night News Editor, coming in at teatime and working through to 1 a.m., making sure late-breaking stories were covered to the exacting standards of what he referred to, only half-jokingly, as 'Her Majesty's *Daily Telegraph*'. He was old-school, meticulous and, on first acquaintance, rather odd, with a sense of humour that convinced him jokes improved only through repetition. Around midnight, as late-shift reporters headed home he would never tire of calling across the newsroom, 'Take the rest of the day off'.

As the paper's rawest recruit I was soon drafted onto the night reporting shift, a post where, it was assumed, I could do little harm. Night reporters answered directly to Silk, as he liked to be known, and I can still remember how nervous I felt when sending him my first offerings. One by one he knocked them back, seeming to take pleasure in rejecting those early pieces. A missed capital letter, an incorrectly used comma, an error in emphasis: nothing was too trivial to stop him sending back my stories. I was an Oxbridge graduate who had not served the traditional newsman's apprenticeship on local newspapers, and I convinced myself he was picking on me out of spite, seeking to put me in my place.

But as months passed of those long and often quiet dogwatches my opinion shifted completely. I learned his criticism was not caustic but constructive. A fiercely private person, he was actually doing something incredibly public-spirited – he was taking time out to make me a better reporter. Ego, ambition and individualism are hallmarks of Fleet Street papers, but Silk showed none of these as he conscientiously did whatever he could to improve the standards of my work and that of the other night reporters in his charge. Over the years, the one question that I longed to have answered was why he had prematurely stopped serving as the paper's 'fireman'? This was one of the great jobs in British newspapers, a role so exciting it made egotistical, ambitious individuals, like me, sign up to be reporters, but for some reason Silk had walked away from it. The answer was linked to Liberia.

One night shift he mentioned that he had covered the 1980 coup but gave scant other details. So down I went to the newspaper's cuttings library to find out more. In those pre-internet days, the work of every reporter was routinely preserved in hard copy. Librarians would carefully cut out and file every piece of work printed by the newspaper under an individual's by-line. I went through the filing cabinets and found the folder marked 'Silk, Brian'. It was empty. Years before he had broken the rules by destroying all his own cuttings. But Silk himself had taught me that no matter how many dead ends you hit on a story, there will always be another way through. So back I went to the library and slogged through the old, bound copies of the paper. Even Silk was not cunning enough to excise these and, true enough, there I found his coverage.

The coup happened in the early hours of Saturday 12 April and the first Silk report, with no dateline, was put together the next day when he was still in London. Scrambled by the newspaper to get to Monrovia as quickly as possible, I could picture Silk rushing around various central-London embassies and airline offices, hunting out visas and tickets, cursing that everything was closed for the weekend. But by the Tuesday he was writing from the Ivory Coast, the former French colony that is Liberia's eastern neighbour, although he was marooned there for several days because scheduled flights into Monrovia had been suspended since the coup. It took several more days for Silk to find a way into Monrovia and I could picture his growing frustration. Nothing irritates a foreign-news reporter more than not being able to get to the scene. But it turned out he got there in plenty of time.

In a front-page report, datelined Monrovia and published on Wednesday 23 April 1980, he described watching the beach execution of thirteen senior members of the administration over-thrown in the coup. The *Telegraph*'s house-style did not allow for hyperbole, making the impact of Silk's opening paragraphs all the more dramatic.

> It was an episode of extreme barbarity and bloodlust by soldiers driven wild with hatred. After the firing party had done its job by firing volleys in strict military order, an orgy of revenge began.
>
> With thousands of people cheering them on, the soldiers fired hundreds of rounds into the lifeless bodies, some using sub-machine guns.
>
> When it was over the bodies were covered with blood and the crowd continued yelling its delight.

He spent ten days in Liberia, and filed pieces back to Fleet Street almost daily, a feat which, in the age before satellite communications when the telex represented the most sophisticated means of transmission, was not easy. Silk eventually returned to London for what, in reporter terms, would have been a hero's welcome but it was what happened after he got back that I found most intriguing. He basically stood down as the paper's 'fireman'.

I had spent almost twenty years with the *Telegraph*, reporting on most of the world's major conflicts, but in that time never did I witness anybody actually being killed. From the Balkans, through Africa, to the Middle East and South Asia I saw many corpses and met many who were soon to die, but not once did I actually witness a killing. I struggle to imagine how I would have dealt with the scenes on the beach that day – the look on the faces of the condemned as they were tied to wooden stakes driven into the sand, the long delay before the arrival of the firing squad, the macabre carnival of a crowd egged on by soldiers mocking the condemned men, the trooper with the megaphone finally calling the mob to order, the silence, the three orderly volleys of rounds and then the bloody free-for-all, broken bodies dancing as magazine after magazine was emptied into them.

Reporters covering conflict are a strange and eclectic group but many have a limit, a moment when they know they have had enough. For Silk, that moment came during that trip to Monrovia, although he was much too private ever to discuss the minutiae of his thinking with me. He died in hospital in 2004 a few years after retiring.

From the bow of *The Skipper* I spotted the beach where the killings took place, just below the headland topped by the Executive Mansion, the old government headquarters where President Tolbert was killed in his pyjamas. The stakes where the men died were long-gone and, like the rest of Monrovia's shoreline, it was littered with rubbish. The sun was strong overhead but there were goose bumps on my forearms as I tried to picture Silk, a man who took the trouble to become my teacher, standing there that terrible day in April 1980.

I recognised other landmarks on the final approach along Monrovia's shoreline. First was the old tower block taken over by UN peace-keepers when they deployed to Liberia in 2003. It was now the mission headquarters, guarded by fearsome-looking women from the Indian army, who had Kalashnikovs and spotless fatigues of plum-purple camouflage. Then into view came the Foreign Ministry, now used by President Sirleaf as her seat of government, while the nearby Executive Mansion was being refurbished. The rumour mill in Monrovia suggested she was in no hurry to move her headquarters back into the mansion because of its association with Liberia's dark past. After coming to power so bloodily, President Doe carried out ritualistic murder at the mansion in the 1980s as a means of shoring up his dictatorship, a tradition Taylor was believed to have continued in the late 1990s. Finally I saw the Mamba Point Hotel where I had stayed in June 2003, killing mosquitoes and time with the hapless Sierra Leonean ambassador. It appeared unchanged, although the wreck of a trawler on the rocks out front must have altered the view from the bar somewhat.

In the bright sunshine the city looked very different from how I remembered it. Many of the buildings were freshly painted, with sunlight glinting off intact plate-glass windows, and there were even some new buildings, including a swanky hotel built near the large American embassy compound. By the time *The Skipper* rounded Cape Mesurado and swept over the same river mouth sandbar that caused the Greenes' drunken fellow passengers to lurch dangerously to one side, I had begun to convince myself that Monrovia might perhaps have been transformed into a normal, functioning city. But when we landed on the southern bank of the Mesurado River and I climbed off the boat, two things happened that suggested otherwise. First, I stepped in the human excrement that carpeted the river mudflats and, second, we were detained by the Liberian authorities.

We had landed in West Point, the most crowded and filthy of Monrovia's city centre slums, so it was through narrow alleyways crammed with children, pedestrians and hawkers that David, Kofi and I were bundled, towards the offices of the immigration authorities. They were ramshackle, unlit and horrendously hot, so sweat soon started to puddle under my thighs as I sat patiently on a bench, answering questions fired from a shifting cast of individuals who kept entering and leaving the low-ceilinged room, none of whom wore uniform.

To begin with, it was all quite amicable and, indeed, reasonable. Nobody could remember the last time two white travellers had arrived in Monrovia by fishing boat so it was worth finding out who we were. Our timing could also be construed as suspicious as we had arrived days before an important gathering in the city, convened by Liberia's president, of leading women from around the globe. Particular care was taken by the officials over whether we might be drug smugglers so our rucksacks were searched carefully. I rather pitied the junior officer to whom fell the horrible task of unpeeling my humming bundle of walking clothes and, in the confinement of the room, I was ashamed of the state of my socks. Close attention was paid to my medicine bag but, fortunately, my tube of Boudreaux's Butt Paste (half-used) and supply of water sterilisation tablets and malaria pills (almost exhausted) did not represent a criminal haul.

Under questioning, I patiently went through our motive for following the Greenes' sea journey to Monrovia and David got out the maps of the route from their books. We showed our passports, visas, the various authority letters I had gathered along the way and our yellow fever certificates, which proved that aside from our rank clothes we represented no major public health threat.

It was all quite straightforward and my spirits were greatly lifted because Johnson had turned up. After his lift to Monrovia with Mr Omaru, Johnson had decided to stay in the city to spend his earnings on corrugated iron for a house he would build in his village, Yassadu, back in Lofa County. By telephone he had arranged to meet us when we reached West Point but, of course, he had not anticipated the long visit to the immigration office. During a lull in questioning he told me quietly but proudly about his building plans.

'I can build a home with the money you paid me so I thought I would buy the zinc here in the city. It is much cheaper here than up country. I got a good price and now I am waiting to find a taxi that will take me and the zinc.'

On our trip he had mentioned he had never owned a house but I had no sense that the sum I handed over would be enough to make him a home-owner. I congratulated him but deliberately made no fuss. As our questioning continued, Kofi was looking increasingly nervous so I slipped three $50 bills to Johnson and got him to discreetly hand them over to settle the debt for the sea journey. The moment they reached the coast, the Greenes had noted how the possession of money can make a person a target for 'taxes' claimed by corrupt officials, and I remembered how taxi drivers in Sierra Leone were routinely shaken down for money by the police, even more so when carrying white passengers. Johnson made sure Kofi got the money without anyone seeing.

But after starting off so casually, the questioning began to feel increasingly like interrogation. As the hours passed the officials began to repeat themselves, bribes were demanded and in Johnson's eyes I recognised the first flicker of nerves. The atmosphere worsened when a stocky, rather sinister-looking man finally entered the room. All the other government employees – the policemen, customs officials and immigration officers – fell silent as the man quietly introduced himself as 'chief of security' and began to go over the same questions as his underlings. Kofi was now so nervous he could not bear to look up from the floor, and the sweat puddles under my legs began to chill. But then something happened that brought the atmosphere back from the edge. The security chief's phone rang.

'Answer the phone, Mother Fucker,' boomed his personalised ring tone. The chief let out a belly laugh, I smirked and the tension was gone. Within ten minutes we were free to go, Kofi shaking my hand and scurrying back to *The Skipper*, anxious to put back out to sea, while David, Johnson and I went for our overdue celebration.

The snapshot I had in my memory of wartime Monrovia was so grim that it was no surprise to find the city much improved. For a start, the dry season made the whole atmosphere appear cleaner and fresher.

There were none of the overflowing gutters I remembered, the crowds of terrified refugees gathered in schoolyards or the overarching smell of decay. Someone had mended the attic floor of the national museum, and the city centre cemetery, where Elizabeth T. Nimley's voodoo-esque gravestone had so unsettled me, was now hidden from view behind a high perimeter wall designed to stop gangs of thieves using the graveyard as a hideout.

The shops were well-stocked and the large numbers of people milling about the streets were no longer searching in the gutters for scraps to sell. There were students heading to university, couriers delivering packages on motorbikes and internet cafés doing good business. And I made a point of visiting the central post office. It was operational once more. The zombie city was coming back to life as a modest building boom was taking place along the beachfront in the Sinkor district of town, funded mostly by various local Lebananese tycoons, so diplomats, aid workers and other foreigners could live, at a price, in some style. Generators provided power for air-conditioning and, for those who could afford it, third- and fourth-floor apartments offered sea views over high security walls manned by locally employed private security guards. This was my first time in Monrovia since Taylor's government had threatened me and, although I was a bit anxious when we arrived, by the time I had walked around the small grid of downtown streets my nerves had largely gone.

David and I spent two days decompressing in Monrovia. He found a swimming pool to lounge by, while I took motorbike taxis to various appointments with a long list of aid workers and contacts I had to thank. The city's roads were not as clogged as those in Freetown, so I buzzed around easily enough and met the individuals – country directors, mostly, of various NGOs operating in Liberia – who had introduced me to Johnson, made available accommodation in Zorzor and provided other helpful gems of advice and support. In turn, they were interested to hear the rare perspective of someone not chained, like them, to spreadsheets and computer screens and who had been able to get an intimate, ground-level view of the country. Back in 2003 the Mamba Point Hotel had almost the only functioning restaurant in the city but, six years later, a much wider range of eateries was available. They included a perfectly respectable Indian curry house and a very smart sushi restaurant, although, after my wobbly moment with the crème caramel, I took it easy when it came to ordering.

True to its promise, the Foreign Office forewarned its people in Monrovia about the Greenes' arrival in 1935 and they stayed at the old British diplomatic mission up on Cape Mesurado, described by Graham Greene as 'a most luxurious & beautifully placed home with lashings of drink'. David and I enjoyed the hospitality of Our Woman in Monrovia, Britain's solitary diplomat currently deployed to Liberia, although instead of alcohol I was happy to make do with lavish amounts of freshly brewed coffee and use of her washing machine.

In many ways it was hard not to get caught up with a sense of optimism in Monrovia. In a city-centre café I found myself flicking through a glossy magazine called *Liberia – Travel & Life*. Produced locally, it was only in its fifth issue but the fact that there was enough money to fund full-page adverts for local businesses including mobile phone companies, insurance brokers and, I was interested to see, a restaurant in the town of Smell-No-Taste, underscored how much better things had become in peacetime. From its pages the title of a feature article jumped out – *Trekking Through Nimba*. When we were up in Ganta staying with Dave Waines we had been 'trekking through Nimba County'. At the time I thought we were quite adventurous, pioneering even in the post-war period, but this article seemed to suggest otherwise. Perhaps there was already a tradition of forest walking near Ganta? I turned anxiously to the piece but found it was simply a photo-spread for shots of a beautiful Liberian model taken in and around the town. In one of the shots she draped herself down the steps leading to the Miller McAllister Memorial church at Dr Harley's mission. In another she poses coquettishly, one leg cocked, on the veranda of Abuja, the restaurant where we had drunk with Dave Waines.

The article might have glossed over Abuja's limitations – I remembered the waitress could not provide us with a single dish from the menu – but the point was that the magazine symbolised a country pulling itself back up off the floor. After the horrors that had gone before during Liberia's long, dark night of dictatorship and conflict, the fact that a photo-shoot could even take place in Ganta was a monumental step forward.

But as I got my bearings in Monrovia, I found the recovery unconvincing. The disconnect between the Liberia I had seen on the trek, a Liberia of Poro-dominated, subsistence farmers living in abject poverty, and the Liberia as represented by city-centre car showrooms and restaurants felt downright dangerous. It was this divide between the haves and have-nots that led to the 1980 coup and Doe's dictatorship. And it was the same sense of injustice that allowed the various rebel groups spawned by Taylor's 1989 invasion to thrive in Liberia for so long.

Since 2003 Liberia has held elections and been relatively peaceful, with some positive economic development. But when you start at Ground Zero is there any way to go other than up? My fear was that the intrinsic problem of the country – a wealthy elite enjoying a life-style unreachable by the vast majority of the population – remained as toxic as ever. For those left behind, those unable to bridge legitimately a gap growing ever bigger, the aspiration I saw on the T-shirt worn by one of my jungle guides remained potent: Get Rich or Die Tryin'. The demons of jealousy and frustration felt a great threat in Monrovia.

Over the weeks I spent with Johnson I came to see him as my post-conflict African Everyman. He had dealt with the war as best he could, surviving in various refugee camps, maintaining an education begun at the mission school in Bolahun, winning the trust of several foreign NGOs and eventually leading his surviving family members back home to Yassadu. He was well-informed, capable and hard-working. When we discussed our children he spoke in language lifted verbatim from the pages of a western pamphlet. I found his words unforgettable.

'I made sure to practise safe birth control methods and had only three children, all spread out two years apart. We cannot afford overpopulation in our country you know, Mr Butcher.'

Johnson had kept his part of the social contract. Like countless millions across Africa he had gone to school, heeded the advice of experts, changed his lifestyle to meet their standards. But what had this got him? Nothing. Before I met him he had no job and after I left Liberia he had no job. Through greed and incompetence, the authorities in Liberia were not keeping their part of the social con-tract. Instead of providing a stable economy, earning opportunities and even the rule of law, they provided nothing.

In the city centre, right next to the government headquarters, I saw a crude poster depicting street lights illuminating a tarred road with white lines painted down the middle. In large letters, the poster declared 'Your Taxes at Work – The Process is On'. It was fiction. I knew from my slow slog through the backwoods of Liberia, past unlit towns, along roads maintained only by UN peacekeepers, past schools funded by foreign aid groups, that the impact of Liberia's central government is almost non-existent. And I knew from my own experience in Ganta that the law of government from Monrovia means nothing when it comes up against the traditional power of Poro. Take away the UN peacekeeping mission from Monrovia and the aid groups with their well-funded budgets and I fear not just for the future of the sushi restaurant in Monrovia. I fear for the future of the entire country.

On the night before we left the city I read a postscript to the army worms health crisis that had led the government to declare a state of emergency just days before David and I set off from Freetown. The dire warnings from foreign health officials had nagged at me for weeks during the trek. I had asked repeatedly about army worms as we crossed into Lofa County and made our way through Liberia but I found no evidence at all of the plague. In spite of this, a local newspaper carried the story that funds had been made available by the Liberian government to provincial health authorities to deal with the crisis. The paper reported all the money had gone missing.

The Greenes were trapped for nine unhappy days in Monrovia before a ship arrived to start them on their route home. Barbara Greene did not hold back when describing her attitude to the place.

> I hated every moment of my time in Monrovia. I was tired, but, what was far worse, I was bored . . . I had said my farewells long ago in the forest and now wanted to leave the whole comedy behind me. This dragging out of the end was inartistic and spoiling the balance of the whole thing.

For the thirty expat – that is to say, white – residents of the city in 1935, drink offered the only escape. They drank gin with their quinine in the morning, beer throughout the day, and crème de menthe, chilled in an icebox, as a digestif. Barbara Greene recalled how appalled her hosts were whenever she asked for something non-alcoholic, and how sickly the expats appeared, with a third of their number struck down by fever during her stay. Both Greenes complained there was simply nothing to do to pass the time. Every Saturday the menfolk would walk down to the sea and entertain themselves with target practice, shooting bottles set up on the beach close to where, years later, Silk would watch the cabinet being shot dead. Graham Greene wrote how the English expats would routinely gather at six o'clock each evening and turn on their wirelesses in the hope of catching the Empire Service from Daventry. But the meteorological conditions on the tropical coast would defeat them each night and the speakers would emit nothing but a background medley of wheezes and whistles.

Graham Greene's opinion of Monrovia was scarcely higher than his cousin's. In his description of the city and its black elite, I detect the same tone of mockery he uses for the seedy white colonials in Freetown. When the cargo steamer that would take them home eventually came in sight off Cape Mesurado, the Greenes' sense of relief was palpable.

I loved getting to know the Greenes during the trip because it changed so radically my understanding of them both. My initial image of Barbara Greene was the one she so self-deprecatingly projected in her writing: a socialite born of the Edwardian era, demurely playing a bit part on a stage rightly dominated by her male cousin. But I had come to see her quite differently, striding through the jungle mile after mile, day after day, clad in her ballooning shorts, keeping the whole expedition going through stamina and wit. And as a reader who knew Graham Greene only through his novels, my view of him as a literary untouchable was also transformed. I came to see him as more of a mortal, an adventurer who got ill, tired and confused – in his diary and correspondence he misspells champagne as champaign – on a thrilling journey embarked on not for selfish, inward-looking reasons but to help the philanthropists of the anti-slavery society.

The Greenes both came to acknowledge the huge impact of their shared adventure in Sierra Leone and Liberia. Barbara Greene, the twenty-something who before the journey had never trusted herself to do much more than float around the London social scene, had not just survived the physical hardship of the trip, she had thrived. Her later life would be complex and not without danger, as she married a German aristocrat and spent the Second World War in Berlin, an English patriot in constant fear of being denounced to the Nazis. Her son, Count Rupert Strachwitz, today believes the 1935 trip was key in making his mother what he called 'an intellectual adventurer'.

After returning to London, Graham Greene was quick to report on his trip to his sponsors at the Anti-Slavery and Aborigines Protection Society, presenting the keynote speech to the society's 1935 annual meeting, specially convened to fit in with his programme. I could find no written proof that Graham Greene reported back to the Foreign Office, although I feel this was highly likely, a foretaste of his closer links with the British government when he spied for MI6 during the war. The true impact of the journey on Graham Greene is perhaps best expressed in a letter he wrote to his cousin in January 1975 on the fortieth anniversary of their trip. Their lives had taken them in differing directions and they rarely saw each other, but Barbara Greene had clearly seen the anniversary as a suitable moment to write to her cousin reminding him of their shared bond and suggesting some sort of celebration. Her note is lost but his reply survives.

> By God! I think you are right. 40 years. I would have loved to split a bottle with you – preferably not champaign! It should be whisky with warm filtered water and squeezed limes. To me too that trip has been very important – it started a love of Africa which has never quite left me . . . Altogether a trip which altered life.

My life was also altered by the journey. I had loved my years as a news reporter but this trek had been so rewarding and illuminating that I would find it difficult to go back to the flash immediacy demanded by modern online journalism. The trip had taught me the value of taking time to savour the true smell and taste of a place and, like Silk, I would leave Liberia with a different attitude towards my career. Within a few months I had left the *Telegraph* to begin a different phase of my life as an author. David also moved on, taking a management job overseas that meant he escaped the world of banking.

I felt a little lost when the pair of us finally set out from Monrovia for the long jeep drive back to Freetown. For many months I had been so intensely preoccupied, anticipating every aspect of the trip – the route, security, border crossings, guides, accommodation – that to have the worry suddenly vanish was odd. The city was soon left behind and within a few minutes we were speeding along a tarmac road. The jungle that had been home for so many miles of trekking was a blur through the windscreen, the leaf definition, contour of the ground, smell of woodsmoke from village kitchens, all lost.

Some time after crossing the border into Sierra Leone, the road filled with people, slowing us to a crawl. It was a political rally by the main opposition party, one led by politicians making the platitudinous promises heard throughout the turbulent histories not just of Sierra Leone and Liberia, but wider Africa: corruption will be crushed, wealth shared, laws respected, hope reborn. The crowd was young, loud and enthusiastic, waving a thicket of palm fronds out of allegiance to the party's official colour, green.

I was tired and distracted but out in the mêlée something caught my eye. Some women were standing in a circle smiling, their heads swaying from side to side as they clapped and chanted. In their midst was a twirling, masked, grassy figure I recognised immediately. The devil was dancing one last time.

The author in Liberia

Bibliography

Graham Greene

Private diary from Sierra Leone, Guinea and Liberia, Jan–Mar 1935, held by Harry Ransom Humanities Research Center at the University of Texas, Greene collection, box 20 item 7

Manuscript proof of Journey Without Maps, 1935/36, same collection, box 20 item 9

Journey Without Maps, 1936, William Heinemann

A Chance for Mr Lever, 1936, Story Magazine

The Heart of the Matter, 1948, William Heinemann

In Search of a Character – Two African Journals, 1961, The Bodley Head

Graham Greene revisits the Soupsweet Land, Observer magazine feature, May 1968

A Sort of Life, 1971, The Bodley Head

Ways of Escape, 1980, The Bodley Head

Barbara Greene

Land Benighted, 1938, Geoffrey Bles (re-printed as *Too Late to Turn Back*)

Works on Graham Greene

Nicholas Elliott: *Never Judge a Man by His Umbrella*, 1991, Michael Russell

Richard Greene: *Graham Greene – A Life in Letters*, 2007, Little, Brown

Julia Llewellyn Smith: *Travels Without My Aunt*, 2000, Michael Joseph

Anthony Mockler: *Graham Greene – Three Lives*, 1994, Hunter Mackay

Adam Schwartz: *The Third Spring*, 2005, Catholic University of America Press

Michael Shelden: *Graham Greene – The Man Within*, 1994, William Heinemann

Norman Sherry: *The Life of Graham Greene*, 1989/1994/2004, Jonathan Cape

W. J. West: *The Quest for Graham Greene*, 1997, Weidenfeld & Nicolson

Papers relating to Graham Greene

Anti-Slavery and Aborigines Protection Society files, 1934/5, Bodleian Library of Commonwealth & African Studies, Rhodes House, University of Oxford; correspondence (MSS. Brit. Emp. s. 19, D3/67 and D3/68), minutes (MSS. Brit. Emp. s. 20, E2/17 and E2/21) and periodicals (100.221 v.16 - The Anti-Slavery Reporter and Aborigines' Friend, Series V., Vol.25. No.3 October 1935)

Foreign Office files concerning Greene's plans to travel to Liberia, 7 to 23 Dec 1934, held by The National Archives, Kew, London. Registry serial J 2957/2957/24. Catalogue serial FO 371/18044

Bolahun Mission Station Visitors' book, January 1935, held by The Order of the Holy Cross, Holy Cross Monastery, West Park, New York

Winifred Harley correspondence on meeting the Greenes, March 1935, held by Rare Book, Manuscript, and Special Collections Library, Duke University, Durham, North Carolina

Charles Evans, chairman of William Heinemann, libel action correspondence, February 1937, held by Random House Group Archive & Library, Rushden, Northants

Secret Service files from Greene's intelligence career, 1942-1944, held by The National Archives, Kew, London. Serial KV 2/2272, The Security Service: Personal (PF Series)

Sierra Leone

Phil Ashby: *Unscathed*, 2002, Macmillan

Philip Beale and Vic Mitchell: *Sierra Leone Narrow Gauge*, 2004, Middleton Press

Tim Collins: *Rules of Engagement*, 2005, Headline

Ross Donaldson: *The Lassa Ward*, 2009, Transworld

Aminatta Forna: *The Devil that Danced on the Water*, 2002, HarperCollins

William Fowler: *Operation Barras*, 2004, Weidenfeld & Nicolson

Christopher Fyfe: *A Short History of Sierra Leone*, 1962, Longman

— *Sierra Leone Inheritance*, Oxford University Press, 1964

Lansana Gberie: *A Dirty War in West Africa*, 2005, C Hurst & Co

Michael Jackson: *In Sierra Leone*, 2004, Duke University Press

A. P. (Peter) Kup: *The Story of Sierra Leone*, Cambridge University Press, 1964

Roy Lewis: *Sierra Leone – A Modern Portrait*, 1954, Her Majesty's Stationery Office

M. McCulloch: *The Peoples of Sierra Leone Protectorate*, 1950, International African Institute

Harry Mitchell: *Remote Corners*, 2002, The Radcliffe Press

John Peterson: *Province of Freedom*, Northwestern University Press, 1969

Simon Schama: *Rough Crossings*, 2005, BBC Books
A.B.C. Sibthorpe: *The History of Sierra Leone*, Elliot Stock, 1868
F.A.J. Utting: *The Story of Sierra Leone*, 1931, Longmans, Green and Co

Liberia

R. Earle Anderson: *Liberia – America's African Friend*, 1952, University of North Carolina Press
Christopher Clapham: *Liberia and Sierra Leone*, 1976, Cambridge University Press
Helene Cooper: *The House at Sugar Beach*, 2008, Simon & Schuster
Anthony Daniels: *Monrovia Mon Amour*, 1992, John Murray
Brother Edward: *'Plenty How Do' from Africa*, 1960, Holy Cross Press
Stephen Ellis: *The Mask of Anarchy*, 1999, Hurst & Co
Merran Fraenkel: *Tribe and Class in Monrovia*, 1964, Oxford University Press
Harry J. Greenwall and Roland Wild: *Unknown Liberia*, 1936, Hutchinson
George W. Harley: *Notes on the Poro in Liberia*, 1941, Harvard University
— *Masks as Agents of Social Change*, 1950, Harvard University
Winifred J. Harley: *A Third of a Century With George Way Harley in Liberia*, 1973, Liberian Studies Association in America, Newark
Sir Harry Johnston: *Liberia*, 1906, Hutchinson
Werner Junge: *African Jungle Doctor – Ten Years in Liberia*, 1952, George G. Harrap & Co
Adam Dubar McCoy: *Holy Cross*, 1987, Morehouse-Barlow
Lady Dorothy Mills: *Through Liberia*, 1926, Duckworth
Mary H. Moran: *Liberia – The Violence of Democracy*, 2006, University of Pennsylvania
Wilson Jeremiah Moses: *Liberian Dreams*, 1998, The Pennsylvania State University Press
William Powers: *Blue Clay People*, 2005, Bloomsbury
Henry Fenwick Reeve: *The Black Republic*, 1923, H. F. & G. Witherby
James L Sibley and Diedrich Westermann: *Liberia Old and New*, 1928, James Clarke
Richard Lane Stryker III: *Forged From Chaos*, 2003, 1stBooks
Stefan von Gnielinski: *Liberia in Maps*, 1972, University of London Press
Esther Warner: *The Crossing Fee*, 1968, Victor Gollancz
Charles Morrow Wilson: *Liberia*, 1947, William Sloane Associates

Misc

Julian Barnes: *A History of the World in 10½ Chapters*, 1989, Jonathan Cape

Dr Cuthbert Christy: *Liberia in 1930*, The Geographical Journal, Vol 77, No 6, June 1931

Joseph Conrad: *Heart of Darkness*, 1899, Blackwood's Magazine

Daily Telegraph: *Ex-rulers executed on Liberia beach*, Brian Silk, 23 April 1980

— *Dark Journey into Greeneland*, Jeremy Gavron, 16 January 1988

Foreign Office, London: *Papers Concerning Affairs in Liberia December 1930 – May 1934*, Cmd 4614,

Sir Harry Johnston: *Liberia*, Royal Geographical Society paper, March 1905

Wangari Maathai: *The Challenge for Africa*, 2009, William Heinemann

Donald MacIntosh: *Travels in the White Man's Grave*, 1998, Neil Wilson Publishing

Sir Alfred Sharpe: *The Hinterland of Liberia*, The Geographical Journal, Vol 55, No 4, April 1920

The New York Times: *Rev. Allen Dies In The Jungle*, 22 April 1929

Acknowledgements

The help I received began long before I set out for West Africa and continued well after I made it home. My debt is substantial and my thanks are heartfelt.

The adventure would have failed completely without the strength and companionship of David Poraj-Wilczynski, Johnson Boie and Omaru N. Kanneh.

And the trail through the jungle would have been lost without the skill of guides Moses Kallie, Amah Karoma, David Jalleh, Selmah Jalleh, Karmah Gayfor, Forkpa Zaza, James Monbar, Peter Sumo, Moses Kollie, Shmay Lablah, Fidel Bofumu, Musa Koroma-Gbembu, Carlo Dunzo and Nathaniel Dean.

Understanding Sierra Leone a little better was made possible through two more Poraj-Wilczynskis – Joe and Huw, Yvette Reyes, Mohamed Bangura, Kelvin Lewis, Alpha Kahn, Yannis Behrakis, Dominic O'Neill, Mark Ravnkilde, Garry Horlacher, Lamine Somparé, Kenneth Jones, Professor Eldred Jones, Marjorie Jones, Marie Staunton and her colleagues at Plan, Fadimata Alainchar and Sarah Smart, Rugiatu Neneh Turay, Abator Thomas, Phil Ashby, Keith Biddle, Simon Lang, Victor Ferrari, the late Tamba Pujeh Gbekie, Peter C. Andersen, Gary Schulze and Bala Amarasekaran and his colleagues at the Tacugama chimpanzee sanctuary.

Similarly for Liberia, I owe much to Dave Waines and his colleagues at Equip Liberia, Mark Chapeskie and Sarah Joy Carlson, Chantal Richey, Marcel Koppejan, Jill Salmon and her colleague at Concern, Jacob Blama, Gillian Dare, Mark Lavender, Frank Foday and his colleagues at the Holy Cross mission in Bolahun, Mark Togba and Mawolo Kpawor, Weegie Freeman, Andy Russ Gborley, Father Gareth Jenkins, Forkpa Duolar, Dr Edna Johnson, Mark Buckland, Dave Buston, Mark Wells-Cole, Mary Jo Loehle, Richard Martin, James Brabazon, Tim Hetherington, Samuel Shevach, Sue Porter and her associates at the Ganta United Methodist Mission, Nancy

Chamberlin and Barbara Tutton, Nick Alexander, Stephen Ellis and Augustine A. Allieu and his colleagues at Plan.

Learning more about Graham and Barbara Greene was made easier by Count Rupert Strachwitz, Nicholas Dennys, Caroline Bourget, Francis Greene, Bruce Hunter, Richard Greene, Colin Garrett, Jeremy Lewis, David Williams, Jeremy Gavron, Donald Macintyre, David Oakley, Helen Threlfall, Drummond Moir, Ziaad Khan, Nikolaus Kircher, Philip Laubach-Kiani, Christopher Munnion, Jean Rose (Random House chief archivist), the staff of Hebrew University social science library in Jerusalem, Lucy McCann and her colleagues at the Bodleian Library of Commonwealth & African Studies at Rhodes House in Oxford, Hugh Alexander and his colleagues at the National Archives in London, Richard Oram and his colleague at the Harry Ransom Humanities Research Center at the University of Texas, Elspeth Healey, Janie Morris and her colleagues at Duke University and Father Adam McCoy and fellow members of the Order of the Holy Cross.

And through the loneliest part of the journey – the writing – I was kept going by the enthusiasm of Camilla Hornby at Curtis Brown, the skill of Poppy Hampson at Chatto & Windus and the vision of her former colleague, Alison Samuel, and the special support of Margaret Hussey, Richard Foreman, Tim and Jacqueline Parsonson, Ruth Fuller-Sessions, Sally Stephens, Stanley and Lisette Butcher and Patrick and Marilyn Flanagan.

Jane, Kit and Tess were with me every step. Their love gave me reason both to go the extra mile and to relish coming home.

Credits

Main map by Paul Simmons
Hand-drawn maps by Jane Flanagan
Hand-drawn illustrations by Sally Stephens
All photographs property of Tim Butcher unless mentioned below

6   Foreign Office memo, courtesy of The National Archives, Kew, London

34   Newspaper advert, from the *Independent Observer*
60   The Greenes in Liverpool photograph, courtesy of the *Daily Mail*
86   German newspaper cartoon, courtesy of Count Rupert Strachwitz
104   Yannis Behrakis self-portrait, courtesy of the photographer
106   Sierra Leone railway photograph, courtesy of Middleton Press, publisher of *Sierra Leone Narrow Gauge*
131   Barbara Greene with bearers photograph, courtesy of Count Rupert Strachwitz
134   Graham Greene walking photograph, courtesy of Count Rupert Strachwitz
152   Excerpt from 'An Arundel Tomb' from *Collected Poems* by Philip Larkin, reprinted courtesy of Faber and Faber Ltd
162   Liberian devil photograph, courtesy of Count Rupert Strachwitz
234   Graham Greene in sun-helmet photograph, courtesy of Count Rupert Strachwitz
284   Hand-drawn map, courtesy of Count Rupert Strachwitz

For more photographs, video and historical material go to
www.vintage-books.co.uk/books/chasingthedevil

Index

www.vintage-books.co.uk